The Pirate Inside

The Pirate Inside

*Building a Challenger Brand
Culture Within Yourself
and Your Organization*

Adam Morgan

John Wiley & Sons, Ltd

Other Wiley Editorial Offices

John Wiley & Sons Inc., 111 River Street, Hoboken, NJ 07030, USA

Jossey-Bass, 989 Market Street, San Francisco, CA 94103-1741, USA

Wiley-VCH Verlag GmbH, Boschstr. 12, D-69469 Weinheim, Germany

John Wiley & Sons Australia Ltd, 33 Park Road, Milton, Queensland 4064, Australia

John Wiley & Sons (Asia) Pte Ltd, 2 Clementi Loop #02-01, Jin Xing Distripark, Singapore
129809

John Wiley & Sons Canada Ltd, 22 Worcester Road, Etobicoke, Ontario, Canada M9W 1L1

Wiley also publishes its books in a variety of electronic formats. Some content that appears
in print may not be available in electronic books.

Library of Congress Cataloging-in-Publication Data

Morgan, Adam.
    The pirate inside : building a challenger brand culture within yourself
and your organization / by Adam Morgan.
        p. cm.
    Includes bibliographical references and index.
    ISBN 0-470-86082-0 (cloth : alk. paper)
    1.   Brand name products–Management. 2.   Brand name
products–Psychological aspects. 3.   Brand name products–Planning. 4.
Creative ability in business. 5.   Corporate culture. I.   Title.
    HD69.B7M665 2004
    658.8'27 – dc22
                                                              2004006448

British Library Cataloguing in Publication Data

A catalogue record for this book is available from the British Library

ISBN 978-0-470-86082-3 (HB)

Typeset in 11/14pt Goudy by Laserwords Private Limited, Chennai, India
Printed and bound in Great Britain by TJ International, Padstow, Cornwall
This book is printed on acid-free paper responsibly manufactured from sustainable forestry
in which at least two trees are planted for each one used for paper production.

For my parents

Contents

Dramatis Personae

All narratives are driven by characters; the following is the list of characters who were generous enough to share their time, thinking, and ideas on the brands they had been involved with. This book would not exist without them.

The Interviewees	Their brand or company (*have since left that brand or company, † has left brand but still within parent company)
Andrew Sanders	Puccino's
Bob Gill	Pringles*
Brian Lanahan	OK Soda*
Candy Tree	Crunch
Charlotte Semler	Myla
Chris Hawken	Skoda†
Colleen Barrett	Southwest Airlines
Dalia Saliamonas	Camper
Dave Hieatt	Howies
Dave Illingworth	Lexus
David Atter	Tango*
David Magliano	easyJet*
David Nelms	Discover Financial Services
David O'Hanlon	independent consultant
Doris Mitsch	independent consultant
Hans Snook	Orange*
Ian Benton	Yorkie
Jamie King	Leo Burnett
Jeremy Kantor	Unilever*
Jeremy Woods	Pot Noodle*
Jim Nordgren	Mountain Dew
John Dempsey	M.A.C.
Kristin Krumpe	Yoo-hoo

Lizzie Palmer	Orange*
Lorenzo Fluxá	Camper
Luke Lewis	Lost Highway
Marina Tosin	Diesel
Merrill J. Fernando	Dilmah
Michael Abrashoff	US Navy*
Michelle Feeney	M.A.C.
Mike Harris	Egg
Neil Munn	Axe
Nick Graham	Joe Boxer
Paula Moss	Hovis
Renzo Rosso	Diesel
Richard Reed	innocent
Roger Kirman	Unilever
Sam Ellison	Yorkie
Scott Lutz	8th Continent*
Shubhankar Ray	Camper
Simon Clift	Unilever
Theresa Fatino	W Hotels
Tim Little	Tim Little Shoes
Tom Birk	Crispin Porter Bogusky
Tom Brown	Yoo-hoo
Tony Margolis	Tommy Bahama
Wilbert Das	Diesel

Where these people are quoted, I have drawn directly on my interviews with them.

I would also like to thank the five interviewees who asked not to be named, but who provided valuable information about other brands mentioned in the course of the book.

The Relationship of This Book to Eating the Big Fish, and The Challenger Project

T he Challenger Project is an ongoing study of Challenger brands, and what it has taken for them to succeed. It is qualitative in nature, and consists of interviews with individuals at the heart of those brands during the key time in their challenge. We have now looked at over a hundred such brands.

The first output of The Challenger Project was the strategic process outlined in *Eating the Big Fish* (Wiley, 1999). Since I wrote *Eating the Big Fish*, the book has fostered a business – **eatbigfish Ltd**. At **eatbigfish**, I and my partners continue to develop the thinking around this strategic process. We nurture our understanding through a continuing commitment to the Challenger Project, which means at least three to four days per month spent researching new Challengers. We also run workshops in which we directly apply the thinking to brands that want or need to think like Challengers themselves.

This book is designed to complement *Eating the Big Fish*, without requiring the reader of *The Pirate Inside* to be familiar with the previous book. *Eating the Big Fish* looked at the commonalities in 50 Challenger brands around the globe, and identified the eight underlying Credos that seem to unite the way that Challenger brands think and behave. In *The Pirate Inside* some of those same themes are revisited but with a much deeper look at the personal qualities and skills required to help Challenger brands and Challenger cultures thrive – sometimes against the odds.

In the third and final book in the series about Challengers, *Fugitive Indigo*, we will look at how Challengers approach Innovation; it will be published in 2006.

If you would like to find out more about how **eatbigfish**, our own company, is working with other brands and companies to apply the thinking in this book and the previous one, you can visit our website at www.eatbigfish.com, or contact us directly on pirates@eatbigfish.com.

Introduction: Necessary Pirates

'It's more fun to be a Pirate than to join the Navy.'
Steve Jobs[1]

Enough. I have had enough.

I have had enough of corporate rules. Of enforced mediocrity. Of doing it this way or that way, because this way or that way is the way we always do it round here. I have had enough of being a prisoner of my category's history. Of being handcuffed by my company's culture. Of being hamstrung by benchmarks and processes and so-called 'best practices' into becoming just another kind of establishment brand.

I read the most depressing article in the *Harvard Business Review* this morning. Apparently some study looked at 340 prime time commercials and found that there was a differentiating message in only 7% of them: 7%. Is my brand really any different? *Really*? My God, what am I *doing* in this job? And why do I feel that much of the time my company's culture is dampening, rather than igniting my ability to change those statistics?[2]

So I want out. Well, kind of out. I want to take the brand out and see what it could do if I had a little open water. I want to try doing things a different way. Try a little liberating lawlessness, frankly. Find my piss and vinegar, and see where that takes me. I look at the great marketing pirates like Jobs and Branson, and I think, yes, I'd like some of that. Some freedom – I could do something with that. The freedom to make up my own rules for a change.

Oh, we have dabbled with doing things differently, my company and my brand and I. We know at one level, some of us, that we have been sailing under the wrong flag, that we have been following the charted course when we should have been finding our own way.

For a while we pushed for Chinos Theory. The belief that the mere act of wearing light-coloured trousers at work would help us think more creatively. That attending offsites and using scented magic markers would propel us magically free from the box we had never previously been able to escape from. We agreed that there is no 'I' in team, and that if we came up with Horizon 3 ideas like retail outlets and theme parks (even if we were a cheese spread), those things meant that we were thinking big.

But now. But now.

But now I keep coming back to that idea of Steve Jobs, that whole thing about being a Pirate rather than in the Navy, and what it really means. Why it really matters.

You see, what is interesting to me is that he doesn't talk about processes; he talks about a *type of people*. He doesn't talk about *saying*; he talks about *being*. And I find those two distinctions interesting and important. The idea that perhaps it's the kind of people that we are or choose to be, individually or collectively, that will make the difference to our futures. Perhaps we shouldn't focus so much on the processes we use, or the tools we have, or the architecture we discuss, or the organizational structure we find ourselves in but on *who we are and how we behave*. If it is people who create great brands, then it is who we are, and how we choose to be – our qualities and behaviour – that count, at any stage in the process.

And I recognize that this is not just an interesting conceptual exercise; I recognize that, for many of us, underneath the flippancy of the word 'fun' in Jobs' celebrated saying lurks the clarion call of necessity. We will *have* to be Pirates, to some degree: we keenly recognize that getting the positioning right is the very least part of creating success – the brand and brand team will probably need to go to market in a wholly different way if we are to create the step change we need. We will need to understand we are going to have to live outside the codes of the Navy, for a while at least: find our own way of keeping clear of the corporate round holes that will slowly blunt all the fine sharp edges of our square peg. We will need to live by a set of rules for what is right for us and our brand at this particular time, and not be confined by the category conventions laid down by the establishment player, on the one hand, or our own internal corporate culture, on the other.

And, yes, we are going to have to be a little less compliant to the admirals if necessary – we are not simply going to salute and follow each order as it comes our way.

And, yes, we are going to have to bring people with us, whether they initially want to or not.

And, yes, that it would be enormously energizing, indeed liberating, for them to sail this different course, and we acknowledge that this degree of energy and commitment, this 'intangible' is going to be at least as important to my success as getting the strategy right.

But.

But. It is frightening, isn't it, the power of that little word? And yet it does rear its head at this point.

Because here's the thing. When I look at who actually said that thing about Pirates, that's where the heady desire to be a real Challenger within the context of my company hits the cold, cold water of reality.

Because the 'but' is this: 'It's easy for you to say, Steve.'

For while we may admire the man, the fact remains that his position and perhaps character are not ours, and his type of company (for better or worse) is not our type of company. He is, let's face it, a charismatic and publicity-hungry CEO of a single brand company, his own company, which seems to have in its very DNA a commitment to difference and finding an alternative way of going up against the Market Leader. And that's great. And we are the first to applaud all that Apple has done to build a desirable brand, even accepting that its perceived functional incompatibility limits its consequent share. But what blunts our enthusiasm about just taking Jobs' philosophy and running with it is that his situation is a long, long way from our own.

We are not the CEO. We may not be in a single brand company. We don't perhaps even have a sufficiently sharp and unified sense of who we are as a brand, certainly not outside the marketing department. We may not have either the large advertising budgets, nor access to the kinds of stage (and therefore forums for publicity) that he seems to be able to reach. *Fortune* magazine is not waiting on the phone to interview us any time soon. And piracy, well, much though we love the romance of the sound of it, we are very process and best practice orientated around areas like research in our world. Talk of Necessary Piracy is going to sound a little too much like unleashing the Beast of Chaos to cut much ice with those above us.

And the result of all these 'buts' is that while we admire the sentiment that someone like Jobs espouses here, when it all comes down we cannot really believe it is possible to live by it in our organization; so while we lock the quote away somewhere and bring it out now and again a little wistfully at offsites or in the bar, its implications are not something we honestly believe we can live and die by in practice. And certainly not something we can use as ammunition to persuade other people to slip their ropes and come with us.

Which brings us to the purpose of this book.

The Purpose of the Book

We are going to take what one could regard as a slight but engaging quote by Steve Jobs and explore it very seriously indeed. The book will explore what it means to be a Necessary Pirate: unpacking the behaviours and personal qualities necessary for individuals and teams of people working on brands who need to be Challengers – and how to use those behaviours and qualities to bring out a more active Challenger culture within our organizations. It is going to argue that if we understand what Necessary Piracy really means, then all the reasons that we find put forward by others about why 'it's different for Apple' and why 'we can't think like that here' are simply excuses – they are, in fact, one of what we will call 'the Six Excuses for the Navy'. And we will look at each of these six excuses one by one, and strip them away.

The book is intended to be useful. As such, it will include at the end of most chapters some challenges and exercises to stimulate fresh thinking and behaviour, and an overview section in Chapter 14 for those interested in applying some of the learning to their teams and brand.

The Articles: The Binding Code of Piracy

I am going to start by suggesting that if we pull this metaphor of Jobs out, then the first problem that marketing 'Piracy' has to overcome is the perception that it is the same as lawlessness. This perception is wrong: in fact, in these situations, where one needs to leave the confines of the Navy (whether one defines the Navy as 'the category rules', 'our own corporate culture' or 'an establishment parent'), one is not moving outside the law, but *from one law to another*. This book will argue, in effect, that creating or fanning a Challenger culture or subculture (if we live within a larger organization) is not, as is sometimes the concern from senior management, about lawlessness but about the deliberate move from one less suitable and successful personal and cultural model to another that is more appropriate to the opportunity for the brand. Furthermore, we will argue that even when it comes to large multi-branded organizations, as long as this transition from one 'model' to another is properly understood by both the parent 'Navy' and the 'Pirate' subculture, both sides will not only be comfortable but can actually benefit from the establishment of such a subculture. What is then critical, of course, is establishing exactly what that new model is. And to understand the transition we need to make, first humour me in allowing a brief discussion about two important aspects of real Piracy.

The first is the fact that Piracy, at its most successful, was not the same as anarchy; it was a way of doing things that had its own code. The reason that we think of it as lawless is because our perspective on pirates is largely formed by Hollywood and Disney, and these two cultural sculptors have carved a very clear (and not altogether unappealing) idea in our minds as to what piracy was like – a life of wild carousing, gambling, fighting, and lawlessness, enjoyed by an ill-disciplined rabble who were held together by the will and pistol of a ruthless despot with a large beard and larger laugh.

But while a romantic and in some ways apparently liberating notion, this idea of simply living outside any law and doing whatever you want, wasn't actually the case with pirates. The great age of piracy in the Western world is usually regarded as lasting from 1650 to 1725: at this time pirates were, in effect, commercially motivated teams of people operating in very high risk, high return environments, and to succeed in those kinds of high risk, high return commercial ventures they needed to have clearly understood rules of their own. These were different kinds of rules from the Navy, certainly, but rules – and fiercely enforced rules – all the same.

These rules were called the Articles, and they bound every participant in the joint venture. Each pirate captain had their own set of Articles, but common across all of them were certain key principles – those governing the distribution of profit, for instance, and certain fundamental rules of behaviour.

The following is an example of some Articles that were used by the pirate Bartholomew Roberts and his crew:

1. Every man has a vote in Affairs of Moment; has equal title to the fresh Provisions, or strong Liquors, at any Time seized, and use of them at pleasure, unless a Scarcity make it necessary, for the good of all, to Vote a Retrenchment.
2. Every man to be called fairly in turn, by List, on Board of Prizes, because, they were on these occasions allowed a Shift of Cloaths: but if they defrauded the Company to the Value of a Dollar, in Plate, Jewels, or Money, Marooning was their punishment.
3. No Person to Game at Cards or Dice, for Money.
4. The Lights and Candles to be put out at eight o'clock at Night: if any of the Crew, after that Hour, still remained inclin'd for Drinking, they were to do it on the open Deck.
5. To keep their Piece (i.e. weapon), Pistols, and Cutlass clean, and fit for Service.
6. No Boy or Woman to be allowed amongst them. If any Man were found seducing any of the latter Sex, and carried her to Sea, disguised, he was to suffer Death.
7. To Desert the Ship, or their Quarters in Battle, was punished with Death, or Marooning.
8. No striking one another on Board, but every Man's Quarrels to be ended on Shore, at Sword and Pistol. (I suppose this is what management consultants would call taking it offline these days . . .)
9. No Man to talk of breaking up their Way of Living, till each had shared a 1000. If in order to this, any Man should lose a limb, or become a Cripple in their Service, he was to have 800 Dollars, out of public Stock, and for lesser Hurts, proportionably.
10. The Captain and Quarter-Master to receive two Shares of a Prize; the Master, Boatswain and Gunner shall have one Share and a half, and the other Officers, one and a Quarter.[3]

You are probably humouring me at this point – thinking we are involved in an entertaining little piece of detail early in the book before getting back to the serious stuff. Well, let us just seriously consider a couple of interesting points here before we dismiss the Articles that quickly.

The first point relates to the nature of this as a contract. The key point here is that the Articles were all agreed with the crew, each of whom was then required to physically sign them before they were allowed to join the ship, and the ship set sail. What the Articles represented was, in effect, a group contract: not just the kind of vertical contract we tend to have in our companies between an individual and some notional employer or superior, but a horizontal one between an entire team embarking on a common goal. One of the lesser known aspects about the pirate ships in the Caribbean, unlike any Western country of the time, is that they were democracies: the crew elected the captain and the crew chose the destination – and the captain could be replaced at any point in the journey if the crew voted so. (As modern democrats, in fact, it has been noted that they pre-dated the French Revolution by over a century.)[4] Hence the need for the Articles, which reflected in turn a different set of priorities from the Navy, one based on the nakedly commercial imperative of the ventures they were engaged on. Pirates were, after all, strictly 'payment by results': if you didn't achieve your objective, you didn't eat.

The second point of interest in the Articles relates to the comparison of the specific points of content in their set of rules when compared with ours. We, after all, also find ourselves engaged in high risk, high return environments, and yet how many of us have a contract that specifies that if we have a conflict with one of our fellow team members that we take it offline and don't come back until we have sorted it out? Or a contract in which everyone knows how the profits will be distributed if the mission is successful? Or one where everyone is forbidden to even talk of doing things in a different way until the goal we have collectively set ourselves has been reached?

In other words, putting both these points together, which kind of contract do you think would give you a better chance of succeeding if you were embarking on doing something different with your brand – the kind you have at the moment, or the kind represented by the Articles? I would suggest there is no comparison: not only do the Articles show that piracy has a different, well-formed way of doing things of its own, but also that this way could be much more useful to us than those we have at the moment. This is because the Articles' objective was to bind a group of people to a common purpose, and treat any act that limits the group's chance of achieving that purpose very seriously indeed.

Pirates and Perspective

I said that there were two key aspects of Piracy we needed to understand before we started. The first was that they had a code and contract of their own. The second is that the definition of who was and wasn't a pirate was always relative to one's point of view: it depended on whether one's government took the view that the individual was acting in or against the national interest. So, for instance, Sir Francis Drake, an English hero of schoolboy history, is known in Spain as 'El Pirata Drake' – 'the Pirate Drake'. Why? Because he filled Queen Elizabeth I's coffers with gold that was taken at swordpoint from ships belonging to the King of Spain. So while one side derided him as a pirate, the other made him a knight of the realm. Technically, in fact, there was a difference between a pirate and a privateer in a case such as Drake's – the difference being that a privateer had a commission from the sovereign (called a Letter of Marque) to attack ships belonging to an enemy nation, as long as the sovereign got a share of the money.

Even within the same side, one's perspective could change. Some pirates proved too hard to catch, and were pardoned in exchange for some of their gains. Henry Morgan (no relation), who made a fine living from being a buccaneer in the Caribbean in the 1600s, who at one point led two thousand men in the capture and sack of Panama City, and who would seem to have been technically a pirate on a number of occasions under international law, was eventually knighted by the British Government. He had made sure that he always set sail with a 'commission' from the Governor of Jamaica, however dubious its validity was in reality and, besides, you can't argue with success. And we will see that of the Pirate/Challengers whom we discuss within large organizations, some were knighted (so to speak), some were effectively suppressed, and some left to pursue their ambitions elsewhere. We will argue that often the loss of such individuals and the enterprises that they have embarked on is a business loss as well as a personal loss to the organization, and we will be looking at a model that supports a more active 'commissioning' of such Necessary Pirates before they begin.

Having drawn out these two aspects of Piracy, I should make it clear that I am not proposing to endlessly play out the pirate analogy throughout the book; although I am sure there is a book that could be written that draws entertaining parallels for marketing with every dimension of parrots and planks, it is not this one. Nor is the intention here to hopelessly romanticize organized crime, or to suggest in any way that Pirates were noble and honest and misunderstood. On the whole, we are simply using Jobs' notion of being a Pirate as a metaphor for being a certain sort of person who finds themselves wanting or needing to be a Challenger, working on a Challenger brand (and in this regard I will be using the terms 'Pirate' – or 'Necessary Pirate' – and 'Challenger' interchangeably in the book). But at the outset we should note three points:

1. The move from being the Navy (i.e. behaving like everyone else in our company, or category) to being a 'Pirate' (i.e. doing what is imperative for the task we have set ourselves, regardless of the 'wisdom' we are offered from those around us) is frequently a matter of necessity, not fun or iconoclasm. As such, the need to be a Pirate in this sense is not in itself an act of defiance, let alone aggression. It is about recognizing that things need to be done in a different way if the opportunity is to be grasped, and getting a team together to start setting that new way of doing things in motion. At the same time this new way may lie outside what your superiors apparently want you to do, and the historical best practices of the brand or company.
2. Success in being a Pirate (i.e. an individual or group who chooses to seek their fortune along a path other than that of the Navy) does not lie in having no rules. It is about moving from one set of rules, one model, to another. One that is more suited for the task in hand.
3. This different model governs both individuals and teams.

The bulk of the book will consist of looking at examples of such brand 'Pirates' and the lessons we can draw from them in each of these three regards.

Six Excuses for the Navy

Along the way we will tackle the six excuses people put up for staying in the Navy – doing just the same as everyone has always done, even if they are not hitting their performance targets in doing this. The six excuses for the Navy are:

1. 'But my consumer doesn't seem to want anything different in the category.'
2. 'But I do not have a large advertising budget.'
3. 'But I am in packaged goods – I don't have a lot of opportunities for brand communication.'
4. 'But my category doesn't reward brand building.'
5. 'But that leaves me very exposed.'
6. 'But I am not in a single brand company with a charismatic founder at the helm. I am in a big multi-brand company with a conservative culture, and I am just another marketing director or manager.'

In attacking these excuses we will necessarily uncover an underlying issue that runs through many of these, namely 'Does one need a founder to be a successful Challenger?' We will see that the answer is that, while it certainly helps, there are enough examples of brands without founders making it work to show that it is not necessary – as long as we have a consistent core team, with this very particular set and combination of personal qualities and behaviour. And as long as you have at the heart of that team what we will come to call a Denter.

The Brands and People Discussed

We are deliberately going to look at a wide range of brands – from luxury cars to dehydrated noodle snacks, from Spanish shoe brands to US chocolate milk. In terms of people, we will move from iconic single brand companies and individuals you will have heard of (Ingvar Kamprad and IKEA) to marketing directors and managers and brands that you will be entirely unfamiliar with. As such, these brands and people are not intended to be a definitive list of modern Challengers or Pirates, but a range of examples across all kinds of categories and company sizes, from the largest advertiser in the world (Unilever) to brands that are, in effect, a single person. We are going to look for common threads across all these varying people and brands, and along the way demonstrate that being a Challenger or Pirate is not necessarily easier (as many think) in a single brand company, and indeed it is quite possible to be one in a large conservative company – as long as we understand how we can maximize our chances of success.

Within these brands we will, particularly in Chapter 2 and onwards, focus on the importance of personal contributions, individual acts, and how they influence the bigger picture. We will draw on success stories we think we know quite well, and see what lies beneath them. Lexus, for instance, we know as the extraordinary US success it has become, and there is almost a temptation to see it now as an inevitable thrust into the luxury category and a success naturally driven by the engineering and sales might of Toyota. But we shall look at two key interventions by individuals along that path which exerted a profound influence on the existence and success of Lexus. On the other side of the Atlantic we will see that the iconic brand Orange might well have been called Microtel if there had not been an individual within the team – and not initially the CEO – who was prepared to fight tenaciously for his vision of the brand. And do we think a brand called Microtel would genuinely have reframed the communications business?

Behaviours that Stimulate Challenger Brand Cultures

Part I will outline a set of four behaviours that we need to commit to as individuals if we find ourselves in the position of wanting or needing to be Brand Pirates – and the standard behaviours in brand building that we will need to think about differently as we move through the strategic development process.

Chapter 1 Outlooking: A Different Kind of Insight Seeking

There are two kinds of Insight a Challenger needs to distinguish between: Insights that frame the problem and task (Reflective Insights), and Insights that identify where we might build the future (Insights of Opportunity). Outlooking is a way of describing how Challenger individuals seem to find the latter, and the first behaviour we need to bring out in ourselves and our team.

Chapter 2 Pushing: A Different Kind of Approval

Their need to stand out and genuinely reframe the consumer's perception of them or the category means that the team on a Challenger brand need to be prepared to 'Push' an emerging idea in order to make it powerful enough. This represents a different kind of 'approval' of ideas emerging in the strategic process: merely being a good idea on brief may not be sufficient – our first questions should be 'Has it gone far enough? What would happen if we pushed it further?'

Chapter 3   Projecting: A Different Kind of Consistency

This chapter explores the behaviours a Challenger brand team should foster in terms of communicating their pushed idea, once it has emerged. It argues that we have far more media at our disposal than we think we do, and we need to use the potential power of each medium by thinking in terms of consistently 'projecting' our identity – evincing a strong sense of who we are and what we stand for – rather than simply relying on the more conventional concept of 'messages'.

Chapter 4   Wrapping: A Different Kind of Communication

This chapter argues that successful Challengers offer a differentiated culture that their consumer can participate in, and proposes that we should develop a new behaviour to propagate such a culture: 'Wrapping' our brand in the belief system, language, customs, rituals and iconography that are the constituents of a distinct culture, and then letting that culture – and the people behind it – be an integral part of our relationship with our consumer.

The Four Behaviours

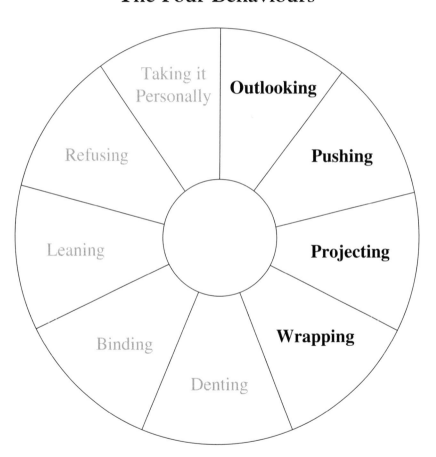

1

Outlooking: A Different Kind of Insight Seeking

Figure 1.1 **Outlooking**

We open on Ingvar Kamprad, the founder of IKEA, at an open food market in China. Imagine the sensory energy of the scene: the traders clamouring for our attention in a language we don't understand, the unusual colours and foreign textures of unfamiliar foods, the rituals and negotiations of money changing hands, the smell of food being cooked at a local stall somewhere just out of sight. Ah, this is what one travels for.

It is not clear what Kamprad is doing there from a business point of view – while IKEA have a restaurant, they don't actually sell food: they are in the furnishings business. But here he is all the same,

and while the market is full of all kinds of produce and people noisily selling all those kinds of produce, what Kamprad is looking at
is plucked chickens. Rows and rows and rows and rows of plucked
chickens.

Now there are presumably a number of questions we could be asking
ourselves at this point if we were in Kamprad's shoes. 'Isn't it about
time for a competitive store visit?' says the consummate professional in
us. 'Where can I check my emails?' says the networker. 'What time is
lunch?' says the *bon viveur*.

But Kamprad isn't asking himself any of these questions; he is asking
himself something completely different.

He is asking himself this: 'What do they do with all the feathers?'

The Two Kinds of Insight

While we probably tend to think of a call to Piracy as primarily about
unconventional marketing and communications, the reality is that we
have to start much earlier in the process than this. The fact is that,
long before we begin developing communications, Necessary Pirates or
Challengers need to find new kinds of opportunities in their categories to
compete and survive. They cannot compete head-on with the superior
firepower of the Establishment brand, so they have to find a territory
that is fresh and new. And to find the opportunities for such strategic
territories, Challenger individuals and teams need to have a very different
way of looking for insights.

Now it can often be hard to find these kinds of new opportunities
for our brands, and this chapter will argue that this is because much
of our searching for insight is consciously or unconsciously an 'Inward'
examination of our brand and the relationships it currently has with the
category and the other brands around it.

But Challengers tend not to look inward in this way, because
such a perspective usually leads to the creation of small or incremental differences, which are insufficient for a brand or individual
with high ambitions and relatively small resources. Instead, they
tend to 'look out', so to speak – to draw inspiration and ideas for
sources of opportunity not from within their consumer's relationship

with their own category, but from all kinds of different categories around them.

As individuals they do this naturally after a while – but we do not, yet. And so, because this may well even run counter to the way we have been naturally taught to do things, perhaps we need to replicate what such Challengers do naturally by the relatively formal assembly of a new lens to look through, which will help inculcate this new behaviour in us; start us systematically seeing things the way Challengers do. We will call this lens Outlooking.

So let's go back to Kamprad and his chickens, whom we have left suspended in that market in China. Why does he ask that question and what does he do with it? Well, the reason he asks it is because he is Outlooking. He is constantly looking for opportunities, because that is the way someone constantly looking to create a highly differentiated consumer offer naturally thinks. And what he discovers when he asks this question is that what the chicken people do with all the feathers is discard them; they are treated as something of no value, as rubbish. And what does he do with that answer? He makes millions of IKEA feather duvets at prices well below duck and goose. A huge business opportunity for IKEA, and a win for the customer. This is something of a habit for Kamprad: in the early days he used to go into wood factories and look at the offcuts – the timber that was going to be thrown away as waste – and ask himself what furniture he could make with that waste. He knew by taking materials that were not just cheap but of no value to its current owner, he could produce not just well-priced products but extraordinarily priced products. Something that would create a very high degree of competitive difference, right from the start.

So our first step as Necessary Pirates is going to be to change our behaviour in terms of how we look for Insight. In particular, we are going to recognize that although we tend to talk about Consumer Insights as if they are of one kind, there are two importantly different kinds of insight we can look for, one which we are probably doing well enough now, and the other which we need to further develop our abilities in through Outlooking. We are going to call these two different kind of insights Reflective Insights and Insights of Opportunity. Let us look at Reflective Insights first.

Reflective Insights

Reflective Insights are those that reflect or shed light on the *current status* of a category, the consumer and the brands within it. Insights that, for instance:

- describe a consumer profile or segmentation;
- outline current market drivers;
- delineate the current relationship with competition;
- unpack a given brand's rational and emotional equities.

The domain of Reflective Insights is within the relationships described by a fairly straightforward triangle, explored in qualitative or quantitative research (see Figure 1.2).

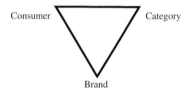

Figure 1.2   **The Reflective Triangle**

Now these are of course important relationships to understand, but they very much reflect the present or the past – the consumer's historical relationship with the category, and the brand's current relationship with the consumer and its competition. As such, Reflective Insights are potentially excellent for:

- identifying key problems in the current relationships;
- framing the overall task for the business, the brand, and marketing;
- identifying the 'Brilliant Basics' that one should consider addressing.

But they are of course necessarily limited by being rooted in the past, and therefore are rarely useful for indicating the way we might want to go forward, particularly if we are looking for large, opportunistic leaps, or even to reframe a profitable portion of the category in our favour.

So let us turn our attention to the other kind of insight.

Insights of Opportunity – Thinking Outside the Triangle

The second kind of insight we need to look at are Insights of Opportunity. Useless at framing the current problem (and therefore being complementary to Reflective Insights rather than alternatives), they instead outline possible opportunities for the brand and category, and in particular how to drive a greater degree of difference between our brand and the competition.

We are going to look at four different examples of these kinds of Insights of Opportunity, each of which comes from looking outwards rather than inwards:

- Emotional Insertion;
- Overlay;
- Brand Neighbourhood;
- Grip.

In a few pages time we will outline what these four are, offer some examples from Challengers that have drawn on insights of this type to develop their brand, and close with exercises that help us apply each in looking for opportunities on our own brand. But first, let us just reinforce why as Challengers it is paramount that we adopt this behaviour in the first place.

The Three Buckets

Let us try the following absurdly crude exercise. Let us imagine that we are going to mentally review all the working projects we have on our real or virtual desk at the moment, and place them in one of three buckets (see Figure 1.3), depending on what they are really doing for our brand: 'Brilliant Basics', 'Compelling Difference' and 'Changing the Game'. I'll explain what these buckets are in a little more detail, and then we can fill them in.

The first bucket we can assign a project to is Brilliant Basics. Brilliant Basics are the core activities our brand and product need to do to meet our promise to the consumer – to maintain the contract we already have,

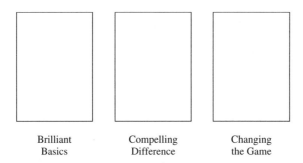

| Brilliant
Basics | Compelling
Difference | Changing
the Game |

Figure 1.3   **Three Empty Buckets**

if you like. These will include regular product upgrading, development of ease of use, ongoing refinement and modernization of graphics and other brand elements, and so on.

It is important to recognize that Brilliant Basics is in no way a put-down. It is an extremely valid thing (or set of things) for us as a Challenger to pursue – as long as it is not the only thing(s) we pursue.[1] We may need to bow to no one in our enthusiasm for difference, but there are still some things in any category that are not actually differentiating, but which still have to be done really well (punctuality in the airline business, for example, or some basic low level stream of fragrance news for household products). They are not always what the category wisdom says they are (the US airline jetBlue made in-seat TV standard, but sacrificed meals completely, for example), but they do have to be delivered on to compete.

The second bucket we can assign a project to is Compelling Difference. This will include anything we are doing that is creating a really compelling difference for our brand versus the other brands in our market (however we are defining that market).

The third bucket we can assign a project to is Changing the Game. Here would go strategic or ideational initiatives that would reframe the whole category in our favour. They will take more time to pull off, so may not be Year One initiatives, but are clearly critical nonetheless. Apple's setting up of iTunes and its pioneering of 'digital hub' computers and the iPod in terms of digital music would be a good example of this.

And for the purposes of this exercise, these are the only three buckets you can choose from. If anything fits into any other bucket than these, it has no place on our project list; innovation, for instance, simply fits into one of these three buckets depending on what kind of innovation it is.

So, as I say, a very crude exercise. But rather interesting. So let's do it. If you have a pencil, actually fill in the distribution of your marketing activities over the coming year across those three blank buckets in Figure 1.3 above. If you are in charge of a brand, do it for your brand. If you work in a communications company, you can either do it for a brand you work on, or for your own company. But just stop and fill it in.

OK. Now the realities of book publishing mean that I am unable to see what you have actually done for the moment, so I am going to make a guess. I am going to guess that, for most of us, the distribution of our 20 or so marketing activities on our brand this year across these three buckets will look something like this (see Figure 1.4). And I am further going to suggest to you that if you work on a brand, a very great deal of what makes up that slender black bar in the middle box called Compelling Difference will lie in communications, primarily advertising.

Now some of you for whom this is true will challenge me at this point. They will agree that communications is the primary filler of the middle bucket, but feel that the size of this bar is misleading – they will feel that they have highly differentiated communications that impart a high degree of differentiation for their brand. My only defence here would be that what goes into this box should be what the consumer sees as compellingly different, and not what we the creators of it see as compellingly different.

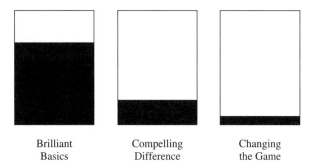

Brilliant   Compelling   Changing
Basics   Difference   the Game

Figure 1.4   **Three Filled Buckets**

Quibbling? Maybe not. The scale of the difference between these two things is illustrated by the results of august studies, such as the one published in the March 2002 *Harvard Business Review* that I referred to right at the beginning of the book, and also by a simple personal test that I mentioned in *Eating the Big Fish*, called The Peanut Test. It put you in the position of the tired consumer at the end of the day, and went like this:

> Sit down and watch an hour and a half of commercial television this evening with a small bag of peanuts. Take as a basic premise that any good piece of communication has to be at least relevant and distinctive. Count the number of ads that fulfill this single basic premise, and mark each one with a peanut on the arm of your chair. Eat the other peanuts.
>
> It may be depressing, but at least you don't go hungry.[2]

The *Harvard Business Review*, or a bag of peanuts – which you put more faith in is really up to you. The point is that if you are the Market Leader, this manifest lack of real difference in your communications is merely a shameful waste of money, energy and talent. But as the Market Leader you are in effect profiting from the status quo remaining as it is, so the effect of such a waste is simply to limit further growth. If you are a Challenger, however, this borders on the suicidal because it allows the status quo to remain the same. Challengers by their very nature have to change the existing order. As Hans Snook of Orange says, the role of a Challenger is not to unseat the Market Leader, it is to reframe the category. Meaning we do not prosper by accepting what the category gives us – we need to get the consumer to see the category on our new, redefined terms, rather than the way they have always seen it. The '7%' revelation in the *Harvard Business Review* illustrates that people are continuing to see and think about the category, and brands in that category, in the same ways they have always done. Which does not give us the platform to grow and challenge that we need.

So my point is this: we leave the creation of difference far too late in the process. Let's not wait to be Pirates until we are further down the path. Let us not allow ourselves to rely on just filling that middle box with 'communication'. We will certainly need any communications to be differentiating, but as Challengers we must not be relying on communications to do it all for us – we have to look for Insights of Opportunity as to how we might be able to create compelling difference in our core offer much earlier in the process. We should in fact look to develop a behaviour that allows us to do the following:

1. Start thinking about the *source* of Insights in a new way.
2. Start thinking about *who is responsible* for them in a new way.

Let us take these in turn. First, the nature of Insights themselves.

Insights of Opportunity

To recap, Insights of Opportunity are complementary to Reflective Insights rather than alternatives. Useless at framing the current problem, they instead outline possible opportunities for the brand and the category. Because they are rooted in the possibilities of the future, rather than reflections on the past, they are less relevant for Brilliant Basics, but key for Compelling Difference and, for that matter, Changing the Game.

While there are a number of these, we said there were four of them that we were going to focus on: Emotional Insertion, Overlay, Brand Neighbourhood, and Grip. Let's go through them one by one.

The Insight of Emotional Insertion

The first kind of insight is the observation that our category is missing a fundamental emotion that is a driver for consumers elsewhere – and that our brand could be the first to put it in our own category. Steve Jobs said in launching the iMac, 'Today we are putting romance into computers.' Now there are many emotions one had associated with one's computer up to that point, but it is fair to say that romance had not been one of them. And indeed subsequently people gave all sorts of rational reasons for buying an iMac, such as user-friendliness, but the real reason most of us bought one was so that we could put it on our desk and kiss it every half hour, just to feel alive. Jonathan Ive, the designer of the iMac, in fact brings a romance to even the smallest details of his design, for example, he talks about wanting to create a surface with the effect of 'a shower mist' on as apparently small a detail as the cable that links the mouse to the computer. And it is the way Ive thinks about the design of an apparently functional tool that in turn affects the emotion we feel in relation to it.[3]

Sometimes the inserted emotions are even more startling introductions than the one represented by the iMac; let's try an emotion at the other end of the scale from romance. In the summer of 2002 London's Science Museum featured the travelling exhibit called Grossology, and one of my sons promptly demanded to go. The first display in Grossology was a Vomit Machine where you used a pump to agitate the stomach until each and every cookie had been duly tossed. We then came to 'Urine: The Game!' before moving on to attack a rock climbing wall made out of rubber 'skin', where the hand and toe holds were made up of zits, hair roots and blackheads. And of course no such exhibit would be complete without a tour of the nose – entering through a giant pair of nostrils and touching the slimy mucus oozing down the walls from the sinuses. Frankly, I am not sure which of us loved it more – and we were not alone. It helped the Science Museum win the award of 'Best Visitor Attraction in London' in the same year (and bear in mind this is a science museum competing against other forms of entertainment and tourism such as Madame Tussaud's, the London Eye, and Buckingham Palace). The emotion? The fascinated and amused disgust of being grossed out. It had understood that small (and large) boys like grossness, and that if one inserted this emotion into science, the former would make the latter interesting. We willingly learnt – and remembered – more about the nature and functions of the human body after that one hour than I for one had done in years of school biology classes.

So both of these players have seen the possibility of inserting a whole new emotion in the category. The emotion was not one that existed within the category at the time, though clearly emotions such as romance and grossness have existed in very different categories around them. Nor was the emotion one the consumer was necessarily asking for at the time. Yet by being the first to introduce, talk about and genuinely deliver against this entirely 'outside' emotion, both of these players have successfully redefined a profitable part of the category in their favour.

The Insight of Overlay

The second kind of insight one sees Challengers drawing on is the related insight of overlay – the idea that one can take the rules of a different category and simply overlay them onto our own.

Take Lush. Lush is a bath and cosmetics retailer that has taken freshness and the colour and sensory overload of the deli and built it into their category. Something that has historically been adversely associated with eating ('you use that word again, young lady, and I'm going to wash your mouth out with soap'), is now made delicious. An Australian beauty writer gushed: ' Lush is just such fun . . . It's like walking into a deli . . . I think people – not just women – want a more holistic approach to beauty. People want products that are sensory as well as good for the skin . . .'.[4] Lush CEO Andrew Gerrie takes the deli metaphor on a little: 'Freshness is key. Ideally we will be like a bakery where the product is made today and sold today.'[5]

Lush plays this out at a product level (the products have the startlingly bright colours and rich scents of ripe exotic fruits, but are cut from large chunks like slabs of cheese or meat) and in the theatre of the store. In Figure 1.5 we can see the products laid out like in a greengrocer's shop, and using the visual device of a chalked blackboard as another cue for freshness. But the deli-fresh overlay carries through to a more profound way in which Lush creates perceived value as well. A shower gel called Slammer is on the face of it just an amusingly described, nicely scented product in a cheap plastic bottle. But if you read down the label, it will tell you who made it ('made by Sarah', for instance), the day on which it was made and when it is best before. By playing the overlay of deli-freshness all the way through, in fact, Lush instils a cheap plastic bottle full of soap with a sense of specialness and value.[6]

This is played out in the theatre of their retail stores: in writing those chalk descriptions on blackboards, they use the language and spelling of an East End of London barrow boy shouting out his wares: this product is described as 'Luverly', that one is 'tisty tosty'.

So we can see with the example of Lush that it is not simply a question of a provocative but slight analogy (as Space NK's founder claimed they were a 'sweetie shop for grown ups', or the notion that hotel bathrooms are supposed to be 'the new minibars') – this is an overlay that has been very carefully worked through in all its serious, playful and theatrical

Figure 1.5   **Lush 'Fruit Stall'**
Reproduced by permission of Lush Limited

implications to genuinely create an experience for the consumer and open up the category in an entirely new way.

Another fascinating example of overlay has been provided by the Sri Lankan-based tea brand Dilmah – the seventh largest tea brand in the world, and the fastest growing. In March 2003 they held a day in New Zealand to launch a new concept in tea – that of the 'single region' tea. We are so used to 'mixed source' tea in tea bags that even the idea of single origin tea (Dilmah is purely from Sri Lanka) is a relatively unusual one these days. But the founder of Dilmah, Merrill J. Fernando, had been intrigued by a booklet he had been given six years earlier about tea and the similarities to wine, and he decided (for reasons we will see below) to explore it further. He recognized that, while he was not a wine expert, many of the things he loved and championed in good tea – mouthfeel, colour, body, tone – were also key discriminators in wine, and was struck that although years ago people had simply asked for a glass of red or a glass of white, nowadays they had been educated to ask for wine not just by the colour but by the country, the region and the grape type. Why could people not be educated to think about and ask for tea in the same way?

Now the sources of those differences in tea were things like the soil, the elevation, the nature of cultivation, just as they were with wines.

And one of the interesting things about Sri Lanka as a tea-growing country is the variety of elevations at which tea is grown – from sea level all the way up to relatively high altitudes. So Fernando took four different elevations of tea watte (or 'gardens' – estates where tea is produced) and compared the mouthfeel and structural qualities of each to its wine equivalent. He established that Yata Watte (meaning 'low-elevation gardens') had the richness and body of a Cabernet Sauvignon, Meda Watte (meaning 'mid-elevation gardens') had the depth and robustness of a Shiraz, Uda Watte (meaning 'high-elevation gardens') had the elegance and liveliness of Pinot Noir and Ran Watte (meaning 'golden gardens') had the bright, supple structure of Champagne.

Drawing on this cross-category model, he produced examples of all four types of 'Watte' Teas and took them to a well-known New Zealand Master of Wines called Bob Campbell. He explained his feeling (as a tea expert) about the analogous relationship, and asked Campbell to taste them (as a wine expert) and see if he agreed. Campbell more than simply agreed: at the subsequent event to launch the Watte Teas in New Zealand he introduced the tea using the rich vocabulary of serious appreciators of fine wine, describing it as 'structured', having 'a hint of figs', being 'chocolatey'. Campbell playfully ventured even further into wine territory, describing Fernando and his two sons as 'tea terroirists' – terroir being an agricultural term used in wine-growing circles to describe the particular limits and characteristics of a growing region that lead to it producing fundamentally different wine to another 'terroir'.

Merrill Fernando's ambition is to push this analogous development for tea even further: once they have introduced the refinement from single origin teas (Sri Lanka) to single region teas (a particular terroir within Sri Lanka), he then intends to take it even more specifically to teas from a single estate within that terroir – effectively the equivalent of a vineyard. It is too early to say at this stage whether this will simply be a provocative piece of Thought Leadership for Dilmah, or a significant step in its pioneering the development of Premium Teas, but what we are interested in here is how Fernando arrived at this Insight of Opportunity. It was, like Lush, from looking at the language, cues and drivers of an entirely different category, and laying them over his own.

The Insight of Brand Neighbourhood: the Insight of Real Competition

A number of the most interesting Challengers in recent times have deliberately set themselves in rather unexpected 'Brand Neighbourhoods' – a set of other brands which they would not naturally be seen by the consumer among or would usually compete against.

Chupa Chups in North America made a conscious effort to remove themselves from their naturally childish neighbourhood of candy by redefining themselves as a brand not for people who like candies but for people with an Oral Fixation. This has influenced their redefined sense of their competition (now encompassing a range of other products outside candy, from things you smoke to things you chew), to their redefined sense of their target (adults – hence handing them out to movie stars at Awards ceremonies), to their redefined sense of their distribution: what other kinds of things to suck can you buy at the till of a grown-ups clothing store? They even persuaded chefs and bartenders at high-end restaurants to use Chupa Chups as witty stirrers in Martini glasses and as decoration for dessert trays.[7] As a nod to their success in this new neighbourhood, *Cosmopolitan* in fact labelled Chupa Chups an 'in' item for 1998, responsible for pushing cigars into the 'out' category.

In the case of Unilever's largest male grooming brand, Axe (or Lynx, as it is known in the UK), the brand owner very deliberately changed the neighbourhood. Simon Clift, the new marketing director, was disconcerted when he took up the brand to find that although his brand was performing well, teens in groups were laughing at his advertising. His first insight was to recognize that their real brand neighbourhood for this target market, the set of brands amongst which Axe had to hold up its head, was not other deofragrances, but brands across a variety of categories that teenage boys had very strong relationships with – Levis, Nike, Reebok, Oasis. The result was to change not just the advertising and advertising model, but indeed the whole way that they thought about their target and indeed went to market (this story is covered more fully in Chapter 11).

This issue of deliberately changing the Neighbourhood becomes even more crucial for brands within larger multi-branded companies, where we have two kinds of Neighbourhoods that we are, consciously or unconsciously locked into: the first being our category set, and the second being the other brands (and the way they do things) in the company we are a part of. In this case a Necessary Pirate will need to see both for what they are, and look outwards for a different, more inspiring and useful Neighbourhood in which to live. We will come to this later on.

The Insight of Grip

In the first three examples of Outlooking, the Insights of Opportunity consisted in importing a set of emotions, behaviours or learnings into our category through our brand. In the last of the four we look at how the brand can see and publicly fix on something outside its category in order to create 'Grip' for itself in its consumer's mind. The manufacture of 'Grip' creates a counterpoint that gives a brand disproportionate salience, one to which the brand is the answer. The brand then uses this 'Grip' to engage the consumer in a new kind of relationship, positioning itself as something that is particularly relevant to the consumer, and particularly now – but something which is outside of the brand's expected remit, and indeed beyond what the consumer has asked for and perhaps even beyond the world of brands. This kind of counterpoint can be an emerging social issue. It was Edward de Bono who made the point that strong new ideas or brand platforms are often born because it is 'the right time and place for them' – that they are perceived to be a 'launch whose time has come'.[8] This happened naturally with the first Mini, which was born after the petrol rationing necessitated by the Suez Crisis on the one hand, and the beginning of traffic congestion on the other. But what we are really interested in here, though, is when a brand needs to *create its own sense* of 'my time has come'. So in launching the new Mini in the USA, 40 years later, it may not have been immediately obvious to the American consumer that this was a product that was relevant to them. It was (in comparison to everything else on the road) an implausibly small car in the only nation in the world where average gas consumption a mile is getting worse because of America's enduring love of large cars, and in particular the SUV. So you have the wrong car for the wrong market; and when you look around the world to see how small cars have positioned themselves elsewhere, you realize that there is only one Global Small Car Strategy, namely 'small on the outside, big on the inside'. Where do you go for Grip?

The brand and agency team found two points of 'Grip': culture points they could couple themselves with to create a sense of particular relevance. The first was the unrest in the Northwest about the effect of SUVs – which the brand and agency team capitalized on by producing launch posters (well covered in the press) proclaiming 'The SUV backlash officially starts now'. They then compounded their brand as a counterpoint to these giants by mounting Minis on top of SUVs and driving them around 21 cities in North America for all to see. The tongue-in-cheek nature of the juxtaposition didn't obscure the serious point, though, that lay beneath.

But this was just the opening salvo. The second key strand of the launch was the championing of a return to civilized motoring with the subsequent campaign, entitled 'Let's Motor': setting the car up as a call for a return to the kind of enjoyable, courteous driving that had long been washed over by the stresses of commuting and road rage. Again, the tone was playful; but again, it caught the imagination through the truth beneath.

Now this was a brand launch which was an array of brilliant ideas, of which these are only two. But central to their initial traction was seeking to find a place to exert a bigger grip on the American imagination than the natural relevance of the car would have created for itself. In a similar way we will later see Camper, a Majorcan shoe company, espousing a philosophy of 'Walk, don't run' as *cri de cœur* against the speeding up of the world all around us.

Sometimes the Grip is to be found in a particular ingrained social attitude or habit one 'needs' to overturn. Coming back to Ingvar Kamprad's company, IKEA have consistently challenged the way we think about furniture and style in cultures all over the world, from Switzerland to the USA. IKEA's most famous campaign in the UK is still 'Chuck out your chintz', a charming but challenging campaign where women all over Britain were challenged to throw out their cheesily patterned curtains and put them in a large rubbish skip in the middle of the street. Again, there is a great insight here: the insight that Middle England was not ready yet for IKEA's aesthetic, on the one hand, and that IKEA was not in a position to tailor its offer to the UK consumer's apparent tastes, on the other. So that if IKEA were to succeed, the brand would not simply have to extol the virtues of IKEA, but puncture the complacencies concerning how the British decorated their homes. And so it set itself up as the counterpoint to 'chintziness', a value representing all the outdated, but sacrosanct embodiments of the way the British live and decorate. It was a challenge, but rendered very charmingly – and IKEA's success in setting up 'chintziness' as a point of Grip in this way was reflected in enormous press coverage and subsequent footfall.

And clearly if one wants, there is an easy Grip to be found in taking as a counterpoint the boundaries of acceptability and taste in one's surrounding culture. The Irish bookmaker PaddyPower is interested primarily in creating PR. One way of doing that is to put up posters of a schoolboy and schoolgirl kissing and apparently offering bets on where the boy's hand will go next; celebrating sexual adventure among school children can always be counted on to get you a certain kind of reaction, if that is what you are looking for, and particularly in a Catholic culture. Again, PaddyPower have attempted to gain a salience for themselves. They are not simply offering new ways to bet on the same things – they are offering new ways (the Internet, in addition to their physical shops) to bet on new things (online alligator racing) as well as the more usual contenders for a flutter.

Archimedes famously said, 'Give me a place to stand, and I can move the world.' But as Challengers, the existing world order isn't necessarily going to give us anything at all: we are going to have to create that place to stand, that point of Grip, for ourselves.

How Diesel Avoid the Navy

Is this list of types of Insights of Opportunity complete? Of course not. You will want to add other examples of Outlooking of your own that I have strangely overlooked. That's good. Just as long as we go beyond looking for the one definitive thing 'the consumer has said' that will show us the way forward. If we find one such Reflective Insight, great. But let's not rely on it.

And this is *everyone's* job, all the time. A key role of research is to outlook; it may be a different kind of research, but it is research all the same. To understand this point, consider how one Challenger systematically tries to constantly keep its distance from the rest of the category. We started with Ingvar Kamprad and IKEA. Let's close with Renzo Rosso and Diesel.

Diesel is a fascinating example of a company that is constantly determined to find the open sea, the unsailed water. They do this through two very simple measures: creating competitive ignorance and looking outside their category. And, interestingly, they have made a more conscious attempt to do this the larger they have become. So, for instance, they have stopped going to Trade Fairs since 1997; Wilbert Das, their creative director, says they 'don't look much at what competition is doing'. And, at the same time, they make sure they look outside their category, in two different ways. First, all the designers are sent out twice a year to rifle through other countries for inspiration: in these expeditions they are not just looking for clothes, although they do go to flea markets a lot, but also photography, objects, art, etc. – anything they can bring back as a source of inspiration.

And the second way they look outside the category is the perspective and example of the founder Renzo Rosso himself. You ask him what kinds of shops he goes into when he's travelling, rather expecting him to talk about other clothing stores – and his first answer is pharmacies, and his fascination with the colours and details of the labels and packaging of the products pharmacies contain. Well, perhaps pharmacies are some particular fetish he has. Actually, no – he goes on to talk about an organic food shop in Tokyo, and his preoccupation with soft drink vending machines and the colours they use – everything but clothes. Diesel was one of the first to pioneer art exhibitions and DJs in store, but now everyone has art exhibitions and DJs in store. So time to move on. Diesel is not watching Levi's, but one might put money on the fact that Levi's are watching them.

Outlooking. It needs to become an intrinsic part of the way we all do everything.

Conclusions

There are, of course, more than four kinds of Insights of Opportunity: we have not talked about product insights, or staff insights or business insights (think Kamprad and his chickens) at all, and how we might Outlook to create Insights of Opportunity in each of these. This area merits a book in itself, rather than a peppy little chapter that attempts to lay out some new ground rules and then leaves the reader to move onto the next topic. And the thoughtful researcher or Consumer Insight Director will feel with some justice that they know this, and can do this (even though they are not usually asked to), and that all these things are discussed at market research conferences, and so on. And at some level they are.

But the bigger world in which that knowledge could operate, and could be applied is not changing, or at least not changing fast enough for the Necessary Pirates among us.

The world is too often looking for opportunity in reflection, and it is devolving the responsibility for that search to a particular function, rather than making it the constant responsibility of the broader team. And if one looks at Challenger organizations of any kind, these two simple but vital shifts are an essential prerequisite for finding new opportunities and a differentiated universe of one's own. But all we are really arguing is that the first step in finding our own path is to recognize a necessary shift:

From	$\longrightarrow$	To
Insight is 'someone else's job'.		Insight is 'our job and their job'.
Insight is insight.		There are two complementary kinds of insight: reflective and opportunistic.
Focus inside the triangle.		Frame the status inside the triangle, but focus on opportunity through Outlooking.

Excuses for the Navy?

The first excuse for the Navy we are therefore looking to strip away here is 'But my consumer doesn't seem to want anything different in the category.' If you are looking for opportunity in the Reflective Triangle, of course they are going to say that. You will need to encourage more opportunistic thinking within the whole team to create real opportunity.

In this, you will be the catalyst – but your whole team will be responsible for the thinking.

And we are also starting to attack the Sixth Excuse – 'But I don't have a founder'. There is a tendency to think that there are two very different kinds of marketing/business philosophies one can live by – there are either companies who are driven by research and the consumer, or there are companies who are driven by vision. Research has no value in the latter, the simplistic view would have it, and nor do insights in the way we usually talk about them. They just have founders who have this Whole Vision Thing.

But what the Kamprad and Rosso stories illustrate is that this is far from true. If you really look at founders, it is not that the Brand Muse one day touches them with her wing and reveals the Whole Vision Thing. They do have insight, and in fact are constantly on the hunt for insight – it is just that they are finding it in a different place, be it a pharmacy in Japan or a food market in China, and asking different kinds of questions when they get there. So the first thing we can learn if we need to be a Pirate, because we cannot afford to stay in the Navy, is not that we should all become gut-driven visionaries, nor that we should wait till the communications to Unleash Hell. In adopting the discipline of the Necessary Pirate, the first behaviour we need to bring out in ourselves is Outlooking – looking for those first Insights of Opportunity somewhere else.[9]

Exercises

As we've said, Outlooking is natural for the Pirates that we have introduced in this chapter. For the majority of us it is not this easy. We therefore need to consciously attempt to adopt this new behaviour before we can move on. So in order to do this more deliberately, let us agree that we are going to try to do three practical things with our teams to force ourselves to Outlook more.

Establishing the Need: the Three Buckets

Ask your brand team to do this exercise together. We have laid out above how it should be done – it is very easy. Make sure you allocate all innovation work honestly, and make sure you allocate all communications honestly (if it helps, do the exercise for last year, rather than this one, with communications that have already been made and perhaps evaluated). What is the shape of your distribution? Why is it the shape it is – because of market or consumer forces, or because of the way your team is doing things? Take two brands you feel your consumer has a growing relationship with outside the category – what would their distribution across these three buckets look like?

Uncompetitive Reviews

We are all doing enough competitive reviews to make us totally fixated with the competition. But perhaps as a complement we should also be doing an Uncompetitive Review once a year. In this Review we would not be allowed to consider or attempt to learn anything from any brand within our category at all. Instead we would have to look at three or four entirely different categories and the emerging brands and drivers in those, and see what it would mean to transfer those to our own.

The Insight Square

At the outset of getting your team together, take a day offsite. Review all the Reflective Insights you have in an hour or so, and use them to frame what needs to be done. Then put them somewhere discreet, on a wall or board of their own.

Use the rest of your time together to work through all four kinds of Insights of Opportunity. You will need to have prepared for this a little – perhaps ask four members of your team to each come back with three initial contenders for each corner. Discuss these, play them out, but also give the team a chance to evaluate more. Make sure you do all four (there may be something that is a combination of two elements) – and feel free to add your own kinds of Outlooking if you feel there are others.

Make no decisions within the session itself – some of the areas you discuss might be initially surprising and strange. Leave it a

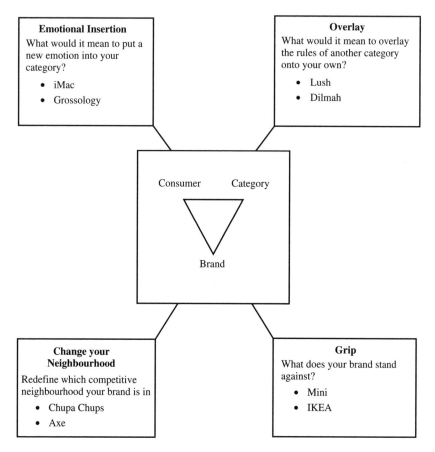

Figure 1.6   **Insights of Opportunity**

week or two before getting back together again to discuss them, and decide which you may want to explore further.

Note: The Brand Neighbourhood Exercise is explained in detail in Chapter 14.

You can get a copy of Figure 1.6 by contacting insightpirates@ eatbigfish.com.

2

Pushing: A Different Kind of Approval

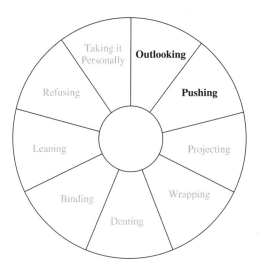

Figure 2.1 **Pushing**

'Push the idea until it breaks.'
Steve Hayden

We cut to the studios of CNNfn, New York. Julian Matthews, the CEO of Discovery Initiatives, an environmentally friendly travel company, is being interviewed about his company, and why it is a Challenger. There are two details that make this a slightly different from the run-of-the-mill interview with a small entrepreneurial business. The first is that Matthews, a Zimbabwean, is sitting at the table wearing a large, dark brown bush hat which is proving an interesting challenge for the studio lighting man, and subject of some flirtatious intrigue for his female interviewer. The second detail is the brochure he has in his hands, which is covered in a coarse, pale brown paper. After some initial chit chat about his company, and its vision (which Matthews describes as 'making you feel like an insider, not a tourist') he passes the brochure cover over to her.

'Mmm,' she says, intrigued, running an elegantly manicured finger over the curiously rough surface, 'what unusual paper.'

'Yes,' says Matthews. 'It's made from something very typically African.'

'What's that?' the interviewer gamely asks.

'Rhino dung,' replies Matthews.

She places the brochure with some alacrity down on the table. And in the animated conversation that ensues Matthews explains that you can make paper out of both rhino and elephant dung because they have very inefficient stomachs, and 80% of the dung is essentially just grass fibre, so holds together very well. Gingerly, the interviewer starts to approach the cover again. And now, merely from what the outside of the brochure is made of, she has a little bit of new knowledge about Africa, a new take on the possibilities of environmentally friendly thinking, and a story about Discovery Initiatives (and this guy who came into the studio wearing a bush hat) that she will take out to three social dinners this week.

And we have yet to mention the effect on the viewers.

Mind the Gap

Dave Trott, the creative director of Walsh Trott Chick Smith in London, once gave a speech entitled 'The Consumer hasn't read the Creative Brief'. His point was simple – in judging a piece of communication we, as the marketing team, know a very great deal about how to interpret the subtleties and nuances of a pack, or a piece of advertising. We know that in accentuating the sunflower a little more on the packaging we are unpacking the new emphasis in our Brand Essence on Naturalness, and that the addition of the green leaves represents the higher proportion of Vitamin D in our product. But the consumer hasn't had the benefit of writing the brief, or compiling the SWOT analysis; they have not the time, background knowledge or interest in interpreting and internalizing cues in this way. They don't realize that your finely wrought tweaks to the packaging are designed to grow your share. They might say nice things in a focus group when forced to think about it for two hours, but at point of sale you have perhaps 1.5 seconds to get them to do it. Perhaps if we DM-ed the brief to the consumer at the same time as the new piece of communication appeared. Trott suggested, they would be able to see more difference in it: those big differences we see, in fact.

The point is that if you really want your target to pick up a difference or a change, it needs to be signalled perhaps more clearly than we might naturally be comfortable with. It is, in short, one thing to have an idea; it is quite another to express it in a form that really drives the idea of difference. In the words of the train announcers, we need to 'Mind the Gap' between *our* understanding and *their* interest and time.

So, one of the characteristics we need to cultivate is an appetite to push for bold differentiation. Sometimes we see this manifested in a blind aversion to sameness – Stelios Haji-Ioannou, founder of easyJet, adopted vivid orange as his chosen colour for the brand simply because no other airline used orange, and it was bright and differentiating, and he needed to stand out. Now one encounters people who are rather dismissive of this kind of simple yet bold differentiation, as being a rather crude way to approach brand building. Not a lot of rigorous brand thinking here, they say – just a visceral rejection of being like anyone else. But let's not get too dismissive. Perhaps that visceral rejection of being like others, and perhaps that appetite for big dramatic slashes of distinction are exactly what we need. It is easy to forget now that over a hundred years ago a newspaper that wished to set itself apart from the competition changed the colour of the paper it was printed on from white to pink, simply to stand out – and now *The Financial Times* is one of the most respected business brands in the world. (It is equally interesting, though, to wonder how pink would have researched in today's groups as a possible colour for the definitive business newspaper were they to be making the change now.)

Which is why leaders of Challenger brands and the teams around them tend to be pushers – people who push the idea and the people developing the idea *further than they would go if left to their own devices.* Renzo Rosso of Diesel is such a pusher. 'In a normal office,' he will tell you: 'the commercial person puts the brake on. But I am in their face saying "Motherfucker, I want more! I want jeans that cost $1000!" I provocate[1] them, I stimulate them.'

So this chapter is about pushing, and its importance in taking an idea further. 'Provocating' the idea developers.

But first, of course, we need to have an idea.

Harry Potter and the Professor of Harvard

In July 2001, the distinguished Business Professor Michael Porter was apparently invited by the Government of Thailand to visit Thailand and spend a single day with them talking about the subject of his most recent book *The Competitive Advantage of Nations*. A natural enough request, you might think. Except that in exchange for this single day spent together, the Thai Government was reportedly offering to pay Professor Porter the sum of one million dollars. For this one day.

The Thai opposition got wind of this, and objected to the cost. In order to justify one million dollars per day, they said, this person would have to be not Michael Porter but Harry Potter. (Which just goes to show that politicians are a great deal wittier in Thailand than they are where I come from.)

But here comes the point: the Thai government had a very interesting response. If Michael Porter, they said, could give them *just one idea* that could significantly impact the way the country thought about itself, or generated wealth, then the investment in that day would have been worth it.

Just one idea.

We all know that simple ideas can change the face of a category. Not necessarily innovations, but ideas – *Glamour* magazine, for example, a female lifestyle magazine whose key breakthrough was to be small enough to fit in a handbag; a big idea, writ small. What this chapter explores though is how far we as a brand group, or as an individual leading that brand group, sometimes need to push the idea in order to really engage the imagination of the consumer.

There are two important underlying concepts here. First, ideas are strategic, not simply the creative expression of strategy; an idea, in fact, can form the basis of a brand's strategic platform. And, second, that pushing that idea until it breaks is a *strategic* imperative for a Challenger, and not simply a creative one. Which means that we will need to think about the notion of approval in a rather different way.

We are going to begin by looking at examples of where this has been successfully done, and what prompted the pushers to push them to a point where they broke through. We are then going to draw together the possible values pushing may have for us – in terms of various situations and benefits, but also over time. We shall see that it has importance across a number of varying brand and category situations – the first of which is where the category itself is in decline.

Reversal: Pushing an Idea to Reverse a Category Decline

'Oh, it's a dead duck in England, wearing hats.
Never see them in London.'

The Old Devils, Kingsley Amis[2]

It is easiest to see how this works where the need is most urgent. Categories in apparent long-term decline, for instance – cigars, coffee, hats – are usually turned around by an idea person who reframes what partaking in that product or experience consists of, in a very arresting way. This is almost always born out of a passion for that category, coupled with a startlingly different way of thinking about it.

Haute couture, for instance, has famously (sometimes notoriously) always been about pushing ideas. But hats have not for many years been a critical part of haute couture. However, Philip Treacy has been widely credited for making hats sexy again – and this was in part due to the fact that he was able to redefine his category by suggesting that the effect of hat-wearing is akin to that of cosmetic surgery.

Here we shall spend some time looking in particular at how with each creation Philip Treacy pushes the idea of what a hat is, or could be, resulting in a dramatic change in the way the fashion business and the public see hat-wearing. Essentially he achieves this through playful exaggeration that engages and creates a reaction from the press and public alike.

His hats have included:

- 'The Ship' – a detailed replica of an eighteenth-century French ship, with full rigging.
- 'The Castle' – inspired by his patron's ancestral home at Doddington, Cheshire, and Ludwig of Bavaria's magnificent palace.
- 'Horns' – a black satin replica of the horns of a flock of ancient Soays sheep.

This sense of playful possibility also extends to the theatre of his shows – he is celebrated for closing off a London street and using a zebra crossing as the catwalk for his first Ready to Wear collection, for example.

So he has prompted a reappraisal of hats from being 'dead ducks' to something chic – and become famous himself through a playful sense of exaggeration, imaginatively pushing his ideas. And there are a number of interesting aspects to the way his ideas get pushed that we can note and learn from:

1. His big ideas always start from very small details. We saw that one of his pieces of Thought Leadership was the hat he created in the guise of an eighteenth-century ship in full sail. The original idea for this came from a little detail his muse, Isabella Blow, had put his way: a passage about the miniature replica ships worn as corsages by the wives of sailors lost in battle from a novel she had given him. He simply pushed and pushed a small idea until it became an outrageously big one.
2. Although the examples I have touched on above are essentially about pushing ideas one doesn't normally associate with hats (from sheep to ships), his sense of pushing the idea to its limits has also at times addressed the *basics* about a hat, such as how broad you can make its brim. In one case he produced a hat so broad in the brim that Isabella Blow simply could not walk in through a door head on when wearing it – she had to turn and walk in sideways. And in doing so she made a much more theatrical entrance.
3. One of the things that is interesting here for us is the relationship and difference in the development of an idea between Isabella Blow and Philip Treacy. Isabella Blow is Treacy's 'Muse', in the sense that she is at once a source of inspiration and the model for his creations.

But she also fulfils another function. Whenever Treacy presents an idea to her, she never says, 'You've gone too far;' she says: 'You've not gone far enough.' As Rosso would say, she provocates him. The ideas person and the pusher in this case are two different people.

4. As a commercial business, Treacy makes his reputation but not his money out of hats of sailing ships and sheep. While we may notice and admire the boldness of what he designs for his muse, what he sells to you and me is something we are much more comfortable with: 'People have this idea that if they come here, I'm going to insist they walk out with an eighteenth-century sailing ship on their head. It's not like that. I want them to find the hat that makes them look great and feel great. Humour is a part of hats, but no one wants to look silly'.[3]

Stagnation: Pushing an Idea to Break Through a Growth Ceiling

Until 1997, Burberry was a profitable but essentially static British clothing brand specializing in two products: raincoats and scarves. The arrival of Rose Marie Bravo and (later) Christian Bailey precipitated a drive for growth, which encompassed two main thrusts – the move from a staid brand to one that could compete in the fashion neighbourhood of Gucci and Prada, and at the same time the transition from a brand reliant on a very small range of weather protection products to one that could also compete in warmer weather and hotter climates.

Central to success here was of course the way they used the check motif. Burberry had used its signature motif as a lining material for a number of years – and yet in many ways the check had become one of the things that made it seem stuffy and conservative. It would have been easy to throw out the check, or redesign it in more radical colours; and yet instead one of the key things that gave the brand the visibility and sense of reinvention following 1997 was the extent to which they pushed the idea of how they used the check motif. Taking it from being a detail to a dominant dimension of the brand, they pushed it into areas that no one had expected.

Burberry started to push. Their 'Dog Show' advertising campaign for Autumn 1999, which featured dogs in Burberry outfits, proved a particular draw to the British press, but the key photo shoot in many ways was the one that took place for the 2000 range. Now the rather masculine image of the brand might have suggested that one first extended across other male products and then, when this was established, extend further into women's wear. But Bravo and her team didn't follow this logic at all. They had produced, for the very practical reasons we discussed before (wanting to be a four-season company, able to sell summer products and compete in warm climates), a range of women's as well as menswear, and had hired Mario Testino to do the shoot, which would feature Kate Moss. It was Testino who suggested that they deliberately overexpose the more unexpected Burberry items parading the check device – the bikini and the dress with the spaghetti straps, for example, which were a long way from what the public had historically thought of Burberry and Burberry users.

The new sense of Burberry that emerged as being playful, no longer stuffy, not taking itself too seriously – all this came from the degree in which they pushed the idea, not just the direction in which they pushed it. We didn't just think, on seeing Kate Moss in a bikini, 'Oh, I see, Burberry are now telling us they sell leisurewear.' We thought, 'I had never imagined a bikini made out of that before.'

Bailey and Bravo continued to push core elements of the brand in the years that followed into unexpected places. The check motif was explored in textured black on black. The belt buckle from the trench coat was taken into handbags, shoes. They make it a driving principle to reinvent their core icons more or less every year.

And the results? The increased desirability helped Burberry's sales surge from £400 million to £1.2 billion in just six years, with less than 50% of its then sales coming from its historical core products of raincoats and scarves.

Adversity and Arrival: Pushing an Idea to Create Impact at Launch

In the case of Crunch, pushing the idea was what allowed them to launch successfully in spite of a functional disadvantage with intolerant consumers.

Crunch is a gym chain that started as an aerobics studio in 1989 in New York's East Village. New Yorkers are not famous for a benign 'live and let live' attitude towards perceived faults in neighbours and businesses, and yet Crunch's facilities were far from ideal – they had erratic air conditioning, no lockers, and inadequate after-hours security. The only way they were going to make it, it seemed, was to genuinely create strong reasons to attract users of the fitness market from other clubs with better facilities.

It is not hard to work out the two key category issues with gyms: one, many are elitist and intimidating, and two, the process of going to a gym is dull and repetitive (I am quietly confident that in future years our grandchildren will find it hilarious that we spent so much of our leisure time walking painfully up a moving staircase that never actually got anywhere. 'Hello? Grandpa? What kind of bonehead idea was *that*?')

So Crunch's idea was to make exercise more fun; not because they were wacky pranksters, but because their commercial survival and ultimate success depended on delivering a reason for coming that was greater than the disadvantages of their facilities. Now one wonders what we ourselves might have done if this was our brief. Imagine that we got a small group of us into a room and started to brainstorm how to make going to the gym more fun. Hire funnier instructors, someone throws out; or change the music more regularly, adds another. Perhaps even have an in-house DJ. We stick these ideas up on the wall and admire them. Not bad, we think. Some novel stuff there. Definitely a start.

But Crunch pushed the idea of engaging workout ideas to a completely different level. Beginning with the likes of Disco Yoga and Underwater Cycling, they moved on to offer courses as varied as Fire-fighter Workouts, Circus Training, and the Goddess Workout (a belly dancing class). In case you think these are just interesting titles for the same old stuff, the Fire-fighter workout asks you to haul real fire fighting equipment over an obstacle course, while the speakers around you play the sound of sirens and 911 calls. The Circus Training ends with the group forming a human pyramid. And the belly dancing class is taught by a 'real-life gypsy'; we are not sure how she might be able to validate this (Certificates? Letters from her mother?), but it seems to be more than a slap of lipstick on the same tired old routines – they in their own way have pushed the reality of the idea as well as the concept of it. And in case you think this is an intriguing niche brand, they built it up to a $75 million business in eleven years, before selling to Bally.[4]

An example with a different kind of adversity to overcome – that of being a minority interest category – is that of the launch of the *O Brother, Where Art Thou?* soundtrack, by the label Lost Highway. Although in principle an obvious spin-off of the Coen Brothers movie, it was not a great time to launch a bluegrass album: sales even of contemporary country music were falling – why would anyone want to listen to something as hardcore as vintage-style bluegrass? But with a promotional budget of just $500,000 Lost Highway and the Coen brothers set out to really push the idea – in a number of key directions.

The first was 'Authenticity'. In producing the album, they recorded it to sound exactly as if it came from the period of the film. Using a 1930s' stage set-up, and just one vintage microphone for all instruments and vocals simultaneously, they created at once an authentic sound and a newsworthy backstory. They used only musicians who would be respected by hardcore bluegrass fans. 'We didn't want to act like a big fat record company coming into their world,' says Kia Florita, the VP Marketing at Lost Highway. 'There's no one on that soundtrack that isn't completely respected by that community. We didn't try to present it as something it wasn't.'[5] And to wrap the sound Lost Highway produced a promotional CD that looked as if it were vinyl and put it in a tin designed to look like 'Dapper Dan's pomade', with a picture of the George Clooney character from the film on the front.

Building on this, the second key strand was the degree to which they were careful to root it in grassroots credibility and word-of-mouth support. Lost Highway's first target was hardcore bluegrass enthusiasts (half of whom in this case were themselves keen musicians) – before the film was even launched, they distributed the promotional CD at the 2000 Annual Convention of the International Bluegrass Music Association in Louisville, Kentucky. Some 2,300 strong, it was important to get their respect. They liked it. The result – speciality bluegrass shops sold and recommended the album.

Next they offered 1,500 copies as an incentive for people pledging money to NPR (a commercial-free radio station in the USA) – at the same time as advertising in 'free thinking' journals like the *Utne Reader* and the *New Yorker*. Word, interest and sales grew. By the time the film rolled out, it was selling over 50,000 copies a week. And by the time the DVD came out, it was hitting 90,000 a week. It spent 22 weeks at number one on the Billboard country music charts, 12 weeks on top of the soundtrack charts, and reached Number 13 on Billboard's top current albums, ahead of J-Lo, with very little airplay on music stations, country or otherwise, and a currency way beyond the audience of the film itself. With a promotional budget of $500,000 it has now sold over 3 million copies worldwide; while the film was a moderate success, the album was huge.

Generic Propositions: Pushing an Idea to Get Beyond the Cliché

So we have seen that adversity is a natural clarion call to pushing the idea, and we have seen that the degree of the idea defines the brand and our reaction to it as much as the idea itself. But all of these have succeeded through pushing an already differentiated idea: it is worth now spending a little time on looking at Challengers that have all succeeded by pushing the *same* idea – and potentially a very clichéd and tired idea (that of putting the customer at the centre of the company) – but in significantly different directions.

Putting the customer at the heart of the company is a concept that is frighteningly easy to pay lip service to. And much less easily done. And, indeed, I can hear a couple of you at the back stifle a polite yawn at this point. Customer service? And we are supposed to be holding this up as an example of Challenger behaviour? Come, come.

There are two pushbacks on this. The first is that our understandable cynicism comes from the difference between the number of people who put it as important in their mission statements and the number of companies that really deliver it. This in many ways is a different dimension to 'Mind the Gap', in terms of the distance between the motherhood stuff we produce at the top, and the realities of how we actually refer to customers at the point of contact (what IKEA rather charmingly calls 'The Meeting'). When it really comes down to it, how many categories genuinely deliver decent customer service? US car dealers still refer to customers as 'Ups'; the now defunct British Railways relatively recently used to refer to its passenger customers as SLF – Self-Loading Freight; a cable operator talks about customers as RGUs (revenue-generating units). Indeed, Hans Snook said that the reason Orange really understood customer service was because he came from an entirely different business altogether – one which did understand service and the importance of really getting things right: the hotel business; most of the customer service disciplines within his rivals were senior communications executives who had never been outside telecommunications. But the point we are trying to make here is that Challengers don't stop where everyone else does. They seem to take everything a stage further, beyond. Push even apparently bland ideas until they become interesting.

So let's consider here three interesting stories of people and brands who found real traction taking the apparently generic idea of putting the consumer at the heart of the company. The first is admittedly a cheat, because it is an example of a company that, although late in the day discovering a strong brand device (a monkey called, well, Monkey), was undone by the poor business model it represented. But it is such an interesting story that it is worth discussing anyway, in case it holds some inspiration for us in the future.

Clarissa – 'What Would the Consumer Think?'

Jeremy Dale became Marketing Director of the ill-fated ITV Digital when the business was already on the way down. Arriving at his first board meeting, he was horrified to find a conversation in progress about hiding a cost increase to the consumer in a rejigged price tariff. Uncertain at the time what to do, he let the meeting run its course and then considered his options.

His basic idea was that as a customer-centred company (supposedly) what they should be doing as a group is asking what they thought their customer would feel about any initiative if they were sitting right there at the table with them. Most of us would leave it at that. Point well made – perhaps we will genuinely bear in mind the consumer from now on.

But Dale pushed the idea. He went out and bought a female mannequin, and dressed it in women's clothes. He brought the mannequin to the next board meeting and sat her in one of the chairs around the table. As the board sat there looking at this new member of the group, Dale's first action was to apologize to the board; he said he had let them down through not speaking up when he had been concerned at the previous meeting. He then introduced them to the mannequin, whom he called Clarissa. He suggested that they needed to have a physical reminder of their customer there at every decision-making point as a board – when making any decision they should ask themselves 'What would Clarissa say?'

Clarissa came to each of the board meetings for the next six months; the consumer, in effect, physically sat in on and influenced the decision-making process.

The Story of Tommy Bahama – 'We Are Our Consumer'

If this sounds entertaining, though short-lived, it is not that big a step from the reasons behind the undoubted success of Tommy Bahama.

We are accustomed to men and women launching ranges of clothing in their own style. Ralph Lauren, Tommy Hilfiger, Donna Karan, even Jacqueline Smith perhaps. And Tommy Bahama is the latest in this rather egotistical trade. Launched in 1991, he has grown his business to over $300 million. Mr Bahama has a very clear set of values, enthusiasms (vintage convertibles) and a very specific lifestyle – golfer, beach lover, bar enthusiast, outdoor guy; he knows what he likes and he spends a lot of time doing it.

The difference between Tommy Bahama and Tommy Hilfiger, though, is that Tommy Bahama does not exist. He is the very detailed creation of three men, a lot of beer and years of conversation.

Bob Emfield and Tony Margolis met during their days working for a jeans manufacturer in 1969, and developed a friendship that resulted in them buying adjoining beachside holiday homes on the coast in Florida. They and their wives took to idly fantasizing on vacation about a guy who never had to return back to 'real life' from this beach idyll – how and where he lived, his lifestyle and enthusiasms. His perspective on life and how it should be lived.

In 1993 they had such a clear idea of the character of Tommy Bahama (as he became called), and the kind of clothing he might represent – elegant, tropical, with a leaning towards silk – that they enlisted a third partner as head of design and launched a clothing brand to suit the character.

The first year was a disaster. Their overheads were too high, they failed to focus on one brand (Tommy Bahama was one of a portfolio of three they launched at the same time), and their distribution target of large department stores wanted large, recognized brands like Nautica and Polo, rather than small boutique brands like Tommy Bahama.

So they regrouped. Refocusing on the Tommy Bahama brand, they switched their distribution emphasis to speciality stores. By 1994 they had reengineered the business, and people were starting to understand the story of Tommy Bahama – because of the way the sales force told his story:

> All of our initial reputation was coming through our sales force, to our wholesale accounts who would then tell these . . . stories to their clients about the Tommy Bahama vision and so it sort of got around that way.

But even though the trade warmed to the story, the partners found it hard to get them to display the brand in the way they felt it needed:

> The first real step that we took in terms of communicating directly with the consumer came about seven years ago, when we started the retail project. And the original thoughts behind that came from the fact that we were a little frustrated because when we went to a trade show we had a trade show booth that we installed that was like an old island beach bar, and instead of there being liquor bottles on the shelves, there was clothing. You walked up to a bar and you sat on a bar stool, and there was a grass thatched roof over it, and the sales force would stand behind the bar as a bar tender, but they'd present product instead of booze. And the message was really clearly delivered; people could tell from 100 yards away what the Tommy Bahama brand was about, and they came to the booth understanding that vision.
>
> When the product got to their stores, unfortunately, they didn't make that kind of investment and they were putting our stuff on glass-topped

tables and chrome rail racks, and mahogany shelves that were there for the traditional brands. And we decided to open a Tommy Bahama store to show them what could happen with the product if it was, in fact, presented in an appropriate environment.

They found a potential location for this first store in Florida, close to their vacation homes – and an interesting and unexpected challenge:

> When we made the first trip to try to find a site, we made a presentation to a prospective landlord down in a town called Naples, Florida, and she was so enamoured with the story we were telling, she said, 'Well, if I made more space available to you at a really good deal, what would you do with it?'

They approached answering this challenge by asking themselves the question of what their mythical character/founder would do. Initially thinking of a juice bar, they felt on reflection that something to eat and a good microbrew would be more the man's style, with a casual, fun, tropical atmosphere – 'Steel drums, full moon, palms wafting in the breeze.'[6]

What would Tommy do? Tommy would open a restaurant – and so, at a cost of $1.2 m, they opened the retail store with a restaurant attached to it over Christmas 1995. The 'browse-dine-buy' idea has proved an enormous success: each half of the concept in Naples was turning over around $7 m a year by 2001, and they have opened five more such combinations, besides 28 stand-alone stores. And 'What would Tommy do?' has become a key filter for every decision in the company:

> This guy, Tommy Bahama, and hopefully his female counterpart, have become real people to our company, and we kind of talk out what Tommy would and would not do. 'Would Tommy go there? Would Tommy drink that? Would Tommy drive that car?'

In some ways this clear sense of Tommy Bahama is not so much a representation of the consumer as a representation of a founder, with his own very clear sense of personal culture and style, and producing a range of goods for others like him. The management at Tommy Bahama do indeed pay attention to the consumer – the cashiers in their stores noticing women were buying extra small men's shirts to wear themselves prompted the company to extend further into a women's line – but that seems to offer a different kind of value to them: perhaps more a question of *where* to take the products, rather than what the style and concept of *what* they are doing should be.

One more piece of learning here. Towards the end of the interview, Margolis remarked, 'At the basis of any marketing philosophy, there has to be a story that's going to be told.' And of course usually in single brand companies the story is the story of the founder and how they started. But Tommy Bahama suggests there is another way to create 'the story that is going to be told' that underlies our brand. And it suggests that to be powerful, before it can genuinely be clear enough to influence decision-making, you have to push this story. Perhaps as far as these three men pushed theirs.

Dancing with Egg: Pushing the Idea Internally

When Prudential set up Egg as the UK's first Internet bank, the vision of CEO Mike Harris for his fledgling company was that a key part of its differentiation was going to lie in customer service. And this is where those scoffing at me before for even mentioning customer service start reaching for something to throw. But hold fire with that sourdough roll: the point of this story (of this chapter, even) is that Challengers don't stop where everyone else does. They seem to take everything a stage further, beyond. And Harris didn't stop at 'customer service' – he had a very particular and new vision about good customer service, and what it was like when done well: he saw it as like a dance between Egg and its customer.

Think about what it means to dance. Two people come together by mutual consent. They move flexibly and comfortably around the dance floor for an agreed period of time. One is leading and the other allowing themselves to be led, but it is subtly and comfortably done – no one is dragging anyone else around the dance floor. They move at the same pace, respecting each other's space – no one treads on anyone's feet. At the end of a certain period of time they break apart by mutual consent, acknowledge the end of the dance, and then return to their previous places. How often they repeat this is again up to them – it can be initiated every five minutes or once a year – that is for them to decide.

And this analogy too would be uninteresting if Harris had kept it to himself. But he made it part of the language and culture of the nascent Egg. So he recruited his key people on the basis of this vision. He then brought in dancing instructors to train his sales teams. And in fact he and they came to feel so strongly about it that they decided that they would make it a key part of interview procedure for all new employees – unless the potential recruit agreed to dance during the interview they would not accept them.

What is our reaction to this? I suspect we are divided. Some of us will find this very strange and flakey; if we were moving into financial services, this would be one to avoid, we think. Dance in an interview? In daylight? Sober? I think not, my friend.

Others of us, conversely, will think this appealing – if we were to work in a financial services company, then this would be the one for us. It shows they have a spark of life, of being different. And they are obviously very different from their large, conservative parent.

How Far is Too Far?

What is the breaking point of an idea? Let me answer the question a different way. Some time ago I went to a day organized by an advertising agency for one of its principal clients, a large multinational personal products company. The day was started by the agency Media Director on the business. He stood up with a large roll of blank paper, a metre deep. 'I have stuck some ads on here for us to look at,' he says, 'Let's have a look at them.' And he starts unrolling the paper.

The roll is a long one, and within 15 seconds it is clear that it is not going to be a solo task. 'Oh dear, I'm going to need a little help,' he says, innocently. He tentatively asks the Marketing Manager if she would stand up and take one end – and she starts pulling the paper away from him. When there is 12 feet of paper covered in ads between them – more than the length of the meeting room table – he asks her to stop. 'OK, it looks like we're going to need another pair of hands,' he says. The Brand Manager volunteers. They pull out another ten feet (they are now running along two sides of the large meeting room table) and the roll of paper still has plenty left to give. 'Um . . .' says the Media Director – and another member of the team offers to do the last stretch.

So eventually there are four people standing up, holding a single piece of paper about 30 feet long, a metre wide, filled wall to wall with colour print ads, running around the back and up both sides of the horseshoe-shaped table. We look at all these print ads and consider them. The Media Director asks, 'What have they all got in common?'

We scratch our heads.

'They are all from one issue of *Cosmo*,' he says. 'Now, do we need a big idea, or a small idea? And do we want it to look the same as everyone else's ads, or do we want it to look different?' It was an easy question to answer.

So we all need a touch of Isabella Blow. Perhaps the first question we should be asking is: does it go far enough? The breaking point is probably further along than we think.

Tough Love

Two final points. The first is that in order to push, you have to have someone who screens your ideas as well – because not every idea is a good one. Lord Leverhulme's famous complaint that he knew half his advertising money was wasted, but just didn't know which half, is dwarfed by the dilemma of the brilliant but troubled writer Philip K. Dick, best known as the man who wrote the story that became the film *Blade Runner*, who complained: 'I have written and sold 23 novels, and all are terrible except one. But I'm not sure which one.'[7]

Now there are two potentially significant variables in the nature of the authors that explains this differing range of uncertainty. First, Philip K. Dick was a creative, and Lord Leverhulme was not. And, second, as far as we know Lord Leverhulme was not a speed addict taking (as Dick claimed) 1000 methedrine pills a week when he made his own observation. But even so, these variables simply make the problem one of degree. What is the solution?

Suggesting people use their head less and their gut more in evaluating ideas is a step in the right direction. But it ignores the fact that not everyone is a good judge of ideas – not everyone has a good gut, in this regard. They may be good at all sorts of other things, but the judging of ideas should be taken away from them and given to someone who really does have the knack. This is a hard thing to do in tight teams, but it is so central to the success of the venture that we are being unfair to the rest of the team – and the brand opportunity – if we do not do so. Training does not necessarily help – to some degree you either have it or you don't.

The second point to close on is that pushing a bad idea doesn't make it a good one. And three pushed ideas at the same time are not necessarily better than one. Moby Grape were arguably the first victims of this: the first example of a brand to be killed by Bad Use of Multiple Pushed Ideas at launch. A technically strong folk-rock group with a taste for harmonization, they had accepted a contract with Columbia in the late 1960s, and the record label were excited enough by their new acquisition to want to make the launch of the first Moby Grape album one unlike anything that had ever been seen or heard before.

Even then releasing a double-A side was relatively unusual, yet Columbia decided to blow that idea out of the water: they would release no less than five singles from the band's debut on the same day. For the citizens of LA they would provide an elephant painted purple – think Grape – that would walk down Sunset Boulevard on the day of the launch at its own magnificently slow pace (when else in the 1960s would you be able to say with a clear conscience you saw a purple elephant without being high?). And, for those lucky enough to attend the launch party of these inevitable future rock legends, there would be bottles of wine with a Moby Grape label on each. 700 such bottles, to be on the safe side.

Forgetting to provide corkscrews to open the wine bottles was perhaps an omen. Only one of the five singles charted at all, and that at number 88. The group did not pass into success and legend as planned, and indeed things really began to unwind when the guitarist ended up taking an axe to the drummer's door under the belief that he was the Antichrist. Small wonder, perhaps, that the bassist subsequently chose to join the Marines and go to Vietnam as a preferable alternative to staying in the band.

Now it may simply have been lack of talent, of course. But one could argue that the launch failed not because they didn't push an idea, but because they pushed too many of them – and that each idea was solely aimed at generating publicity rather than communicating a key quality about the band or generating an intense relationship.[8]

Summary: A Different Kind of Approval Process

Successful Piracy depends on not just having an idea; it's about our behaviour with that idea once it appears – and in particular our preparedness to really push it. To recognize that even small ideas can become interesting if they are pushed as far as they can go. This represents a very different kind of idea review from the normal approval process, so we need to be very deliberate about the order in which we ask our questions: let's not ask 'Is this too much?' until we have asked 'Is this enough?' Remember the gap. Remember the gap. If you are not a natural pusher, work with someone who is.

And bear in mind that consumers get comfortable rather too quickly, even when initially stretched. The things that make us at first gasp in surprise – 'a lime green computer!', 'a Burberry check bikini!' or 'a communications company called Orange!' – are all too soon things that we take in our stride. There is a story about the 'King of Diamonds', Harry Winston, putting a new ring on the finger of Vala Byfield, a Russian beauty married to an American hotelier. When the woman gasped at the sheer size of the enormous square cut stone in the diamond ring on her finger, Winston replied reassuringly 'Don't worry, Mrs Byfield. You'll see it gets smaller the more you wear it.'[9] He was right, of course: shortly afterwards her husband was signing the requisite cheque. We get used to it; what seems initially very different is soon something we become very used to. We must size our new rings for how they will feel in a few months, rather than how they feel on the first time of wearing.

And the Excuses for the Navy we have tackled here? The Second – 'But I do not have a large advertising budget', and the Third – 'But I am in packaged goods'.

Exercises

Clarissa

Have a three-dimensional mannequin of your consumer sit in your meetings with you. Give her or him a name, but not a face. Ask them how much of what you are doing in your marketing plan they will genuinely notice, up to and including their three seconds in front of you at the point of purchase. Make them tired and intolerant, and then ask the question again. Use them to remind you of how little time they think about you; how big and how visible your idea will have to be before it catches their attention.

Tommy Bahama

What is your brand's story? Where could it start from? Who is the protagonist? What is the world they live in? What matters – and doesn't – in this world? What are the emotions and objects that most vividly bring this world and protagonist to life? And so on.

3

Projecting: A Different Kind of Consistency

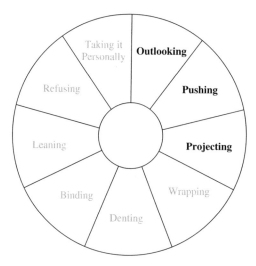

Figure 3.1 **Projecting**

Points of Projection

F or all that we talk about using a variety of media to communicate with our desired customers, most of us are still remarkably conventional in how we see and use those media, and indeed what we see as a medium at all.

This is largely influenced by the size of our budget. In terms of mass market advertising, for instance, if we have over X million doubloons to spend, we regard ourselves as a TV advertiser. If we have under X million but more than Y million doubloons, then we are a print advertiser. And if we have less than even that, we put a brave face on it and do some tactical outdoor advertising at times of key seasonality, together with some ingenious linking-in with shopping trolley placards (to show we really are right on the nail when it comes to thinking this whole thing through from soup to nuts). And look forward to the day when we work on a brand that has a really big budget.

While I understand we are sensitive to the nature of the medium and the kind of conversation we want to have, much of this is in reality driven by a notion of 'what we can afford'. While we have intriguing excursions into ambient and viral marketing, for instance, for most of us they are titillating flirtations on the side, a diverting relish beside the meat and potatoes of what we are really serving up.

Yet the most interesting consumer relationships are being built by the people behind Challengers who cannot afford very much at all. And who are in effect using media that are not currently regarded as media much more powerfully than some of us are using advertising.

Consider, for instance, the following two requests for customer feedback, both from coffee chains. The first is a circular card titled:

'. . . Because we value your opinion!'

Underneath these words is a request to rate their drinks, service, prices and cleanliness on a three-point scale – excellent, average, poor. There are a couple of other questions (what we bought, whether we are a regular customer, and so on), a Freepost address to send it off to, and then a close:

'Thank you for your patronage!'

This was on the counter of a coffee chain in South London that serves a good cup of coffee. And we understand that they mean well because they have resorted to using punctuation (always a worrying sign) to convince us that they really are being sincere. But the chances of us really filling in whether we rate their coffee or food as 'excellent, average or poor' and sending it off to a black box in Birmingham (unless we plan to sue them because the damn stuff is too hot) is next to nil; this little circular card sits dutifully on the counter and looks at us, and we briefly look at it, but it is, for all its earnest punctuation, a piece of paper that they have to produce and we have to respect in some small way, and that's it. It does nothing to build a relationship with us.

Now consider exactly the same kind of request, but from a company that is using every medium it has to project its sense of who and why it is. It too is on a white card. It reads:

I think comment cards are silly.

They're analysed by weirdos in ivory towers.
My name is Sandra, I'm the General Manager of Pret at Kingsgate. My team and I meet every morning. We will discuss the points you've raised … the good, the bad and the ugly. If we can deal with it ourselves we will. If we can't, I will forward your card to Julian Metcalfe at the office. I know he'll do what he can.

Either way, thanks.

I suggest to you that if we got a hundred people into a room, showed each of them this card, and asked them to write down, with no other knowledge of this company or its conventional communications:

- What the company's values were
- Who this company was for and who it was not for
- The degree to which it cared about its customers
- The degree to which it cared about producing a quality product
- Whether they were interested in having a further relationship with this company or not

Then, not simply would they be able to write all this down, but also what each of them wrote would be pretty similar to what the person next to them had written. And yet all this piece of paper is apparently trying to be is a request for customer feedback, a request such as 75% of B2C service companies in the world have.

So what's the point here?

Well, the last chapter was about Pushing – the behaviours that we needed in order to make sure the 'what' of our idea is made big enough to be noticed in the way we need it to be noticed. This chapter is about Projecting – it looks at *how* we project the identity we attach to that sense of brand opportunity, once we know what it is, at each individual point of communication. As such, we are changing our thinking from being about 'communication experts' to 'projection experts': we are not trying to put across the brand message at each interaction so much as we are trying to engage the consumer with a provocative or intriguing projection of our identity and idea.

So the first point of this example of the two feedback cards is not, of course to suggest that the future lies in how we ask for customer feedback, but to make the far simpler point that Challengers do not seem to see media in the same way as those of us with conventional media budgets do. What they realize is that if one regards a medium as *any vehicle for building or nurturing a relationship with an existing or potential customer*, then we all have far more media at our disposal than we think we do; we are simply not regarding them as media at the moment. And it is therefore essential that we reconsider our potential range of media. This broadsides the old status-driven 'her budget's bigger than my budget' – because if everything is a potential medium, our currency needs to be ideas, not money. And we need to see our job as being constantly to project our identity, rather than just be graphically consistent in the way that we use it.

Let us look at another two examples of this. First, in another service brand, and then in a packaged goods brand.

As this book was going to press, you might have been forgiven for thinking that the coffee thing was now all sewn up. Starbucks have redefined the category, and shown everyone else how it needed to be done: passion, sophistication, romancing the bean and the brew on the one hand, and the creation of that famous Third Space in which to meet or kick back on the other – this is what coffee is all about now, surely. And there is an everyman sophistication in that pure white cup with its mermaid logo and that row of little boxes on the side, to remind them and us of how we have customized our own particular order. So if you want to succeed as a brand in this market, these are now the rules of the game: you romance the coffee, offer a sophisticated multisensory experience, create a little new language and, boom, you're there. And indeed a whole variety of me-toos have been taking up arms and doing exactly the same.

So let's not take Starbucks but a Challenger to Starbucks. A coffee Pirate. The number four in the UK, and in fact until recently the only one of the top four to be profitable (more on this later).

A Journey through Puccino's

First, a little bit of context. If you talk to Andrew Sanders, Puccino's Marketing Director, he will tell you there are two parts to the brand's success, and both hinge on the imperative of customer loyalty. The first part of driving loyalty is to only locate themselves in high traffic areas where the same people pass by each day – railway stations, for example, but not airports. And the other part of driving that customer loyalty?

Well, let's approach that from a customer's-eye view. Let's abandon our daytime disguise as sophisticated marketers of the world, and slip into our leisure selves as just ordinary people responding to the world and the environment as it passes by.

God, that feels good.

Now, more specifically, I'd like us to imagine that you and I are in need of some caffeine, and Puccino's is a coffee shop that, although previously unknown, the two of us stumble across in our hour of need. Scarcely looking at the menu, we order two large lattes, and sit down.

Figure 3.2 **Puccino's 'Kiss Me' Cup**
Reproduced by permission of Jim Smith and Puccino's Ltd

Figure 3.3   **Puccino's Moccacheena Cup 'On Being Well Over It'**
Reproduced by permission of Jim Smith and Puccino's Ltd

The first merciful gulp inside us, we start to look around. You look at your cup. It does not have the austere white distance of Starbucks, though it does have its equivalent of the little boxes for customization on the side. But this cup is a light blue, and it talks to you: 'Kiss me', it says, but then warns 'No tongues' – this is a first date, after all (Figure 3.2). And those boxes for customization on the side? Well, it certainly has those, but they seem not to mention decaf or shots or milk type at all. Instead they say:

No Drum and Bass

Sprinkling of Irony

Anchovies

Ceiling tiles on top

You look over at my cup, which is pink. On one side it launches into a plangent lament about 'overitness' – people reaching a point in their lives when they are suddenly 'over it' – but it does so in a very particular way (Figure 3.3).

Huh.

You sip the coffee. It is pretty good, but you decide you need the sugar rush as well as the caffeine hit. So you go over to the sugar counter, grab a handful of sachets of brown sugar, and buy a couple of biscuits at the same time. As you start to tear open the first sachet, you notice the words on the side. 'Don't diet', instructs the first. 'Sprinkle on shoulders of enemy' suggests the second. 'Put in coffee and shut up' commands the third (Figure 3.4).

Figure 3.4 **Puccino's Sugars**
Reproduced by permission of Jim Smith and Puccino's Ltd

Well, okay. And the description of your biscuit? (Figure 3.5)

We look a little more closely at the place the two of us have just walked into. Above the coffee bar where we have been served is a large

Figure 3.5   **Puccino's Biscuit**
Reproduced by permission of Jim Smith and Puccino's Ltd

sign showing me where everything is. This way, the way we have come in, offers, we are told: 'Crackly radio ... false ceiling ... quite nice staff ...'. And written on the wall behind the counter as an apparent reminder to their staff are five key instructions:

'Things to remember when heading out'

- Smile
- Clear nostrils
- Stop swearing
- Apply factor 15
- Act all professional

And so it goes on. Is this a trade-off because the coffee isn't up to scratch? They can't serve coffee so they might as well be funny? Well, no. The humour is a part of their strategy, but it is not at the expense of the product or the quality of service, both of which they are very proud of.

They have a serious reason for being funny: Andrew Sanders of Puccino's will tell you that humour is a necessary and fundamental part of their identity because they grew up on rail stations (we saw at the beginning that the traffic patterns of rail travellers were a key reason for their profitability). And those of us familiar with British rail services will know that they have historically had a rather informal relationship with punctuality – so that if one is waiting in the driving rain of an English winter (or indeed the driving rain of an English summer) for the cancelled 7.35a.m. service to London Waterloo, offering someone a smile as well as a good cup of coffee is an excellent way to start building a relationship with them. A smile while commuting in the wet of a London autumn is an unmet consumer need, if you like.

A by-product of all this – of having cups that say Kiss Me and sugar that talks – is that it depositions Starbucks just a little. Just a little, but enough. God, you think, it makes me realize how seriously The Big Brand takes itself. Maybe it could do with a little lightening up.

But the learning that we need to take from this story is not the need to be funny, but rather the meaning of consistency for a Challenger. In Puccino's case, it is the fact that this sense of the brand's identity is *constantly* being projected at *every* point of contact with the brand (even those as apparently pedestrian and insignificant as inch-square packets of brown sugar), that creates such a strong sense in us of who this brand is and whether we want to have a relationship with them. This is not a consistency of message in the conventional sense of 'the proposition being taken through the line'; it is, however, a much more surprising and engaging kind of consistency: that of a brand that has such a clear sense of itself that it simply cannot help showing that in *everything* it says and does.

Furthermore, this spirit of constant conversation is not simply part of a consumer-facing company 'image', it is a spirit that is taken through to their staff. When Puccino's started, they didn't want to recruit staff who had been through catering school, because they wanted their people to be genuine in the enthusiasm with which they served, and they thought that catering school killed genuine, friendly service. So they advertised for staff in *The Stage*, the weekly for out-of-work actors. For a while this produced a good flow of enthusiastic, big personalities. But the trouble with using out-of-work actors is that occasionally they get jobs – not very often, but frequently enough to be an issue as Puccino's grew bigger. So now they spend more time in making clear to a broader influx of staff and franchisees what is expected of them. And they produce a book iterating the five principles of service that they whole-heartedly believe in.

Now bear in mind before we look at two of these principles and how they are expressed that great service is something Puccino's are very, very serious about. Their whole business model is based on repeat purchase, coming from customer relationships rooted in customer service.

So one might have thought the temptation for Puccino's was to be playful on the outside, but deadly serious on the inside.

Not a bit of it. Here are two of the five principles, as outlined in the internal book (see Figures 3.6 and 3.7).

Now there are some very serious points embedded here – the fact that they want Puccino's staff (unlike any other retailer I have ever met) to happily give out change for the car park; the fact that they want them to know train times and help carry things (besides telling well-covered business men that their zip is somehow undone). But it is done in the manner of the brand. They live on the inside what they project on the outside. They have even created a new word, 'Helpfulosity', to playfully capture the particular kind of attitude towards service they are after.

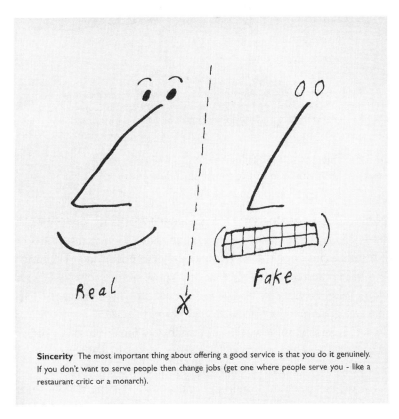

Sincerity The most important thing about offering a good service is that you do it genuinely. If you don't want to serve people then change jobs (get one where people serve you - like a restaurant critic or a monarch).

Figure 3.6 **Puccino's 'Sincerity'**
Reproduced by permission of Jim Smith and Puccino's Ltd

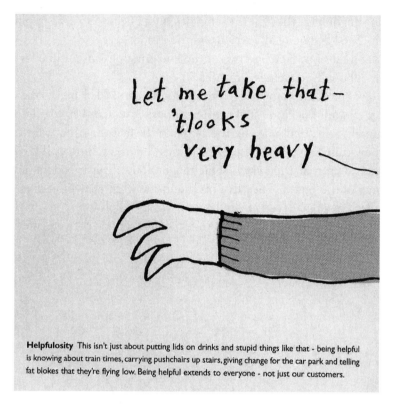

Figure 3.7 **Puccino's 'Helpfulosity'**
Reproduced by permission of Jim Smith and Puccino's Ltd

Now doing it in this way is somewhat polarizing. There are some franchisees who look askance at this – they have been to catering school, and, frankly, this isn't the way one does service training. Training is a serious matter and no time for jokes: one's profitability is at stake here, for heaven's sake. And that's fine as far as Puccino's are concerned – these people can go and buy a franchise with someone else.

But, conversely, some potential franchisees are enormously drawn to this way of talking, because it reflects their own personality and personal style – and this sense of personal alignment is exactly what Puccino's is looking for, because such an alignment means that the people working behind the counter will naturally be more inclined and more likely to deliver the Puccino's brand in serving the customer.

So Puccino's is a good example of the power of projection – in everything they do and say. They show that:

- Everything can be a medium, if you think it is. Think brown sugar.
- Everything can project.
- Great design in a Challenger is not about consistency of graphics and typefaces. It is about consistency of projection.

To make this happen, Puccino's have an in-house creative called Jim. Jim's sole job is to write the copy. And he writes all the copy. And everything is copy. So they project Puccino's identity, as expressed by Jim, in everything they do.

Excuses for the Navy

Ah, but this is a service brand. I can understand how they in reality have more media than they think they do – service and retail brands have an enviably broad range of signage and places to project themselves. But I am just a packaged goods brand. All I have is the pack – and most of that is for the contents and the legal stuff.

'But I'm in Packaged Goods – I Don't Have a Lot of Opportunities for Brand Communication'

The obvious counter to this is innocent. innocent is a UK smoothie brand that was started in 1999 by three 27-year-olds who had been friends at university, and wanted to make it a little easier for people to do something healthy for themselves. They themselves were three years into careers in advertising, marketing and consultancy respectively, and were working and playing at the kind of pace that one does at that stage in one's career. So they decided their target was not going to be people who live healthily already, the people who wear open toe sandals, eat lots of bran and go running. It was to be a brand for people who worked too hard, too late, who drank too much and ate far too many curries.

In doing so they recognized that while they were creating a health product, the health food category itself was very, very dull: all brown rice and earnest, dry-mouthed homilies. To make their brand successful, they felt, they would not only have to have a delicious (as well as healthy) product, they would have to demonstrate that healthy didn't mean dull.

They started selling their pure fruit smoothie in a clear plastic bottle with a paper label. Lacking the budget to advertise, even if they had wanted to, they used the packaging instead to project this sense of putting fun into doing something good for yourself. The clear plastic bottle had its moments (printed on the bottom of the bottle are sentiments ranging from 'Open other end – it's easier' to 'Stop staring at my bottom'), but the key was the way they used the labels. Let's look at a typical example of just half of the back of the label – i.e. a quarter of the whole.

Thou shalt not commit adultery.

You said it big guy. That's one guideline we follow religiously; our smoothies are 100% pure fruit. We call them innocent because we refuse to adulterate them in any way.
Wherever you see the dude, you have got our cross-your-heart-hope-to-die promise that the drink will be completely pure, natural and delicious. If it isn't, you can ring us on the banana phone and make us beg for forgiveness.

Amen.

Why not say hello?
Drop a line or pop around to Fruit Towers,
6 The Buspace, Conlan Street, London W10 5AP

Call the banana phone on 020 8969 7080 or visit our online gym at www.beinnocent.co.uk
® = Religious-experience

Reproduced by permission of innocent Ltd

If you were entertained, you might turn the bottle and peruse the rest of the back. 'Shake before opening' it would tell you, 'and not after'. Next to the list of ingredients you would see an asterisked note that 'Separation may occur*'. You would follow the asterisk down to the bottom of the bottle and find it read '* But Mummy still loves Daddy'.

A well worked-through label, you might think. Nice detail.

But here's the point. When they started, they offered four flavours. Each flavour had on it three different versions of the pack copy, and they changed all the pack copy every three months. That is to say that they were producing 48 *different versions* of the copy every year – just for four flavours. But the result is that not only is the innocent packaging a delightful read, and one that projects their identity in many and unexpected ways – from the ingredient list to the bottom of the bottle – but it also embodies a constantly changing little conversation with me.

And for the more hard-nosed among us, some results: based on the relationships they built on the outside of the bottle, and the excellent product they delivered on the inside of the bottle, innocent has risen to market leader within four years at a price premium of 20%. There is a business value in projection; it creates loyalty to the brand.

Now to make all this pack copy happen, innocent have an in-house creative called Dan. Dan's sole job is to write the copy (for both the packaging and the weekly newsletter). He writes all the copy, and everything is in effect copy. So they project innocent's identity, as expressed by Dan, in everything they do.

Hmm, that last paragraph seems curiously familiar. Perhaps there is some kind of pattern emerging here.

'But I'm Not a Single Brand Company . . .'

Well, yes, they are a single brand company, and the founders have obviously created such a strong culture that the copy more or less writes itself. But I am just a candy bar, within an enormous international company. How can I possibly be expected to be able to project in this way?

Yorkie is a chunky confectionary bar sold by Nestlé in the UK. Originally launched in 1976 with advertising featuring happy truckers with forearms the size of girders, chewing as they drove, the brand was initially very successful in carving out a strong and profitable share of the market. But the brand idea seemed to inherently tire, and sales slowly halved over the following 15 years.

The brand's strategic positioning had always effectively been 'Yorkie – it's for men'. In conjunction with Interbrand, the Nestlé and JWT brand team flipped this strategy to 'Yorkie – it's not for women' – and then, critically, *pushed* it a stage further to the deliciously un-PC, 'Yorkie – It's Not For Girls'. Now of course, with the wisdom of hindsight we can reflect on how naturally this plays to an insight about 'the rest of the confectionary market drifting towards feminine indulgence', on the one hand, and 'men being confused about the role of masculinity in society', on the other. And how naturally this strategy flows out of those two insights. But let us ask ourselves a much simpler question: if we knew, as they did, that 47% of our brand's purchasers were female, how enthusiastically would we have championed that strategy? Within an organization like Nestlé?

But let's play it out. So they have arrived at this really interesting strategic positioning – an intriguingly pushed idea: what a wonderful advertising brief this would make, we think to ourselves.

And here's the point: the brand team started projecting the idea well before the advertising. First, they gave this idea of 'It's Not For Girls' a logo of its own. Then they put the logo on the pack, in the middle of the brand name (Figure 3.8).

Figure 3.8 **Yorkie Pack Shot**
Reproduced by permission of Nestlé UK

They imprinted the logo at the centre of their extra large bar for 'sharing' but actually only allowed one small segment to be given to the female of choice – this particular chocolate square was the single square at the bottom right-hand corner of the bar that had 'one for the birds' imprinted in the chocolate. Brand Manager Sam Ellison:

> Once the icon was developed, it was clear that it communicated the proposition instantly and had to be exploited. By being so single-minded, the ideas just kept pouring out. What an obvious link with beer cans . . . (Figure 3.9).

Figure 3.9 **Yorkie Beer Can**
Reproduced by permission of Nestlé UK

We also ran a limited edition Pink Yorkie pack as a challenge to women and changed the letters on pack to Blokie [playing off the slang expression 'Bloke' to mean a man] for another limited period (Figure 3.10).

They distributed 'It's Not For Girls' stickers in men's magazines like *FHM* and *Maxim*, so that readers could peel them off and stick them

Figure 3.10   **Yorkie Blokie Bar**
Reproduced by permission of Nestlé UK

to things in their life that were, well, not for girls. The PlayStation, obviously. The TV remote, ditto. And as for the rest – well, it depends how feisty you were feeling, really.

And, of course, they did take the idea very powerfully into advertising – advertising that walked a nice line between wit and provocation (Figures 3.11 and 3.12).

Figure 3.11   **Yorkie 'Do Not Feed the Birds' Poster**
Reproduced by permission of Nestlé UK

The result was a 20% sales increase in 12 months, without launching a single new product, and winning for them in 2002 Nestlé UK's Innovation prize. And the interesting thing about them winning this prize was that they had not launched a single new product; they were essentially innovating around the core, by projecting a pushed idea through every medium available.

Figure 3.12   **Yorkie 'Save Your Money' Poster**
Reproduced by permission of Nestlé UK

'But My Category Doesn't Reward Brand Building'

Let us launch ourselves against one last reason why one might not be able to project – namely when one finds oneself in charge of private label products. But the riposte is that private label is also brand building, and good private label packaging also says something about the retailer. Look, for instance at two examples of the packaging for the pharmacy retailer Superdrug (see Figures 3.13 and 3.14).

We understand what the products are, but we also get an intriguing sense of the brand.

So, no excuses for the Navy.

The New USP

Project, then. Only Project.

Another exercise. What if we were to change our title from 'Marketing Whatever' or 'Important Brand Person' to something with a rather different emphasis – call ourselves 'Ubiquitous Sticky Projectors', for

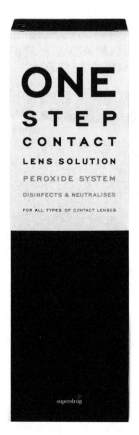

Figure 3.13   **Superdrug Lens Care**
Reproduced by permission of Superdrug Stores plc

example. A Ubiquitous Sticky Projector (USP) is a person whose job it is to:

- Project
- Everywhere
- In a way that creates attention and engagement at each point, with a sense of the brand's identity
- Resulting in an overall stickiness (as the Internet retailers used to say): a sticky loyalty between our brand and consumer.

A USP, therefore, in a very different sense from the one the initials were originally used to connote, but one that is more pertinent to the

Figure 3.14   **Superdrug Pregnancy Test**
Reproduced by permission of Superdrug Stores plc

current marketing world. And ask ourselves this: if this were our title, and we were to review our brand mix, how would we have fared this year? Would we have hit our targets? Would we deserve our bonus? What are the most glaring areas of neglect? Where should we start next year?

And if we think we might not hit those targets, or have deserved those bonuses, then next year we need to be briefing our design partners for projection, not simply graphic consistency – there is no point in evaluating ourselves against something we are not briefing for. Which brings us onto the interesting subject of needlework.

Briefing for Needlework

At the end of the interview with Richard Reed, one of the three founders of innocent, we leave the little meeting room where we have been talking and emerge into the central corridor of Fruit Towers (innocent's headquarters). In the middle of the corridor's long wall there is a notice board, on which are pinned all the unsolicited pieces of communication they have had from their customers – the brand's fan mail, if you like. Reed points to one piece in particular – a piece of needlework on which an elderly lady has embroidered the little innocent logo of a head with a halo over it. 'That's my mission,' he says: 'To inspire people to express themselves through the medium of needlework.'

It's a joke, of course; and yet he isn't smiling.

So what if we were to give our design company two briefs next time? The first is all the usual brand stuff; you can do that in your sleep. And the second is to ask them to inspire our consumer through this packaging to want to express themselves about us in a piece of needlework (or perhaps, if we were being a little more accommodating, the medium of their choice). What is the packaging they would give us then?

Summary

In the Navy, the size of the budget matters. Spending a lot of money with your agency? You're an important person. As a Pirate, because we are viewing everything as a medium to project our little brand, and at the same time deposition the other or others, size of budget doesn't matter at all. It is our ability to see everything as a potential medium that matters. And the constant behaviour of converting the tedia into media that count.

As such, we are going to think about consistency on our brand differently from the way the Navy thinks about consistency – we are going to think about consistency of projection rather than consistency of design. Our primary interest is not to make sure the same logo is being used in the same typeface; our primary interest is to make sure the brand is projecting a sense of itself in a provocative or intriguing way at all key points in the interaction with the consumer. And we are going to be constantly looking for those places to project who we are, rather than being the 'Graphics Enforcer' that the Navy seems to implicitly define as one's role.

The Two Excuses for the Navy

We have obviously been quite explicit about tackling the Second ('But I do not have a large advertising budget'), and the Third ('But I am in packaged goods – I don't have a lot of opportunities for brand communication'). Look at innocent – the riposte for any such feebleness.

Exercises

You don't need to be the person that comes up with all the ideas. But it is up to you to make people see the brand and all its physical expressions as potential media in this way. And to understand what the brand means clearly enough, of course, to make turning them into media possible.

Tedia-media Circles

Get the team together. Put every expression of the brand up on a wall. Everything – packaging, pack copy, price coupons, leaflet drops, competitions, trade information, internal information sheets, everything. Which of them are a medium, and which are bits of tedium? Come up with two ideas to turn each of the tedia into media.

Brown Sugar

Take the smallest and apparently least significant part of your brand (the cap of the toothpaste tube, for example, or the inner lid of a coffee jar). What would it take to turn that into your most powerful medium?

Briefing for Needlework

Ask your design company to produce some exploratory packaging that doesn't simply communicate, but stimulates the consumer to respond spontaneously back to you (in a good way, I need hardly add) in return, because of the way that you make them feel.

And finally . . .

A last story for those of us who hunger for the kind of customer enthusiasm that needlework embodied for the team at innocent. We tend to think of popular hysteria about musicians beginning at the start of the 1960s with Elvis and the Beatles. But just under two hundred years ago after the Italian composer and violinist Niccolò Paganini played in London, 300 members of the public were actually hospitalized after reportedly suffering from 'over-enchantment'. Paganini: now there's a brand to aim for; Nike famously wanted 'fans' rather than 'customers' – but Paganini had 'the enchanted'.[1]

4

Wrapping: A Different Kind of Communication

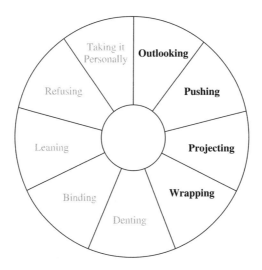

Figure 4.1 **Wrapping**

> 'Identity' these days is a fashionable term. But it is not very meaningful unless one can show how it manifests itself in behaviour. What makes up a culture is not simply works of art . . . but the unwritten codes, the rituals and gestures, and the common attitudes that fix the public meaning of these works and organize the inner life of a society.
>
> *Orlando Figes*[1]

W hen two of us went to interview Hans Snook, then at Orange when the brand was on the brink of taking market leadership of the UK market, he arrived for the interview carrying in his cupped hands a mug of coffee. Although he was at the time the CEO of one of the most extraordinarily successful (and imitated) brands in mobile communications, now in 19 countries around the world, Snook had never been much for the formal trappings of the other mobile telecom providers – he had achieved a certain fame at his press conferences, for instance, for holding them on a double-decker London bus dressed in a leather jacket, rather than in the grey suit and polished wood of a telecom boardroom.

He smiled genially and sat down. We explained that we were interested in asking him what had made Orange as a brand and a company so successful. Snook paused, and then drew his hands away from the front of the coffee mug he was carrying. Written on the curved glaze of the china were the words 'Snook Doggy Dogg'.

'It all starts with the coffee mugs,' he said.

Pirates, Brands and Countries

What do we use to define a strong brand, over and above its name and performance? It is usually some combination of conceptual elements (positioning, rational and emotional consumer benefits, personality) and executional elements (consistent and integrated communications, a clear and directional brand book, for instance).

How, on the other hand, do we define or characterize a country, over and above its name and geography? Through some combination of:

- Their beliefs – what they hold important that differentiates them from other countries and peoples
- The way they speak/their language
- Their culture and customs
- What characterizes their citizens
- Their funny little habits
- The things they have no one else has
- Their iconography

To try this out, I am going to fill these in for a given country, without naming it, in the hope that you would have a good idea of their 'branding' before we get to the tell-tale iconography at the bottom.

This is it:

Their Beliefs
That good food, wine and culture are to be unhurriedly enjoyed (and vigorously debated) by all walks of life; that they are the best – and only real – creators of these three desirables in the world.

The Way They Speak/Their Language
Of course, they have their particular and untranslatable words, like the one that roughly means 'sophisticated know how', but their language is as much characterized by *how* they speak – a regular shrugging of the shoulders and a 'bof!' of air expelled through the lips.

Their Culture and Customs
It is customary for all male politicians to have a mistress, and for the mistress to attend their funeral when they die, even if the wife is there as well. Particularly, perhaps, if the wife is there as well.

What Characterizes Their Citizens
An enthusiasm for gesticulations, especially in traffic; among the men, a conviction that they are great lovers, who do not need care in their personal appearance or familiarity with a shampoo bottle to make them irresistible to the opposite sex; among the women, that they personally are the epitome of fashion. Among both, a general love of sharing the smoke of unfiltered cigarettes with the people on the restaurant table next to them.

Their Funny Little Habits
Cycling. Long and painful hours of cycling in groups up mountain roads on seats the width of razor blades as a pleasant way to spend one's free time.

Things They Have No One Else Has
Terrific breakfast pastries: the best in the world. Hot chocolate served in *bowls* – how great is that?

Their Iconography

The Eiffel Tower, the beret, the striped matelot jersey – need I go on . . .?

Voilà: I don't have to name the country, but you recognize it, and you recognize why it is special, why we have some of the feelings we have about it, and indeed why the world would be utterly impoverished if it disappeared beneath the Atlantic tomorrow.

So here we have, as I say, two different kinds of models: that of brands and that of countries; and we are going to suggest that iconic Challengers have more in common with the second of these than the first of these – certainly within single brand companies, and sometimes within a larger organization. Because what underlies both countries and iconic Challengers is a sense of a highly differentiated culture. Not highly differentiated lists of brand values, handsomely bound on glossy paper, but a differentiated culture that is manifested in the way that they speak, and behave – from the big gestures to the little details. And this is the point that Snook was making when he talked about his coffee mug: strong Challengers need to be clearly differentiated cultures, more than just brands, both inside and out.

In this chapter, then, we are first going to look at examples of how strong Challengers themselves evidence all these characteristics that we will normally associate with a country. We will then look at a key reason why that is important: because a strong sense of a differentiated culture emanating from such a brand also gives a sense of the people behind it. And we will end by suggesting that what this way of seeing Challenger brands offers is a fresh way to think about where we (as one of those people) should be projecting our identity.

Let us begin by playing out our model of the various kinds of 'country' differentiators and looking at how Challengers deliver against them.

Their Beliefs – What They Hold Important that Differentiates Them from Other Countries and Peoples

The *Pocket Oxford Dictionary* talks of a country being 'an individual with opinions'.[2] And we can see belief systems and the opinions coming out as a key definer of many of our Challengers, their cultures and their consumer relationships.

Lorenzo Fluxá, founder of the Spanish shoe brand Camper, now in over 50 countries and with almost 4,000 distribution points, sums up the brand's philosophy in three words: 'Walk, don't run'. Camper dislikes the 'speeding up' of everything, a life running too fast, symbolized by the global explosion of McDonald's and the Internet. Camper's ambition is to have not simply commercial success, but a cultural influence – they invite people to join 'The Walking Society', a movement that slows down and savours the world around them, in food, in play, in relationships. They don't believe in the instant buddydom of the Internet; they believe instead that, in their words, 'The Med[iterranean] is the Net': that the old kinds of relationship building that have existed for centuries in Mediterranean culture are still the models the world should follow.

M.A.C. cosmetics was born in Toronto in 1985 and is now the number two selling brand in the USA after Clinique. Founded by two gay men, Frank Angelo and Frank Toskan, it grew out of the drag scene, holding at its heart a belief in 'The celebration of individuality'. In the words of CEO John Dempsey, M.A.C. has no preconceived notion of what beauty is:

> Our motto is 'All ages, all races, all sexes, all matter'. So whether you're fat, thin, tall, short, black, yellow, green, male, female, straight, bi, gay, goth, makes no difference. The only preconceived notion is that this is a place that's creative, that's open, that's diverse, a place that has created an environment for which the celebration of the individual is germane. Whatever your choice is that day – *and it can change* – come on in.

Perhaps the most visible and famous expressions of this belief are the strikingly different personalities that M.A.C. chooses as spokespeople for their Viva Glam range. The convention in cosmetics advertising is to use the face of young white heterosexual females, without very strong personalities of their own; M.A.C., on the other hand, chose personalities rather than faces, and personalities that offered almost a direct counterpoint to the conventional blank canvas. After successfully launching the Viva Glam range with the drag artist RuPaul (who isn't white and isn't technically female), they have since used the singer k. d. lang (who isn't heterosexual, and doesn't wear make-up), and most recently the outspoken hip hop divas Mary J. Blige and Lil' Kim – each decision being made based on their core tenet about beauty and the individual.

The US retail brand Anthropologie believes in discovery. To ensure that they genuinely deliver this sense for the visiting consumer, Anthropologie creates an environment that invites them to discover the joys of the store for themselves. Going against the conventional wisdom of store display, which dictates that all products must be clearly visible and uniformly arranged, Anthropologie invites the consumer to rummage through drawers, to take things out of wardrobes, or to open books with secret compartments to find an assortment of brightly coloured buttons or other hidden treasures. To fuel this carefully designed theatre the people who work at Anthropologie understand the importance of maintaining fresh eyes, continually open to the possibility of everyday discovery – on the agenda of their regular staff Monday morning meetings each individual shares their stories of personal, political or culture discovery.

As we have seen, these beliefs are often made visible. Sometimes this is a straightforward wearing of one's heart on one's sleeve, as when Camper stamp their four core beliefs on the side of their shoe box (see Figure 4.2) but sometimes these beliefs act as more of a provocation. Howies is a mountain bike and skateboard clothing company from Wales, a company whose ethos is all about getting out there and doing stuff. On the bottom of the Howies T-Shirt bag is a small piece of type that looks like one of those normal pieces of nonsense you get on the bottom of any clothing bag. If you read it, however, it says:

WARNING
Each day comes with 86,400 seconds and you have just spent 42 of them reading a bag. Tick tock.

Whether these beliefs are directly stated to the consumer or not, they act as the kernel around which every other aspect of wrapping develops – which of course makes them visible in their own way.

Figure 4.2   **Camper Shoe Box**
Reproduced by permission of Camper

The Way They Speak/Their Language

So, for instance, one's own particular way of seeing the world is also displayed in the language one uses, and how it differs from the language and vocabulary of those around one. Japanese, for instance, apparently has a single word for 'to try out a new sword on a passer-by'. While I imagine this is used less often today than it was three hundred years ago, the existence of the word does give an insight into one aspect of the culture of a country then dominated by the samurai tradition.[3]

In brand terms, product nomenclature is obviously a good starting point for a different language. If one buys a pair of Tim Little shoes, for instance, his names have a deliberate romance beyond the descriptor of the style and colour. A particular style of loafers is called 'Whiskey and Women'. Another is called 'Slidewinder'. A pair of oil-tanned boots is called '40 days and 40 nights'. We do not know if there is a backstory to all this exoticism or not at this stage, but we sense there is a different and consistent way of thinking, and perhaps more importantly, of *feeling* about shoes here that is different, that we may or may not find intriguing.

Consider the US soda Mountain Dew, number four in the US market, and a high caffeine brand which is positioned all around energy, adrenalin and 'the rush'. How many of us, if we are really honest, when asked to come up with a name for a new cherry variant would have come up with an adjective that romanced it a little: 'Radical Cherry', perhaps, or 'Cherry Rush'? But the Mountain Dew team nicely subverted the whole notion of romancing a flavour – they called the new variant 'Code Red' – the language we associate normally with a military warning that something unpleasant is about to happen. (And of course, in the youth culture where Mountain Dew is king, perhaps that *is* romancing it.) This is something much more interesting than being playful and provocative in naming – we are starting to see the beginning of a language that helps define us as being intrinsically different from anyone else.

Of course, the style of language one uses here has to be appropriate to the brand. So, for instance, the point where cars drop off departing passengers at Nice Airport is called 'Kiss and Fly'. And when one arrives at Nice Airport to drop or be dropped, this seems deliciously appropriate for the South of France. Oh yes, I think, that's exactly what I'll do to the gorgeous suntanned little thing that is dropping me off – and I'll probably throw in a 'Ciao, baby' or two to show what a sophisticated *homme du monde* I am when I am down here. Very little of the above, conversely, would be true for Cleveland, or Schipol, or Glasgow (a 'Glasgow Kiss' is a particularly swift and violent head-butt to the face designed to break one's opponent's nose: one shudders to think of the kind of mess all that blood would make over those nice BA seats). Conversely, calling a product an unusual name by simply crashing a chain of words together is not necessarily speaking in your own language – Z Bigatti Re-Storation Deep Repair Serum (this is a genuine product) is simply a descriptive set of adjectives attached to an odd name. It is hard to feel a sense of underlying persona or culture here.

Now we may be tempted to look at these kinds of examples as flippant embroidery: a bit of fun, but not really something on which strong brands are built. However, while they are moments of playfulness, for Challengers they have a more profound role in reflecting a very particular and differentiated belief about the category and how they feel it should be seen or enjoyed. Look at the following description of ingredients from a Ben and Jerry's pack:

A crazy concoction of chocolate ice cream mixed with fudge brownies and gobs of Chocolate Chip Cookie Dough.

Gobs? What kind of word is that? Can you imagine Häagen-Dazs using such a word to describe their ingredients? Absolutely not – and that's the point: Ben and Jerry's have a much earthier gusto, which is a key part of the personality of their brand. And we as consumers and fans of Ben and Jerry's know this is not because of the words on a brand essence map, but because of the language we hear them use.

This differentiating language can be directive as well as descriptive: as with US bank Washington Mutual talking about branches as 'stores', to mark a real move away from the old-fashioned formality of old-style banking (their stores can include a concierge, kids play area, and areas where customers stand next to tellers and watch as their accounts are opened or managed on the screen in front of them). When Sephora called their staff 'priests and priestesses' of beauty, it accompanied a move away from commission-based sales, and the fostering of an atmosphere of the sensorial elevation of the customer rather than the hard sell.

The idiosyncrasy of such a personal language creates a different relationship with the brand than that with the all-too-easy-to-understand brand leader. What are we to make of the following Diesel label on Type RR55 jeans, for instance?

Diesel Industry Denim Division. Registered Trademark. Superior Quality jeans. Ideal for works and pleasure. Regulated.

Don't these guys have access to a decent translator? Or just a spell-checker? And what's with this regulated thing? Regulated by what? When Diesel originally starting writing this eccentric copy, their Creative Director Wilbert Das says, it was because they had an Italian graphic designer, and they didn't speak English very well. Then – well, people liked it, because it gave character and seemed real: 'People at that time thought it was very, very funny; they didn't really like it when we got the copy right, because they loved the mistakes.' So then it just became a part of the way they did things. The language they spoke.

This language can also be in advertising, naturally. Orange talked in print advertising about their offers as having no 'eek in peak' and no 'ouch in voucher', this being the linguistic opposite of 'no unpleasant small print in our offpeak low rate tariff and plan', and a language that reflected the refreshing and honest humanity of the brand. However, we should be careful about simply thinking that 'language is something we must talk to the agency about': much of what we are talking about here gains its traction from lying outside the obvious opportunity to create in advertising – on pack, in copy, on a website, even in internal manuals, as we saw earlier with 'Helpfulosity' from Puccino's.

Now, as we know, vocabulary is a very important delineator of non-brand-specific subcultures, such as skateboarding and biking. 'Ollies', 'goofy footers', 'candy bars' – whether one understands these or not defines whether you are a part of this highly developed subculture, this world-within-a-world that has its own gods and rituals and kinds of honour. And one of the primary roles of language here is to make some feel part, and to make others feel outside.

But once one is 'inside' the brand or subculture that one has joined, vocabulary is also perhaps a part of creating intimacy. Linguists call such 'private languages' between couples or families 'idiolect' – they reflect shared experiences and private understandings that are part of the special bond between them.

And, in the case of brands, such idiolect can be a key part of what makes them different – and our relationship with them different – from the other players in the market: 'We speak a totally different language from Levi's', remarked Wilbert Das of Diesel, when noting that they referred to their underwear range as 'spare parts' – something Levi's could never do.

Clearly 'the way they speak' extends beyond verbal language to the visual grammar and structure of packs and magazines: note how *Maxim* and its sister music magazine *Blender* 'speak' in the way they lay the whole magazine out – an archipelago of short snippets, charts and bite-size snacks of information, for the male with an appetite for the new and a short attention span to explore on his own terms.

The comedian Steve Martin in one of his stand-up routines is playing the dumb tourist discussing Europe. 'France, what an amazing country,' he enthuses. 'You know something interesting I noticed about France? They call a hat a "chapeau", they call a castle a "château"' – he pauses, as if in wonder, before going on: 'It's like they have a different word for *everything*.'

Their Culture and Customs

A number of these brands have their very own particular culture and customs – ways of doing things which, as we interact with them, influence our own relationship with the brand. So we looked in Chapter 2 on Pushing at the entertaining exercise concepts offered by Crunch gyms – one of the most recent famous courses they have offered has been a pole dancing class, at which Jennifer Aniston was reportedly seen. And as the creators of Disco Yoga, with a philosophy of 'No Judgements', they have consistently had a culture born out of their desire to be more accepting on the one hand, and more appealing on the other – a culture that has successfully mixed new ways to enjoy taking exercise with the usual mix of high quality regular equipment. So there are two things going on here – on the one hand, they understand people are bored with the usual ways of sweating and offering novelty, but at the same time they are also creating a country with its own sense of what is possible (and indeed usual) and not.

innocent smoothies mix their happy, healthy naivety with moments of surprising precision. The eyelashes on the headlights of their cow delivery vans are complemented by the exactness of their ingredient list: on their 'blackberries and blueberries' flavour, they will tell you exactly how many of each you get in your bottle – 11 crushed blackberries and 43 crushed blueberries. As we will see later, the details one seems to place importance on as a brand indirectly communicate much about the culture of the people behind the brand: 'If they are *that* exact about how many go in, they must *really* be particular about the recipe and the fruit.' And this perhaps communicates 'quality' and 'care' and 'people I want to buy food from' far more powerfully than some idiotic line about 'passionate about berries' – the kind of lazy 'passion statement' one sees too frequently elsewhere.

Sometimes the visible culture of the brand is more obviously playful. Look at the way Tsubi make jeans. A group of Australian designers (who are also, it seems, 'rock musician-poets') have their own particular way of distressing their denim to perfection before it gets to you. Before sale, each and every pair is:

Handled by dirty hands, beaten by beat poets, dragged through the street and exposed to extensive noise.[4]

It is perfectly possible that by the end of this the denim is distressed to the point of being positively anxious, yet it introduces us not just to an 'innovative' way of distressing denim, but a playful brand and an imaginative culture behind it. And if we like that, it is the beginning of a bond between us.

Sometimes the culture becomes almost a consumer culture in terms of the habit or rituals it creates. Consider Altoids mints, and the ritual of putting that tin down on the desk in front of you, rather than being furtive about your roll of breath-freshening mints in your pocket; you pass them round, like a treat, making the taking of them a sociable rather than a personal activity. And also adopting, in effect, some of the cues that cigarettes might have had 40 years ago.

Their Character Traits/What Characterizes Their Citizens

Lexus set themselves the task when they launched of 'treating the customer like a guest in our own home' – an extraordinary jump for a car company in 1989, even one playing in the luxury arena. There is one story that is still famous within Lexus exemplifying the degree of commitment some of their dealers gave to this sense of service in the early days. In this case, the customer had received their Lexus back from being serviced only to discover that a nut had been insufficiently tightened after the service, and oil had leaked onto and stained a small area of their garage floor below the engine. The Lexus dealer in question came to them and fixed the problem – though you would expect that. More importantly, the dealer paid for the floor to be taken up and relaid *at his own expense* so that it would be just the way the owner wanted it again: a pristine and unmarked surface on which to park his Lexus. Lexus talked in advertising about the passionate pursuit of perfection – what was unusual about their 'citizens' was that they did actually pursue it, not simply talk about it.

We noted earlier that M.A.C. has chosen to communicate a particular belief about beauty and the individual. Over and above their advertising M.A.C. also ensured from the beginning that this was embodied in the people they chose to represent the brand at the make-up counter. Thus two characteristics that set M.A.C. cosmetics counter staff apart in Nordstrom in the early days were the way they were dressed and the way they looked. At a time when the overly-made-up women representing the rest of the industry wore what appeared to be white lab coats, M.A.C.'s 'artists' dressed all in black, as make-up artists in entertainment did. And each was allowed, and indeed encouraged to express their individuality with tattoos, dyed hair and facial piercings. The characteristic black has now been borrowed by others in the category; the more expressive elements of character have not.

The UK wine merchants Oddbins encourage the staff to enthuse about the product they are selling. About a particular region – one might find 'We are the Cape crusaders' loudly written on the store window promoting a South African wine offer – or indeed about individual bottles: throughout the store one finds handwritten cards from the individual members of staff of that branch enthusing about this or that wine. My God, you think, how refreshing. These are not 'staff': these are people, with opinions of their own. That they are eager to share.

And sometimes these kinds of characteristics are altogether more colourful and exotic. Consider the label for 'Luscombe Devon Apple Juice'. Besides all the normal lists of ingredients, we find two pieces of information that engage us. The first is the detail of the apples it is made from:

Fresh pressed old Devon varieties such as Tom Putt, Pig's Snout, Tale Sweet, Devon Crimson, Oaken Pin, Quench. . . .

I have never heard of any of these varieties, but is hard not to hold up the contents of one's glass and view it in an altogether more affectionate way – the world is somehow a finer place now that I know there is an apple variety called Pig's Snout in it.

It is the second part of the label copy, however, that cements my relationship with the brand. It reads: 'The apple pumice is fed to the organic dairy herd which graze the farm, encouraging Dung Beetles and Greater Horseshoe bats.' Hmm, I reflect: so these are people who like Dung Beetles and bats, and apples with curious and wonderful names. Well, now that I know that, I want to spend more time in their company. In their country. (Some people may not, and that's fine – there are plenty of other apple juice brands for them to choose from.)

Such citizenship characteristics are obviously not always about individuality or self-expression; sometimes they are tied to the very real commercial imperatives that all who work on the brand need to engage in to survive and prosper. easyJet foster what they call an 'above the shop' mentality in everyone who works there. This sense of the importance of a constant awareness of the commercial imperative for their low-cost brand and business is played out in their five core values:

- Lean and mean
- Up for it
- Sharp
- Passion
- Push boundaries.

8th Continent, the US soy milk brand created by General Mills and DuPont, similarly established six core values that drive their team's individual and collective behaviour:

- Direction (purpose)
- Courage
- Trail blazing
- Open communication
- Passion
- Accomplishment.

However, these values were made visible in a slightly different way – represented by a set of six beads strung on a leather cord that the brand team wore around their necks. A significantly different emphasis, presumably, from the natural values of either of the new Challenger's parents.

Border Control[5]

One of the great things about national and cultural diversity, of course, is that there are some countries one is drawn to more strongly than others; and by the same token there are those I would actively choose not to spend time in. This person loves the rude, red-blooded chaos of Italy, and needs to go there twice a year to feel alive; that person finds it infuriating and prefers to rediscover their serenity in the quiet decency of Canada.

So your country will be attractive to some, though not everyone. There is a wonderful (though surely apocryphal) story about the Inklings, a group of writers in the 1930s who used to meet in The Eagle and Child, a pub in Oxford, to read to each other from their works in progress. Two of these writers were in the process of developing their own worlds: C.S. Lewis, who was writing the extensive *Narnia Chronicles*, and J.R.R. Tolkien, who was creating *The Lord of the Rings*.

The story goes that as Tolkien stood one afternoon to read to the rest of the Inklings his latest chapter from Middle Earth, C.S. Lewis was heard to mutter from his corner 'Not another fucking elf . . .'[6]

So, not everyone will want to be a part of this country, and indeed from our side we shouldn't want people who would not be good citizens of it. To some degree, in fact, we should be practising a kind of border control that goes beyond skills or category experience levels. Thus, Kristin Krumpe, Marketing Director for the US chocolate milk brand Yoo-hoo, recognizes that she needs not just good soft drinks people but people who will be in sync with her brand's personality, on the one hand, and her budget's need for resourcefulness, on the other:

Me, I'm a little less interested in somebody's background as a beverage guru. I am much more interested in where they like to spend their time – what kind of music are they into, and whether they are naturally curious about wanting to live on the Internet, and doing all sorts of kind of guerrilla research on their own.

To offer a more extreme example, TGIF were said at one point to have interviewed candidates while making them jump up and down on a trampoline to see if they were 'TGIF people', and in Chapter 2 we saw Mike Harris doing much the same with dancing in the early days of Egg.

The Detroit punk-blues band The White Stripes sent out the advance press promo copies of their fourth album, *Elephant*, only on vinyl. When asked why, Jack White (one of the duo making up the band) replied: 'We didn't want any journalist who didn't own a record player to write about us – it was a way to weed them out.' This reflects a belief of the band – namely, that 'analogue equipment isn't a retro idea, it's the pinnacle of recording technology that was never surpassed'.[7]

Once we have allowed people past the border, there are sometimes initiation rites. Everyone who is about to work on PepsiCo's Gatorade brand, for instance, has first to go through 'Gatorology', a course in the science of hydration at the Gator Institute in Florida. This is not a PepsiCo thing – it is because Gatorade as a brand has a serious underpinning of science as its foundation, and you as a member of the brand team need to know and respect that.

OK, so in exploring this alternate brand model for Challengers we have so far looked at belief systems which, even when not overtly communicated to the consumer, are still manifested in language, culture and customs, the characteristics of their citizens and the way they recruit or repel potential citizens at the border.

Now we're going to look at how that belief system and perspective play out in physical cues and iconography.

Things They Have That No One Else Has

Uniqueness is a word that is often used in marketing, but a concept which in reality most people are afraid of – do we really dare to be entirely unlike anything else in the marketplace in this or that regard? Isn't that rather dangerous? However, one of the most important facets of such brands/countries is precisely the unique dimensions they offer. These take a number of different forms.

(i) Sense of Offer

jetBlue adds to their safety information a collection of yoga poses you can do without even leaving your seat; one of which, the Bidalasana, puts passengers in touch with 'an astral plane where pillows are no longer necessary'. I have yet to be offered this in my travels on any other airline.

(ii) Physical Product Artefacts

The relaunched VW Beetle famously featured a flower vase; this was not just a whimsical touch of the Martha Stewarts – it was a reference to its flower power roots. Staying with cars, the first Mini included generous side pockets in its two front doors, because Sir Alec Issigonis, its creator, believed that they should each be able to hold a bottle of Gordon's gin.

(iii) Sensory Cues

The blue Terra chips passed around in-flight on jetBlue, or the iPod's instantly recognizable white headphones.

(iv) Currencies

In the nineteenth century companies building the infrastructure between the seaboards of the United States (Atlantic and Gulf Railroad, for instance) actually issued their own currency and bonds at the time; they genuinely did have the trappings of nationality. The legal ability to print one's own money is now unfortunately a thing of the past – but it still persists in other kinds of currency we see in more recent strong brand cultures, whether internal (the 'bean stock' of a company like Starbucks), or consumer facing (Club Med and the little plastic beads one wears around one's neck).

(v) Internal Artefacts

Jeff Bezos has a desk made out of a door bought from a hardware store – as does everyone else around him at Amazon. The reason for this is the rejection of his previous experience at Bankers Trust, where if you were really important you were given an office with a credenza (a credenza is a desk, Bezos says, with a drawer just deep enough to hold one sheet of paper).

And think of Mary Kay famously giving her most successful salespeople one very visible and specific kind of reward: a pink Cadillac.

Their Iconography

We noted above (Figure 4.2) that Camper stamp their four core beliefs as icons on the side of their boxes. Let us briefly unpack them:

'Contact Earth' is of course what shoes do, but it is also a belief that each of us should remain grounded; never lose sight of the fact that I'm just, I'm just Jenny from the block.

'The Med is the Net' is the belief that for Camper it is Mediterranean culture, the old kinds of relationships that define the glue between people and the societies they live in – not the absent immediacy of the Internet.

'Walk Don't Run', we have already discussed. And, finally, 'Imagination' is of course important to Camper, but it is the simple imagination of a paper dart, not the complicated brilliance of a motherboard or microwave.

Such iconography obviously goes beyond the constant brand stamp that is the logo. Iconography, in fact, is not always constant in a brand, though the country that it represents always is. Tommy Bahama's designers, for example, constantly change the iconography – sometimes a palm tree, sometimes a sailfish, sometimes the word 'relax' to evoke the multifaceted but consistent world that 'Tommy' represents.

Taking Stock

We started the chapter with the assertion that strong Challengers had more in common with countries and the different layers of nationhood that countries evidence than they do with the more formal definitions of brand elements that we were raised on. We have gone on to look at examples of brands that demonstrate this, both single brand Challengers and those within larger companies.

We can see that such brand 'countries' reflect a different kind of brand consistency than the one we are used to. And I suggest in fact that we will see the emergence of two different kinds of brand consistency in the future. The first type of brand consistency is the worthy (but perhaps rather sterile) one of the Global Brand Book and the logo police, where the emphasis is on making sure that every element of brand representation is produced in every location in the approved way. While this has its place, it can in effect be the enemy of a live culture rather than the champion of it. And the second is a more organic kind of consistency, delivering a consistency in the mould of a Camper or a Diesel: a consistency of depth and layering, rather than a policing of the surface. And it can do this because what unites the brand is a perceptibly rich and different culture behind the brand.

Wrapping – The Idea Behind It

But what do I do with all this? It all seems very interesting, this 'brand as a country' business, but how on earth would I start to use it? To evidence it?

Let's try this: substitute the usual communication model of 'a message communicated through different media' with a new communication model of 'wrapping' the brand. Wrapping the brand and its emerging sense of itself or culture with some or all of the different layers we have noted above – *each of which projects the culture in its own way*. Let us group some of these layers together to create six layers to Wrap around the kernel brand vision. (There is a visual representation of this at the end of the chapter on p. 113 as a template for the first exercise.)

The kernel is:

Our beliefs – what we hold important that differentiates them from other countries and peoples. Our point of view about the way the world is or the way it should be.[8]

The six layers of Wrapping are:

- Our culture and customs – the way we do things. What characterizes our citizens internally – the kinds of border control we practise. Our particular habits and rituals that emerge from all of this.
- The way we speak, verbally and visually – our language and iconography.
- The things we have that no one else has – the sense of offer, the physical and sensory cues to the consumer, the internal artefacts that represent what we believe and what makes us different. Snook Doggy Dogg.

- The manifestation of all of this in experience
- The manifestation of all of this in folklore
- The manifestation of all of this in communications

These first three are in effect a clustering of the different ways in which a culture or country expresses itself that we have been reviewing so far. The next three are the manifestation of this underlying sense of 'Being your own country' in the more conventional marketing arenas of brand experience, the creation of folklore about the brand, and indeed in communications.

Manifestation in Experience

Yoo-hoo offers a number of ways to get free chocolate milk at their stand on the Warped Tour. Two of them are Shoo-hoos and Cutlets. A 'Shoo-hoo' is free to you as long as you are prepared to drink it out of a shoe (Figure 4.3). Fair enough, you think – it is simply a question of introducing my stomach to my foot; I'm sure they can get on in the interests of free chocolate milk. But there is one drawback to this otherwise generous offer – it has to be drunk out of someone else's shoe. When one considers that the owner of the shoe in question is going to be one of your fellow concert goers, who has been standing or dancing in it for some period of time before it acts as your glass, one can see that this is a very different way to experience drinking chocolate milk than the way your little sister does. You don't trust your friend's shoe? Well, let me offer you a Cutlet (Figure 4.4). A Cutlet is where you lie on the grass while those around pour chocolate milk all over your body and clothes; when they are finished, you roll in the grass until the stickiness of the drying chocolate milk has persuaded various grass clippings, twigs and the occasional insect to stick to your skin. 'It is', remarks Kristin Krumpe, the Marketing Director, on the brand, 'not too hard to spot someone walking around who has had a Cutlet. It becomes almost a badge of honour ...'

Manifestation in Folklore

Virgin Atlantic has consistently manufactured a stream of PR ideas that express their positioning as the irreverent underdog taking on

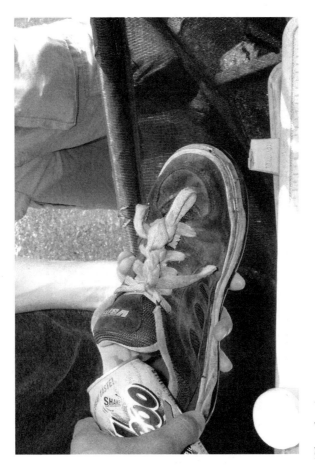

Figure 4.3   **Yoo-hoo 'Shoo-hoo'**
Reproduced by permission of Yoo-hoo Chocolate Beverage Corp.

Figure 4.4   **Yoo-hoo 'Cutlet'**
Reproduced by permission of Yoo-hoo Chocolate Beverage Corp.

British Airways. Sometimes these ideas reflect genuine product offers (the option for the busy businessperson to be taken to their Upper Class flight on the back of a motorbike should they want to beat the queues on the road to Heathrow, for example), and sometimes they are simply entertaining ideas: when BA announced the introduction of beds in Business Class, Virgin Atlantic responded by announcing that they would be introducing double beds in Upper Class, with curtains around them and 'no questions asked'. How much of this last idea did they really implement? Not a lot. But it created a lot of amused conversation among their target market, and positioned them once more in their desired place as the perpetual bushwhacker of BA.

Manifestation in Communications

Of course we will do this in advertising, if we can afford it. But let's think of communications Wrapping as embracing *every single piece* of communications. Let's look at Tango, the hugely successful orange soda brand owned by Britvic in the UK, and the way their brand team treated something as dry as legal copy. Now legal copy is not usually regarded as a playground for creativity. Indeed, when looking at pack copy for a promotion originally, the sales promotion company advised the brand and agency team that one was legally required to have a statutory set of rules and disclaimers on pack that amounted to half the available pack space.

The Tango team's first step was to question this. On further exploration they discovered that this was no longer true – one no longer had to have all the legal copy on the pack: it was possible to shortcut a great deal by creating an address and telephone number whereby consumers could contact Tango if they wanted all the legal details.

So the next question was – how to make what legal copy they did need funny? How to give it the spirit of Tango? They broke it down into pieces and rethought each piece. What if, for instance, instead of simply writing the customary bit about 'employees of the company can't enter', they substituted something along the lines of 'If you win, write to us and say "I've won", and you can't, because you work at Britvic'? What if instead of writing 'If you would like a copy of the full list of rules and entry requirements, write off to XYZ', they wrote 'If you are the kind of anorak that wants to know the full list of rules and entry requirements, write off to XYZ'? And so the agency copywriter set to work.

Well, we applaud the effort and tenacity, but is all of this kind of thing really worth the effort? Did anyone really notice this? The answer is yes. When running the so-called '£10 Bribe Promotion', a consumer wrote in to say that the legal copy on the pack had been put up on the staff notice board in the Ford Plant in Dagenham because the riveters thought the legals were so funny. The legals, for God's sake. As we will see later, it is often the detailing on the brands that reveals the people behind the brands. That shows it is a brand with its own culture. By people for people, rather than just 'another successful megabrand brought to you by the House of Behemoth'.

And we should note that two of the last three examples have all been from subcultures – brands within larger organizations. You do not have to have your own company to be your own country.

Finally, it is no accident that as Challengers we have left advertising until last. Amy Curtis-McIntyre of jetBlue:

> Advertising is the last thing you bring to the mix. You start by getting your product right, getting your attitude right, getting everyone internally understanding the mission. Then you move to telling the story through PR. You build the advertising last, and that way you can live off realistic budgets.[9]

And part of this will lie in leaving leaning on the advertising till late in the process – mentally, if not chronologically. It is not that advertising will not be a powerful tool if we can afford it; it is that pushing it to one side will force us to think through the other layers of Wrapping and start to develop them first. Wrapping means changing the way we think about the destination for marketing, and, indeed, how we add value. We have come to think that the way we add real value in marketing is to interrogate and tweak the centre (the insight, the strategy) – in fact for many of these examples the way people have added real value is by wrapping richness at what would normally be thought of as *the edges*.

Blackbeard's Fuse: The Little Things Are Sometimes the Big Things

And why should we bother doing all these little things? Because the little things are sometimes the big things. Think about a pirate who was himself a brand – Blackbeard – and note two interesting things in particular. The first is that few of us remember his real name (Edward Teach): his nickname is what lingers in the memory. And for the second, consider the following description of him:

> Our hero, Captain Teach, assumed the cognomen of Blackbeard, from that large quantity of hair which, like a frightful meteor, covered his whole face and frightened America more than any comet which has appeared there a long time. This beard was black, which he suffered to

grow of an extravagant length; as to breadth it came up to his eyes. He was accustomed to twist it with ribbons, in small tails . . . and turn them about his ears. In time of action he wore a sling over his shoulders, with three brace of pistols, hanging in holsters, like bandoliers; and stuck lighted matches under his hat, which, appearing on each side of his face, his eyes naturally looking fierce and wild, made him altogether such a figure that imagination cannot form an idea of a Fury from Hell to look more frightful.[10]

What do you remember? Well, the beard, obviously, and its intriguing ability to frighten America. But also, I would suggest, the 'matches'. (We should note that a match in this sense is not a small wooden stick for lighting fires – it was a word given to a length of hemp cord, designed to burn slowly, usually used to prime cannon.) We are struck by that strange little detail, that makes him unique. We don't remember his real name, and we've seen a number of good beards in our time, but that thing with the matches? That really captures our imagination.

In a sense, what Blackbeard with his matches represents is an obsession with what the fashion business calls 'detailing' – specifically, an obsession with emotional as well as physical detailing. Why does detailing matter? Because it shows the love. It shows the love of the people behind the brand for what they are making and doing. Ben and Jerry's doesn't *need* its own way of describing ice cream ingredients; it is just a natural reflection of their own particular depth of affection for what they do. innocent don't need to put eyelashes on the headlights of their cow vans – but they do. It shows the depth of their affection for the brand. And that is something we feel and respond to.

The Culture Economy

It is striking that a number of these brand owners are resistant to talking about themselves as 'a brand'. The former CEO of sandwich retailer Pret A Manger, Andrew Rolfe, notes in *Uncommon Practice*: 'Although our proposition has been very clear from day one, I wouldn't describe Pret as a brand . . . the minute you try and separate the brand from the business it becomes artificial.'[11]

And we also see this caution in the co-owner of a packaged good Challenger, Richard Reed of innocent:

> Maybe brand is slightly the wrong word to use because a brand to me is restricted. [Creating a brand means to me that] a lot of people will work out what somebody wants to hear and then tell them that, irrespective of whether it is actually true or not. We are what we are, and that's why the door is always open, that's why our photographs are on the wall and our emails and our website ... I think marketing can only ever be an amplifier of what is really there.

In other words, instead of seeing themselves as a business producing a product or service on the one hand, and then separately cloaking it in a brand image on the other, brands that Wrap see it all as part of the same thing. A way of doing and thinking that unites the way one behaves, both externally and internally. I don't mean this in terms of simply an *invisible internal* culture that reflects the brand positioning. I mean a *perceptible* culture, a culture that is visible from the outside – a brand where, in fact, what one is visibly and deliberately offering is one's own culture.

So while I feel a little worried looking to replace such well-argued concepts as 'The Entertainment Economy' and 'The Experience Economy', I actually don't agree with either of them. I would suggest instead that what we are about to see is the Culture Economy; of course, those cultures will need to offer experience and express themselves in engaging ways, but they must, above all, offer perceptibly self-confident and well-layered cultures that burn from the inside. And which recognize, perhaps, that getting the inside right first is the most important step – just as Orange's point of view about those France Telecom-owned companies in new geographies which they have been through the process of rebranding is that: 'You have to be Orange on the inside before you can be Orange on the outside'. The internal culture has to be got right before you start expressing it externally.

Which brings us by a different route back to one of the starting points for the book, namely that brands are about people – because what makes up the perceptible culture behind these brands is exactly that: the people. Shubhankar Ray of Camper believes that people engage with you as a brand when they can see the people behind the brand. And this is evidenced by the aspects of the brand or the experience that genuinely are born out of the personal culture – or even the whims – of the people involved. Renzo Rosso of Diesel agrees; when talking about the purpose of Diesel's advertising, he says: 'We are not trying to convince them to buy clothes. We want them to say "I like these people".'

One had the same sort of feeling about Orange for a while: that one could sense (and one liked) the people on the other side of the brand. And that this was an important part of why one warmed so strongly to them.

And this idea of engaging with the people behind the brands is another reason why the little details we have talked about before are important: they give away small clues about the people behind the brand, whether they care, and what they care about. Let's go back to those Tim Little shoes we noted above, on display in Barney's or Saks or Selfridges. If you ask Tim Little himself why those shoes have those names, he will tell you two things. First, it reflects the way he first saw the shoes: 'I thought of them as little individuals, who have their own character. So I thought it would be nice to give them a name.' And when he says a name, he meant a name: not just a style number or a word denoting some sterile old-world town like 'Chatsworth', the way some of the traditional establishment shoe companies had gone. But names. And in particular names of blues songs – because, well, he loves the blues. 'Whiskey and women' is a John Lee Hooker song, as is 'Boom boom'; '40 days and 40 nights' was most famously recorded by Son House. We may or may not know enough about the blues to pick this up, but we do somehow pick up a sense of care and culture behind the brand which, even if we cannot exactly define how, allows us to sense something of the people behind it and how they feel.

Summary

This chapter is the last of the group of three looking at how a Necessary Pirate approaches the development of the idea and its manifestation in brand expression – Pushing, Projecting and Wrapping.

Wrapping is effectively how most of these Challengers seem to bring such a sense of richness and love for their brand to their side of the relationship that it creates real engagement in us – or the relevant tribes of us. How they offer a level of *participation* in the brand and the brand's particular culture that the competition doesn't. So perhaps our role as Necessary Pirates is not just selling a brand; it is selling a way of seeing life – one whose boundaries are so clearly demarcated that it has its own language and beliefs and customs to the point where it becomes its own self-referencing 'country'.

Let's leave the chapter by panning out – taking in a wide shot of the broader universe of branded entities. Because this idea of self-contained (and self-referencing) worlds being sources of a strong relationship is not confined to brands, or at least brands of consumer goods or services. Looking to explain the success of the White Stripes, one rock magazine wrote:

> The best groups live in their own universes, laden with reference points … One can easily imagine living in a White Stripes kind of way, occasionally holidaying in Mississippi, filling one's flat with stuffed animals and rusty candelabras, alternating between Robert Johnson and Stooges records while reading the novels of William Faulkner by the light of a paraffin lamp (and, naturally, wearing white trousers).[12]

Whether or not you yourself actually want to live this way is besides the point; the writer is able to articulate a rounded world of its own, into which he slips – and enjoys slipping – when cranking up the White Stripes.

Looking at film, one can see the idea of powerful brands occupying self-referential and detailed worlds taken into those clichéd, gravel-voiced opening words of US movie trailers: 'In a World Where …'. Yet how few of those films really create that kind of world? And the ones that genuinely do never have to use that phrase. James Bond, Lord of the Rings, *The Matrix* – those entertainment properties who really have successfully created subcultures of their own, who are their own countries, never begin a trailer with 'in a world where …'; they don't have to. They have indeed created their own countries or worlds, but one sees this through their language, beliefs, cultures, rather than their having to signal it so crudely.

The Most Dynamic Brand in the World?

Finally, let us test this 'country as a model for branding' thesis against what has, arguably, been the most dynamic brand in the world over the last three years, in terms of growth, opinions and appeal. So, here we go, then – the most dynamic brand in the world from 2001 to 2004 as its own country. As with the very first example, I am going to do it without telling you what the brand is.

Their Beliefs

That white magic is healthy and good. Something that should be taught in schools.

The Way They Speak/Their Language

The dog Latin of "Expelliarmus!" Occasionally the language of snakes. Describing the rest of us as Muggles.

Their Culture and Customs

Those courses: Defence Against the Dark Arts, for instance. Big dinners at the end of term. The Sorting Hat as a form of Border Control.

Characteristics of Their Citizens

Four houses. Not speaking The Dark Lord's name.

Their Funny Little Habits

Playing a sort of aerial football on broomsticks. A preoccupation with broomsticks and wands in general, in fact. Using owls to carry messages.

Things They Have No One Else Has

Self-shuffling playing cards. Platform $9\frac{3}{4}$. Invisibility cloaks. Howlers. Mandrakes, Dementors and Hippogriffs.

Their Iconography

That scar. Those broken spectacles with the little bit of sticky tape holding them together.

Yes. That seems to fit.

The Excuse for the Navy

As with the last two chapters, we continue to burrow away underneath the Second and Third Excuses for the Navy. Small budgets and being in packaged goods are not the issue. Wrapping need not be expensive; but it does take time and a different kind of behaviour, inside and out.

So once we have identified our opportunity and strategic idea, fight to stop the continual fiddling with the centre. Redefine how the team are to add value – wrapping richness at the edges.

Exercises

The Wrap Map

To help change the way we think in this way, here is a 'Wrap Map'; I accept, of course, that this is a perfectly hideous expression – but I am banking on the fact that, like Blackbeard, the 'cognomen' will at least help keep it salient for you (Figure 4.5). Note that it is not about what the brand's essence and personality are, but about how the brand is expressing itself. Nor is it supposed to be anything more than a piece of stimulus – it is not another box to prescriptively fill in.

Looking at how your brand offer fits into this map, where are the glaring gaps? Where are you over- and under-devoting your energies? Note that most of these brands did not come to all this richness overnight – it grew as they went along. But that doesn't mean we can simply put it all to one side. You need to Wrap over time.

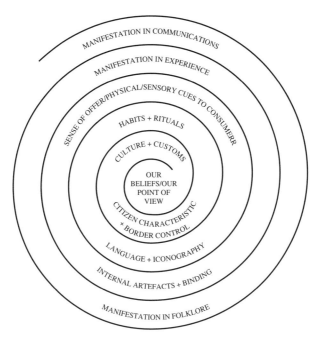

Figure 4.5   **The Wrap Map**

There are a number of exercises one can derive from the examples in this chapter. But here are two more to get you going.

Camper

What do you champion, and what are you against? Make this more than obvious stuff; being for sin and against motherhood has much more potential for stand-out than being for motherhood and against sin.

Write these down as two lists, side by side. Which are the two or three that really define you?

Gobs

Take the four most common words you use to describe the category and the product. Ban them. Building on your outputs from the Camper exercise, come up with four new words that actually reflect how you in particular see and feel about the category.

Personal Qualities that Foster an Internal Challenger Culture

Part II outlines a set of five personal qualities that we need to bring out in ourselves and those around us if we are to succeed in fostering an internal Pirate brand culture.

Chapter 5 Denting: A Different Kind of Respect

The first personal quality that a Challenger individual or team needs to have is the ability to 'Dent': to drive the brand vision forward, and interpret the word 'No' simply as a request for further information. This chapter explores some of the most important characteristics of a Denter, such as their perception that they are employed by the brand rather than by the company, and their acceptance of internal tension if it is necessary to avoid dilution of the vision. As such, Denting represents a different kind of respect – a primary respect for what is right for the brand (and therefore the shareholder) rather than the historic practices of the company.

Chapter 6   Binding: A Different Kind of Contract

This chapter explores the quality of 'Binding': how Challengers create singularity of direction across a team. It argues that one does not need a single individual at the helm of a Challenger brand, but one does need a singular vision, and it looks at how Challenger teams have created agreements or 'contracts' between themselves and their partners in order to bind everyone in that team to delivering that brand vision.

Chapter 7   Leaning: A Different Kind of Commitment

Being a Challenger will require a level of personal exposure to risk – certainly internally, and probably externally. This chapter looks at why this is necessary, and argues that rather than flinch from such exposure, we will profit more from the commitment that comes from accepting and leaning into it.

Chapter 8   Refusing: A Different Kind of Passion

What a Challenger individual refuses to accept defines them as powerfully as what they have a passion for; in particular, refusing to accept that the key issue on their brand cannot be overcome, or that their category is not open to brand building. This chapter focuses on examples of how such constructive refusal overturned apparently inevitable commoditization in two very different categories.

Chapter 9   Taking It Personally: A Different Kind of Professionalism

This chapter is about the imperative for a Challenger individual to personally commit to the brand they are working on – a commitment that goes beyond the normal confines of what we call 'professionalism'. It looks at the reasons why, unless they can take their brand challenge personally, that brand probably will not be fuelled by the standards, fight and spirit it will need to succeed.

Chapter 10   Brand-centricity

There is a centre to all these qualities and behaviours: not the personal agenda of the individual, but the opportunity for and nature of the brand. This chapter looks at this notion of Brand-centricity, and discusses how that will be taken through into the idea of subcultures within large organizations (Behemoth, Inc) in Part III.

The Five Personal Qualities

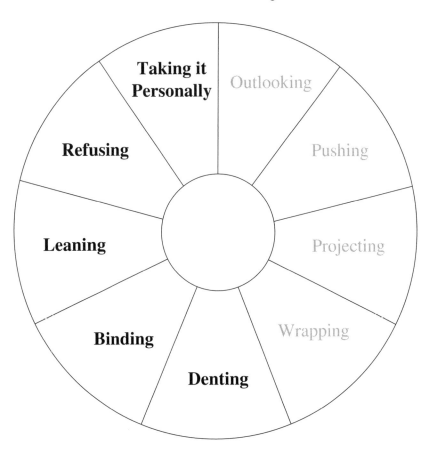

5

Denting: A Different Kind of Respect

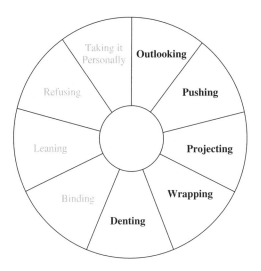

Figure 5.1 **Denting**

> I thought tennis had had enough of manners. In Chile, if the crowd didn't like what was happening, they threw coins and seat cushions. I thought that was a step in the right direction.
>
> *John McEnroe[1]*

When Mikhail Gorbachev came to London a few years ago, an evening was arranged for him to speak, accompanied by two leading UK political figures. One of these was David Steel, the former leader of the Liberal Party, for long an ineffective and fringe centrist force in British Politics – always reasonable and considerate, and never elected. Steel stood up to speak prior to Gorbachev, the sweeping reformist and architect of perestroika, and confessed to feeling a little out of his league in such company. During the last rally of the faithful, he joked, that he had attended as leader of the Liberal Party, his rousing back and forth with the politically centrist crowd had gone something like this:

'What do we want?' he had asked them theatrically;

'Gradual change!' they shouted in answer.

'And when do we want it?'

'In due course!'[2]

A core theme of this book is that building great brands is not really about processes, important though those can be. Great brands are about people. Not necessarily about founders. But ambitious and impatient people: people who want to make significant change, and make it now.

Central to all the cases we looked at, whether single brand companies with a founder, or brands within multi-brand cultures, was a type of individual who, in the words of one of our interviewees 'wants to put a dent on the world': a Denter. Denters are so important to the success of Challenger cultures or subcultures that we should explore their role, nature and impact in more detail – first here, and then more specifically within the second half of the book in terms of their role within multi-brand cultures. They take an important part of the role of the founder in some way. Not completely, but significantly.

Denters may initially sound simply like rebellious mavericks, but in fact they share a number of important common qualities:

- They are on a personal mission to drive the brand vision forward.

And, in doing this:

- They see themselves as employed by the brand, not the company.
- They are therefore doing this job for this job, rather than for the one it will get them afterwards.
- They are happy to embrace tension within the organization rather than dilute the vision for the brand.
- They do not easily accept the answer 'no' – from inside or outside the company.

Let us look at Denters and Denting in terms of each of these five qualities in turn.

They Are on Some Kind of Personal Mission to Drive the Brand Vision Forward

Some of those starting their own companies just want to do something for themselves – even if they are not quite sure what. Richard Reed of innocent talked of 'quieting the voices' that murmur in an entrepreneur's ear.

> Certainly for me, it was about quietening the voices. Trying and failing – that's so much better than not having tried in the first place. Instead of just always thinking 'Well, I wish I had done . . .'

When beginning the interview with Charlotte Semler of Myla, the luxury sex brand launched in 2001, and which was featured in *Vogue* editorial every month for the first year of its life, she asked me where I wanted to start. I replied at the beginning – when she had the idea for the company. She replied that having the idea wasn't the beginning. The beginning, she said, was knowing that she wanted to do something *other than what she was doing at the moment* (working in a large advertising agency), and recognizing that she needed to stop doing that job in order to work out what she wanted to do instead. At the Tesco Christmas party (Tesco was her client) she was standing in a queue for the ladies loos, and found herself next to one of her clients, Nina Hampson; Hampson asked Semler what she was up to, and she replied that she was leaving to do something else, though had yet to work out quite what. Hampson immediately asked if she could join her – and they agreed in that queue to take the jump into the unknown together. It was only some time later that they worked out what it was they were actually going to do.

Clearly, founders can have idealistic ambitions, and quite large ones: Merrill Fernando of Dilmah has a huge ambition – he wants to dramatically improve the life of tea pickers in Sri Lanka and ultimately the economy of the whole country. Fernando is hugely disturbed by the fact that most Ceylon tea plantations are losing money – they sell the tea to large multinationals for less than it costs to produce, resulting, Fernando says, in the workers having minimal pay, and the country subsidizing the profits of the world's big tea brands. Fernando's solution is to promote a Ceylon brand of premium tea – Dilmah – that cuts out the middleman, and creates more money to put back into the living conditions of the plantation workers and their families. He is very open about this mission: he shares it with customers of his products through printed letters that he puts in each packet of tea.

This kind of ambition might seem too high a stretch for someone working within a larger organization. Yet even here, I suggest, the difference is to some extent simply one of degree: even where one has a Denter within a larger organization, what drives them to dent is that they have first a belief that this is the right thing to do. In their own way, they want to make a difference.

Paula Moss of Hovis, for instance, describes the recognition that there is something in the brand itself that needs to be taken head-on, and a determination that you are going to be the person to do it: 'We are here to make a difference. You have to ask yourself in a situation: am I going to take the issue, or duck it?'

Scott Lutz describes his sense of what his embryonic brand could be about, and how it required him to battle against a view from above him to go with what seemed to him an unsuitable name. The reason he fought so hard for '8th Continent' and not 'Zoy' as a name was because he and his team believed this brand stood potentially for more than Soy Milk. Yes, they had a fantastic product that (in his words) 'blew away' the market leader 80:20 in taste tests, but Lutz and his team felt that what they had embarked on was not about producing a great soy milk brand, but about enabling people to be more 'wellness active'. Create a more profound change in their consumers' lives than simply switching soy milk brands.

Sometimes a significant part of the motivation is a desire by the Denter to make a larger impact on the organization as a whole. Let's consider at this point a 'Pirate' (in our sense) in a real Navy – the US Navy. Commander Michael Abrashoff took over command of a destroyer called the USS *Benfold* in June 1997. He inherited a ship that was one of the worst performing ships in the Navy with a crew retention rate of just 28% (i.e. less than a third wanted to sign up for another two-year tour of duty when their current one finished). In 21 months Abrashoff turned the ship around; during the course of the book we will look at some of the less conventional things he did in this process. By the end his crew was leading the Pacific Fleet on measures such as readiness indicators and gunnery scores, and the crew retention rate had increased to almost 100%.

What motivated him? He wanted to make a significant impact on his world and his men.

> I wanted to be the best leader in the industry. I knew I couldn't get there by doing things the same old way.
>
> And I had an overwhelming sense of responsibility to my people. I wanted to provide all 300 of them with an incredible work experience that they could use for the rest of their lives.

Denters sometimes use this sense of the bigger impact to recruit their fellow team-members. Let's go back to Scott Lutz. Lutz was historically an innovator (he had launched Go-Gurt in a previous life), and this was a part of his passion for agreeing to set up the cultural experiment that became '8th Continent' in the first place:

> I did it because I felt the company needed to think about innovation in a wholly new way. When I was interviewing people I didn't ask them would they like to come and work on a soy milk. I asked them how they felt about ensuring the future of innovation at General Mills.

This scale of ambition, of course, drives such Denters to really want to make a significant impact – internally as well as externally; in many ways, in fact, they derive their energy precisely from the scale of the challenge. Chris Hawken described taking the challenge of turning round the reputation of Skoda as 'a joy'. I am not sure there are many other people in the automotive market at the time who would have described it in those terms.

And Denters need this emotional energy to overturn stuck underlying thinking in the organization, and to feed and warm them during That Difficult First Year (see Chapter 15).

They Are Employed by the Brand First, and the Company Second

Denters see themselves as employed primarily by the brand and the vision, and only secondarily the company.

Ken Kutaragi was the person who fought for Sony to enter videogames, and eventually persuaded them to set up a whole separate division dedicated to it. His own personal epiphany came when he bought his son a Nintendo 8-bit game machine; although it was basic and certain aspects like the sound quality were poor, 'I realized . . . that in the future, computers and computer science would change our lifestyle, the way we played and lived.'[3]

Kutaragi initially tried to get Nintendo to use Sony sound components, so that at least Sony would have a foot in the market (and his son would have a more rounded gaming experience). When that initiative broke down, he pushed a reluctant Sony into thinking about entering the videogames market. The organization's resistance dispirited him, but he remained loyal to his vision: 'I was very sad. But I had a strong passion, so I decided to create my own space to make my vision a reality, even if that meant leaving Sony.'[4] This willingness to leave the company is very unusual in Japan, which tends to be a risk-averse business culture in this regard. But in the end Sony gave Kutaragi the space he had fought so hard for, and together they created PlayStation.

This sense of being employed by the brand first and the company second leads them to be enormously and primarily loyal to the people who come under the brand's wings: the brand team, the sales team, factory people, and so on. Jeremy Woods led the team on Pot Noodle, a dehydrated noodle snack brand which was acquired by the much larger CPC; for Woods, protecting the brand's identity and success within this larger, more conservative environment meant seeing his primary loyalty as being to all the people who worked on his brand – in whatever discipline:

It was demanding, but we did it at the time because we passionately believed in the brand. I was trying to protect the people that worked on the brand, the hundreds of people that worked in the factory whose life relied on Pot Noodle, and the people that had come across from Golden Wonder who depended on Pot Noodle, and there was almost no other mission apart from looking after Pot Noodle from these nasty people, these big corporate people that had just bought it.

They Are Doing It for This Job Rather Than the One It Gets Them Afterwards

Returning to Commander Abrashoff, when he was asked how he got around the 'we don't do things like that around here' mentality within the Navy, he replied:

> As for the people above me, I didn't ask permission. I figured 'What's the worst they could do to me?' It's careerism that keeps most people from taking risk. It could have backfired but it didn't. Not once.

What allows many of these people to do it so successfully is, frankly, that they are not afraid of losing their jobs. And if you ask them what would have happened if it hadn't worked out, they shrug their shoulders and say 'I would have probably been fired. But I'd have found something else.'

Careerists are the opposite of Denters in this sense – they see themselves as employed primarily by the company and secondarily by the brand; and, as such, make very different kinds of commitments and very different kinds of decisions at the critical moment. Bob Gill of Pringles, who was responsible for the team that took the potato chip brand from 100 million cans to 1.3 billion cans in ten years, describes how he saw the priority for his loyalties working on Pringles, and for all the team (including the plant):

> I saw my role as being the leader of a business, and I would do what's right for the business and the plant. Obviously one doesn't want to hurt the parent company, but essentially I saw it as a financial resource. There are some corporate policies and procedures you should think about, but frankly if that stuff doesn't deliver for the shareholder, then change it.

The Ability to Embrace Tension

We are all taught that consensus is the way to move a team forward. And there are times when that is true, and even appropriate. Yet if one is trying to move a brand that is stuck or even static, one will encounter people who do not want to move as fast as one does, or indeed who are guardians of processes that need to be changed in order to allow one to move in the direction one wants, at the velocity one wants, and who are more concerned with protecting the process or system than in building your brands. The question here, then, is what one does with the tensions this creates.

Sometimes these tensions are because other parts of the organization fundamentally disagree with where you want to go. The quote that follows is from Yoshio Ishizaka, talking about a meeting with the Chairman of Toyota in Japan. Ishizaka was at the time the Senior Executive Vice-President of Toyota Motor Sales in North America, and had been briefed by his superior to come back with plans for how to market a new car as a flagship for Toyota (known as 'Project F'); he and his closest colleagues, however, felt strongly that this was not the best way forward for the product, and that in North America an entirely new brand would need to be created through which to properly market the car. As though persuading his superiors of this wasn't going to be difficult enough, he also knew that he would need two cars to make a new brand credible. So he decided to ask for three:

> I made my presentation: we believed that the LS 400 should not be the flagship vehicle for Toyota. We felt to successfully market this car would require an entirely new franchise. In addition, we also knew that the franchise would need not one vehicle, but at least two at launch.
>
> This created many what we *now* refer to as 'Discussions'. The engineering divisions were less than positive and suspicious of our ability to build another franchise. There was great tension from TMC on whether or not the LS 400 should be a Toyota flagship, and no one in the room wanted to build anything beyond the LS – well, except us.
>
> Looking back, I was pretty persistent, in fact, so much so, that in typical retail fashion, I asked for a third vehicle – which would go on to become the SC.
>
> I was sure my career was on the line.[5]

Ishizaka persuaded the Chairman, and the new franchise soon acquired its own name: Lexus.

Sometimes the tension comes because someone refuses to back down in front of one's superiors. Bob Gill was a sufficient thorn in the side of one P&G CEO that he was actually fired by the man at one point. He went to his immediate boss and asked what he should do. His boss replied, 'Look, Ed [the CEO] is leaving in a couple of months. Stick around, but just don't let him see you.' The CEO left, Gill stayed on, and the brand grew. Chris Hawken of Skoda was only able to turn the brand around by almost severing his relationship with his own European Head of Marketing. He dropped the internationally preferred advertising agency, against the express instructions of his European boss, and appointed an agency instead with no footprint in Europe outside the UK. The agency's creative work was fundamental to turning the brand around in the UK, but the tension with his superior persisted: the first of two key flashpoints being when Hawken actually had to get permission from his estranged superior to shoot his new commercials in the factory in the Czech Republic (the commercials, of course, that the man didn't want Hawken to make in the first place), and the second when Hawken ignored the European Advertising Guidelines for the layout of his print ads. What gave him the confidence that this relationship was a price worth paying was the conviction that the brand needed the quality and talent of his new agency team and their work, and the constant support of his local MD.

And sometimes the tensions are because the other people you bump up against in the organization just don't seem to understand that things need to be done differently on this brand in order for it to succeed; that it needs a wholly different model. Jeremy Woods of Pot Noodle again:

> Within a very rigid multinational, where there's pack design manuals, advertising approvals processes, teams of lawyers – well, of course, every-thing we did was a problem. For one thing, we had advertising that didn't fit the CPC model; it was a problem: the legal people would not sign it off, and the commercial director did not like it. It did not go through the testing procedures at all. Everything that we did, did not work according to the CPC model.

So here I was, absolutely adamant that we had this great campaign that was going to work, and yet it was completely against the principles of marketing as CPC understood it. We had T-shirts that said 'I need a fork . . .', but it was written in such a way it could be misconstrued. These were banned by the lawyers. 'Oh,' they said, 'you can't do that.' I did it anyway, and of course they were circulated and there was a great big hoo-ha. People were walking around in the T-shirts: we gave them to the sales force, and we gave them to the grocery retail buyers, and they loved them. And then, of course, the buyers starting saying, 'This is fantastic, the way you guys bought Pot Noodle, it is great, the way you are marketing it', and of course the Sales Director and the Commercial Director knew nothing about it, so I got in trouble.

It is interesting to note the frequency within this interview with which Jeremy Woods uses the expression 'of course'. He is supremely confident that he is right and the others are wrong, and that it will turn out the way he sees it.

He goes on:

Introducing instant win promotions was another source of disagreement. On Pot Noodle we used to spend a fortune on instant win promotions all the time – that was part of snacks marketing then. And CPC's attitude was 'You cannot do that, we will all end up in jail.' And I said, 'I don't give a toss, we are doing it', and of course every time they were forced to back down. We had vending machines which we put in garage forecourts and we just started the business with these things that dispensed hot water to make a Pot Noodle. Well, the Head Accountant walked into my office and said, 'I'm going to close down your vending operation . . . no, we cannot do that, no, no, no . . . capital equipment . . . blah, blah, . . . very complicated, legal liability . . . blah, blah . . . I want you to shut down the whole thing.' Again, this was a huge part of the fight that I had, when the Chief Accountant in Europe wanted to close down my operation.

Sometimes the tension comes because one is trying to create a culture that really pushes and challenges its own rules and thinking. David Atter of Tango: 'Far from being bad, conflict when properly orchestrated is good, because it causes people to continually challenge what has been said.'

If you interview Denters, and ask them if there is anything they regret about the way they drove their brand forward, they always say two things. The first is: 'Yes. I wish I hadn't pissed quite so many people off.' And then there is a brief pause before they add: 'But I don't know if I could have done it any other way.'

What Do You Do with the Word 'No'?

Of course, one always has to punch through external barriers. Dave Hieatt of the biking and skateboarder brand Howies:

> When one of Britain's most influential bike shops repeatedly kept turning us down, we asked if we could keep coming back to see them. We asked them to make appointments with dates and times for the next ten years. They thought we were joking. But we got out a ten-year diary and asked them to give us some dates. At that point, they looked at me and saw I wasn't joking.
>
> They went on to stock Howies. It is now their most profitable clothing line and the guy who was running the stores now works for us.

He adds: 'Beware the man who believes in what he is doing.'

But perhaps more difficult for those of us within larger organizations is the internal, rather than the external 'No'; because we are surrounded by the fellow prisoners of our brand and company's history; it's just that they haven't all realized it yet. Freeing ourselves – and our fellow inmates – will take more than just having a great idea.

Chris Moss is a serial Denter. An early Marketing Director of Virgin Atlantic, he went on to be a key shaper of Orange's identity as its Marketing Director at launch; and at the time of writing he was leading the most successful of the directory enquiries Challengers to BT, with some justly famous advertising behind it. Moss says the key question you have to ask yourself is:

> What do you do with the word 'No' when you get it? Does it make you go back and start again? Or does it simply make you more determined to prove the other person is wrong?

Hans Snook, his CEO at Orange, and a visionary founder in his own right, tried initially to reject the name Orange when Moss proposed it, preferring Microtel, which had been registered by their parent Hutchison. But Moss didn't accept the answer. (By the same token, in Moss's view, what makes a great CEO – or boss above a Denter – is not that they spot a great idea straightaway. It's that they have the ability to change their minds and support it with the same level of intensity they rejected it.)

Bob Gill of Pringles shared Moss's view on what to do with 'No' when you get it from your boss – you should basically just regard it as a request for further information:

> Well, you listen to them, and then you repeat their concerns to them, to show them that you've heard and understood them. Then you basically act on the basis that they don't really mean 'No' – they just haven't understood it as well as you have yet. You basically treat the word 'No' as a request for more information. They're not stupid, of course, they're just coming at it from a different place.

I was discussing this with a friend, who said they had been to a conference where the guest speaker, a man from 3M, had introduced himself as 'the person who had killed the Post-It development project. Seven times.' They just kept coming back, he said, until he couldn't kill it any more.

Denting Doesn't Necessarily Mean Direct Confrontation

W. Chan Kim and Renee Mauborgne have done some consistently fascinating work into people and organizations that have changed the rules in their favour. In an article for the magazine *Fast Company* in 2003 they chart the success of Bill Bratton, currently Chief of the Los Angeles Police Department, previously the Police Commissioner of New York and earlier still responsible for running the Massachusetts Bay Transit Authority. The story goes that one fine day in Boston Bratton finds himself faced with a situation where the MBTA Board decide to buy smaller squad cars to save money. He believes this is unacceptable, and he needs to reverse this situation – yet he doesn't control the budgets.

What Bratton does not do, though, is make an impassioned or angry plea to the Board; he approaches it in a rather different way, by inviting the MBTA's general manager to tour the district with him. Bratton picks up the GM in a car as small as the proposed new squad cars, but overcommits a little to the GM seeing things his way – before he picks him up, he jams both the front seats as far forward as they will go, and then stuffs the car with every conceivable tool of the policeman's trade. With the GM already uncomfortable, Bratton then chooses a two-hour tour which curiously seems to take in every pot hole that Boston and its suburbs possesses. At the end of the tour the GM cannot wait to get out, remarking to Bratton that, 'He couldn't understand how Bratton could stand being in such a cramped car for so long, let alone if there was a criminal on the back seat.' The Board subsequently reverse their decision and give Bratton the cars he originally wanted.[6]

Sometimes one has to push the idea to make a personal breakthrough, to create a relationship that will be critical to one's own trajectory of success. The chef Jamie Oliver, whose show now appears in 39 countries, set himself the task (when he was still very much an unknown) of learning about pasta and bread. So when he left college, he went to work at Antonio Carluccio's in Covent Garden as a pastry chef, hoping to meet another chef who worked there called Gennaro Contaldo – the man who apparently made the 'best pasta in the world'.

It was a good, fun place to work, but there was one problem every time I asked for permission to get near Gennaro they put this big wall up.

They got it into their heads that I wanted to steal his secrets . . . That kind of attitude always annoyed me, because cooking is not just about knowing the right recipe, it's about getting off your arse and finding the best butter and the best flour and giving it all the attention it needs. Recipes are only half the work.

I said to him, 'Gennaro, I keep asking if I can come and help you make bread in the night and they keep saying no.' He said, 'It's because they think you're going to steal my bread recipe.' I was really annoyed because I didn't want to nick it, I just wanted to work with him and learn from him. But Gennaro said he couldn't undermine Antonio, and that was that.

But I wasn't prepared to leave it there. I started thinking how I could make Gennaro soften to me, this new, young boy in the kitchen. Because I was the pastry chef I was first there in the morning and left last at night. It meant there was an hour, between about midnight and 1a.m., when our shifts crossed over and so I decided to commit to memory what I saw him doing. After a while I started doing bits of it myself – weighing out his flour, getting his trays ready, getting the oven fired up. It basically meant he didn't have to come in until about half past one.

The new arrangement meant that I was working from 10a.m. to 1a.m., then from 3a.m. I did another four hours of voluntary bread-making. I did that every night for months until my dad said I was looking ill. But I loved every minute of it. It's like a different world at that time of night. My thinking was, if I did an hour's more work, he (i.e. Gennaro Contaldo) would get an hour's more sleep and he'd be a happy man. Or happier with me, at least. When I got his trays ready I used to dust them with polenta, or with stale breadcrumbs.

So this is an interesting thought. But here is how Jamie Oliver actually breaks through:

I used to rack up about 200 of these trays, and on every 10 trays I used to draw rude things and write dirty messages in the crumbs. I thought to myself: 'The man's on his own all night, he's probably really lonely. The least I could do was give the man a giggle.' Believe it or not, it was a tactic that paid off. He said to me that he didn't care what the restaurant said – I could do whatever I wanted and he wasn't going to stop me.[7]

(Reproduced by permission of The Guardian)

Denting – he refuses to accept the answer 'No' – made successful by pushing. A great idea, pushed in a really engaging way, based on an insight into the individual, to make it impossible to continue being refused. How often do we really see that?

So Denting is not simply about cojones, or the preparedness to confront. It is as much about imaginatively finding the most compelling way to help your internal audience feel the same way about your objective that you do.

Some Overrated Virtues

The title of this chapter is 'Denting: A Different Kind of Respect'. Let's consider some of the traditional civic virtues of being a part of a large organization that, for us at least, could use a little questioning.

'Respecting the Parent Organization, and Your Superiors'

One of the difficulties with the word 'No' is when it comes from something the organization is corporately reluctant to do. Bob Gill of Pringles draws the distinction here between what you need to understand and what you need to respect.

What you need to *respect* is whether the action you want to take – or are currently taking – is good for the shareholder or not, and what it requires of the business to deliver that. What you need to *understand* is how to help people who have issues that are nothing to do with the shareholder overcome those difficulties. So, for instance, the Chairman and CEO of P&G at one point was very resistant to the continued use of competitive advertising for Pringles, because at one industry dinner the CEO of a competitor, whose product was being knocked in the advertising, took him to one side and lobbied him to stop – essentially on the basis that they should be respecting each other as companies and brands, not denigrating each other. So he came back from one of these industry dinners and told Gill to stop doing competitive advertising against this competitor.

But Gill knew this was a key factor in the brand's growth at the time – it was, in essence, doing great things for the share and therefore the shareholder. And he also knew that this competitor had made a little rug of the Pringles character and put it as a door mat inside the front door of their building, encouraging everyone to wipe their feet on it as they came in. So Gill resisted changing the advertising, but instead gave his CEO a talk sheet and told him what to say the next time this came up at an industry dinner: 'Essentially it said: "What about the goddam rug in your reception ... where's the respect in that?" The other chairman shut up and didn't open his mouth about it again.'

'Respect Your Peers and Internal Experts'

Of course, there are all sorts of experts within the organization, who have all sorts of useful advice to impart. And historically we are taught to respect that expertise. Yet what comes through with all of these stories is that the one thing you have to respect most is the opportunity for the brand – everything else comes second. Look at Yoshio Ishizaka pursuing his vision for a new brand even though the engineers were against it. To paraphrase Lorenzo Fluxá: 'Of course I respect you. But first I respect the brand.'

'Stay in Your Own Space, and Respect Other People's Space'

A number of the people one speaks to advocate noise, lots of it, and in fact deliberately marketing yourself internally as a key part of making the impact you need on the rest of the organization. Jeremy Woods had a large costume of an animated Pot Noodle character called Ned; he used to get his team to take it in turns to dress up in it and go round the rest of CPC:

> The quickest win, I think, is to disrupt the status quo of the large organization you are seeking to influence, and you have to do that in a very noisy way – you create a *lot* of noise. So, we did mail drops for employees, we sent samples, we got Ned Pot Noodle wandering around, we built this massive great truck to go to rock festivals and parked it in the car park, you know. Everyone is pissed off because that took up about ten spaces, but we did that kind of 'internal noise' generally and that gives you the quick win, because it makes people think. People who are not necessarily directly involved in the business sit up and take notice.

'Respecting the Way Things Have Always Been Done'

Commander Abrashoff tells the story of the USS *Benfold*, at sea in the Persian Gulf in 1997, grappling with the time requirements for launching a Tomahawk missile. They found that these requirements were too ambitious: they could not complete the necessary US Navy Standard

Operating Procedures in the necessary time – and nor, extraordinarily, could any other ship in the fleet.

One of his seamen, unprompted, reviewed all the procedures. The man found that although the missiles had been updated, the Navy's procedures had not – and that by combining some of the key steps and eliminating others altogether (now possible because of the upgraded equipment), it would be possible to meet the time requirements and launch the missile safely. He informed Abrashoff, Abrashoff informed the Admiral, and the revised procedures were adopted throughout the fleet as 'The Benfold Procedures'.

Abrashoff made a point of not blindly following rules and regulations without exploring if there was a better way. We may not want or need to launch Tomahawks at the competition, but we may want to find entirely new ways of thinking about packaging, for example. We will not find those, however, if we blindly respect the way it has always been done.

'Copper Bottoms'

There will not always be copper-bottomed certainties as one tries to do new things. You can look for them, but they won't always be there – on the contrary, there will almost certainly be more risk involved, and that is something the team needs to accept and embrace. In launching Axe in the USA, the team looked at creating two launch commercials that centred on an irreverent take on pornography. It was a difficult thing to pull off, and they were expensive commercials – a potentially risky mixture. Neil Munn, the Global Team Leader, went to his national team and told them it was a good bet: 'I told them that we had a launch mix on the table that scored 9 out of 10; if we got this right, we could take it up to 12 out of 10.'

At one level, the bet did not come off. The ads were shot, but they did not work well enough to be part of the launch. But Munn would do the same again:

> The effort was not wasted – more important than finding an alternative way to use the work, we established a way of working that said that risk will be part of how we manage the brand agenda moving forward.

The ads subsequently proved the basis for a successful viral campaign.

*'Accepting Useful Input from Large Groups
of the Great and Wise'*

Bob Gill of Pringles used to encourage his team not to be afraid of Big Rooms. Big Rooms with Big Tables are there to be filled up with people commenting on what you are doing:

> One of my bosses said, 'Remember, Bill, the purpose of strategy is to never discuss strategy.' In those big rooms we discussed everything except strategy. Because in big rooms like that everybody tries to sound real smart, with the Chairman and all these functional heads. Thirty people go to these strategy meetings and none of them except the team, namely six guys, really know the business, but they all want to sound smart in front of the big bosses, and the board and all that, and so you don't ever want any real decisions to be made there.

The last sentence is of course the key point. One cannot stop the meeting happening, but don't ever allow the real decisions to be made there. Gill's solution to this was, in essence, twofold: first, if you find yourself forced into one of these meetings, and it is a two-hour meeting, then bring a four-hour presentation deck. Then, if people insist on talking anyway, feed them samples of new products until they are unable to speak.

Losing the Eighth Passenger

Bomber crews in the Second World War had a crew of seven (pilot, co-pilot, bomb aimer, navigator, rear gunner, and so on), but they sometimes referred to 'the Eighth Passenger' – an additional member on board each mission whom they were all aware of, and who influenced to a greater or lesser degree how well they performed their assigned task on that mission. The Eighth Passenger was Fear.

A primary role of Denting and the Denter, is to lose this Eighth Passenger. While I am in no way comparing the scale of the danger in what we do to the personal danger faced by an airman or woman in battle, we have this Eighth Passenger on our journey together, all the same – in fact, emotions of many kinds sit in rooms with us as invisible passengers, and they influence the way the team performs. Fear of what our boss will think. Fear of going up against the international category guidelines. Fear of failing in front of our peer group. Fear of how this might impact our career. And one of the functions of the Denter, and their preparedness to expose themselves in the ways we have explored above, is to help the group as a whole shrug off those unwelcome and inhibiting passengers.

Summary: Sailing Under the Flag of the Brand, Rather than the Flag of the Corporation

Denting – and having a Denter in a team – are absolutely critical to the success of any Challenger brand, whether in a single brand company or in a larger multi-brand organization.

But Denting is not about being an obstreperous renegade for its own sake. It is about loyalty – but to the brand and the brand team first, and the company second. It is about respect, but respecting what is right for the brand and what needs to be done, rather than a blind respect to the way the world order around us currently falls. And it is not that one is going to do something that is detrimental to the company; it is just that recognizing what it takes to deliver the brand opportunity – and therefore the optimum value to the shareholder – will mean not accepting the word 'No' as anything other than an invitation for further information and some inventive persuasion.

Our discussion of Denting is the beginning of nailing the Sixth Excuse for the Navy: 'But I don't own the company and we don't have a founder.' The nature of the team you need around a Denter, and therefore a fuller answer to this excuse, will come in Chapter 11 (Red Pill, Blue Pill).

Denting is a personal quality that needs to be front and centre in the team. If we do not have those qualities ourselves, we need to make sure we have someone at the core who does.

Exercises

There are no exercises for practising Denting. You either do it, or you don't.

6

Binding: A Different Kind of Contract

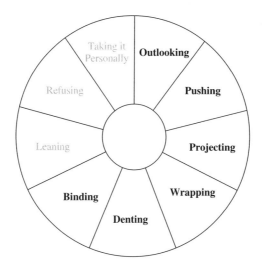

Figure 6.1   **Binding**

A pure vision is the single most important thing in making anything. And when you make a big commercial movie, that vision becomes clouded because there's so many people involved.[1]

Billy Bob Thornton

Can one be a Challenger without a single individual at one's heart? A single founder? Billy Bob Thornton's observation about the need for a singularity of vision is reflected in, for instance, the achievement of Samuel Johnson, the famous lexicographer, who wrote what is remembered (wrongly, as it happens) as the first dictionary of English – all 43,000 words and 114,000 supporting literary quotations of it. Bill Bryson observes that in doing so Johnson 'had achieved in under nine years what the forty members of the Académie Française could not do in under forty'.[2] No doubt part of this was also due to the fact that he was only being paid £1,575 to do this (spread over those nine years), which included paying for his assistants; he could not afford to overrun – he had to hit that nine years or he would die hungry. The 40-strong Académie Française, conversely, knew that they could debate the niceties of the spelling of 'fauteuil' for 20 years and still rely on a good dish of *coq au vin* when they returned to their *maisons* every evening. So it took them a little longer.

And of course all the famous Challengers have charismatic individuals at the helm, don't they? And everyone knows that camels are horses designed by a committee.

And yet, and yet. And yet it is too easy to fall into this comfortable little excuse for why we cannot do it ourselves. This is just another excuse that we create that allows us to stay in the Navy. So let's ask the question the other way around: 'When is a group not just a committee?' And what can we learn from the groups that have turned out to design racing thoroughbreds, not camels?

First, we should note that you do not need to have one person to have a singularity of vision. In many of these Challengers there is not always a single individual at the helm – often there are two (M.A.C., Myla), sometimes three (Tommy Bahama, innocent), and now and again much larger still – as with the so-called 'Group of 99' that started Saturn. What you do seem to need, though, is a *singularity of vision* forced on you by the scale of the challenge or the opportunity, and an understanding of how to bind other people around you to that vision. This singularity can come if the Challenge is clear enough. It is easy to forget now, as Lexus dominates the US luxury car market, how steep the cliff wall they had to scale must have looked in the beginning, as a Japanese luxury brand launching up against Cadillac, BMW and Mercedes. Their initial aspiration was to try to build up to selling 80,000 vehicles a year in the USA; they now sell three times that.

Or it can come if the opportunity is big enough: 8th Continent was formed because General Mills and DuPont estimated that the soy milk market was likely to be worth $1 billion by 2005 in the USA and they wanted to be a significant player in that market.

When Is a Group Not a Committee?

In talking of groups, we could say at this point that we were simply going to look beyond the individual – at innocent and its three founders, perhaps. But in many ways it is more useful for us to look beyond brands where the founding groups are the owner-drivers. I think it is safe to assume that very few of us reading this book are founders in search of a 'how to' manual; I am going to assume that we are mostly individuals within an organization of which we do not have sole leadership, and who have to find a way of binding together a large group of people around us. In which case even looking at groups of two or three founders is cheating. Because while there are more than one in this unit, they are still owners; they still have complete control over the company. So let us instead look at Lexus.

First, just pause a moment to notice what an extraordinary accomplishment Lexus is. A Japanese company, Toyota, known for reliable and good value – though not at the time stylish – cars, creating a luxury brand that overtook Mercedes and BMW in the largest luxury automotive market in the world. Within just 12 years. One of the most extraordinary stories of Challenger success anywhere in the world, there are a number of inspiring dimensions to how they created their success – like building over 400 prototypes for the first car in the line, the LS 400 (to the point where the Chief Engineer's health suffered) in order to be absolutely confident that the launch product would be superior. But the part we are most interested in here is how they created a vision over and above the product of success and what it would take.

They wrote a covenant. The Lexus Covenant. Between themselves and between everyone who was to be involved on the brand. It went as follows:

> Lexus will enter the most competitive, prestigious automobile race in the world. Over 50 years of Toyota automotive experience has culminated in the creation of Lexus cars. They will be the finest automobiles ever built.
>
> Lexus will win the race because:
> Lexus will do it right from the start.

> Lexus will have the finest dealer network in the industry.
> Lexus will treat each customer as we would a guest in our own home.

> If you think you can't, you won't . . .
> If you think you can, you will!
> We can. We will.

I am very familiar with this Covenant now, having had the pleasure of working with Lexus a little, but I find it, although at one level very simple, still a very powerful piece of writing, and a very powerful promise. It begins with an acknowledgement of the scale of the challenge. It moves through their credentials to their intent: to build the finest cars ever built. It outlines briefly the three key strands of why they will win, building to the critical concept of treating 'each customer as we would a guest in our own home' – a revolution in service delivery which would make Lexus's ownership experience unrivalled for years. And, finally, taking head-on the issue of self-belief and will – challenging the listener or reader to believe they can deliver it, and ending with those four immensely confident words: 'We can. We will.'

The story of the Lexus Covenant is an interesting one, for the nature and power of it as a touchstone developed over time. In the spring of 1988 Dave Illingworth, then GM of Lexus (and bear in mind this was a division at the time that had yet to have a finalized car, and would not be launched until 18 months later), saw a brochure on Saturn, on one page of which Don Hudler had laid out the mission and philosophy of that company. Illingworth, who had already been working on what would become Lexus for a year and a half at this point, felt that Lexus would also benefit from setting down its own ambition and mission, though he wanted something briefer. He went to his assistant and just started dictating – and it came. At this point, it consisted of the first two paragraphs of the version above.

He liked it. It seemed to capture what he was looking for. He tried it on some other people, and made a couple of minor changes, but essentially it was there – the ambition and how they were to get there.

The new 'covenant' remained in this form for 18 months. Then in August 1989 Illingworth and his team had to address the dealers, at the time of the formal launch. A key part of the theme of the speech he wanted to make was about 'conquering Everest': 'It was really about being successful, because so many people said it would never work – that Japanese cars would never mean luxury.' Looking at the Covenant again, Illingworth felt he wanted to add a positive, upbeat end to it that would reinforce this sense that it *was* possible, and that the team behind Lexus *was* going to do it. So he and his team added:

> If you think you can't, you won't . . .
> If you think you can, you will!
> We can. We will.

And at this point the words remained a powerful part of a powerful speech for most of its audience – there was no way of knowing yet how real a touchstone it and the Covenant would be for the future.

That moment of knowing only arrived when they had their first setback. One morning in December, a few months into the launch, Illingworth's Service VP, Dick Chitty, walked into his office and told him they had a problem: over the weekend a customer had found a fault in the cruise control.

> At first we thought for a second: 'What are we going to do? Do we just find out about this specific problem?' And I think we probably thought about it maybe two or three seconds and we both said, 'You know, we've got to do the right thing, do what the Covenant says.' So we put together a recall on every car.

This was a big decision. Not only did they have to recall all 8,000 cars sold, but they had to effectively suspend sales until they had corrected the problem – a two-month hiccup at a critical time for the brand. And yet there was little or no hesitation in doing so for the two men in the room, because the spirit captured by the Covenant led to only one course of possible action.

It was in fact the recall that turned the Covenant into the powerful embodiment of Lexus's spirit that it became. In producing a video about the recall and how it was to be managed, they invoked the Covenant. They then got everyone working in the Lexus division to sign their names to it, and carved both the Covenant and their names into a large stone block, which they placed in reception – so that everyone who worked at Lexus had to walk in past it every day. Past the Covenant, the commitment they had put their names to. It was distributed on cards for Lexus employees to carry around in their wallets. And in dealerships it was read out in the regular dealership meetings.

Being tested in adversity had brought power to the Covenant:

> It was probably in the spring, about three or four months after we had executed [the recall], people started talking about how well it was handled, and how it was enhancing our reputation. I think it was then that people started saying, 'Well, what we did was centred on the Covenant. We did what the Covenant said and maybe that Covenant means something after all . . .'

The scale of the task prompted the development of a key part of the Covenant, and the challenge of the real world helped it become a real and powerful credo to live for everyone who worked on the new brand.

Now at which point in this process would we or our organization have naturally stopped? In writing a 'Covenant'? In sticking to it in adversity? In asking people to sign their names to it? In carving it in stone? In distributing it to everybody who delivers the brand in whatever way?

We saw in the Introduction that the Articles represented a different kind of contract – a horizontal contract between a group of people embarked on a common goal. The Covenant isn't written as a contract, but it was a statement of a common goal, and what it would take to deliver that goal. And it did come to act as a powerful unifying force.

So the point is that we don't need a single individual, but we do need to create a unit. One that hunts as a pack. And we do need a way of articulating the challenge that binds that unit together and reminds them of it every day. And perhaps in these two things lies the difference between a brand group and a brand committee.

Keeping Them Together

Binding is not something that happens once, at the beginning, and then can be relied on to keep the team together. It is a behaviour that we need to continue constantly through the journey together.

Scott Lutz and his team at 8th Continent developed a physical way of reminding the group of the bond between them. Each of them was issued with dog tags (in the military sense), tied to a piece of leather that one could wear around one's neck. The more one wore the leather the darker it became as it absorbed the oils of the skin. 'After a while,' said Lutz wrily, 'it was pretty easy to see who was hardcore about what we were doing on The Continent and who wasn't.'

He also instituted 'Deep Breath' meetings – team meetings that would take place just before major decisions or key steps in the brand's life were about to be taken. Part of the value of these meetings lay in discussing the risks in the decisions ahead and giving everyone a chance to air their thoughts, concerns and ideas. And part of it lay in team building – getting the team to learn to play the bongos together and then put on a show in the evening, for example. Continually binding the team to each other and the common goal.

The Right Kind of People

It is not surprising to hear the importance that was placed on getting 'the right people' for the brand opportunity. What is interesting, though, is exactly what this meant.

'Right people' doesn't necessarily mean 'the most experienced available people'. Bob Gill, in fact, didn't always choose the most senior in each discipline around him to make up his team; he chose the ones he thought were temperamentally right (and after a year changed those he still wasn't happy with). David Nelms, the CEO of Discover Financial Services, went further: in one case he put temperament and personal qualities actually ahead of expertise in a particular discipline. In developing the Discover 2GO® Card, he put people with little experience of product development in charge of the product development side of the team – because he felt he needed a certain kind of attitude and energy in that area, above all, to overcome the considerable multi-disciplinary difficulties they faced in bringing it to life.

A Recruitment that Never Stops

Within the team, and indeed enlisting those beyond the team, there is a sense of understanding what it means to *recruit*, rather than simply to create understanding and conceptual buy-in. The two are very different, and as Challengers looking to create a unit behind a common purpose or vision, we are only interested in the former.

There is a very simple but interesting construct by Leslie de Chernatony and the consultancy MCA, looking at the nature of buy-in that a team or individual can generate to accompany their vision within an organization. The MCA Matrix in Figure 6.2 points out that there are two different kinds of buy-in that one can engender – an intellectual one, and an emotional one. De Chernatony offers four different degrees of enlistment for you and your brand vision, depending on whether the individual has a high or low degree of each of these kinds of commitment.

Thus, if one has high intellectual buy-in, but low emotional buy-in, one is a Bystander. This is surely the type of commitment one finds too commonly among senior people on projects within large organizations; they have conceptually agreed to it, but are not prepared to rock the boat: they will wait and see what happens before they emotionally commit.

If one has high intellectual buy-in and high emotional buy-in, one is a Champion – and this, frankly, is the only currency that we as Necessary Pirates are interested in.

There are also, however, two other interesting kinds of people on the grid. The first are those who have a high emotional buy-in but a low intellectual grasp of what the challenge and vision are ('I'm really up for shaking things up around here – now what was it exactly we were trying to do again?'). These are the 'Loose cannons'. These are the people who give Necessary Piracy a bad name, and we don't want these either.

Finally, there is the person who is neither intellectually nor emotionally engaged. De Chernatony generously calls these people 'Weak links',

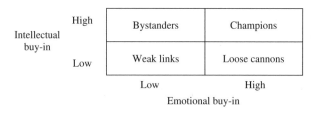

Figure 6.2   **MCA Matrix**
Reproduced by permission of Westburn Publishers Ltd

but in reality they can be much worse than this. They can in fact be practitioners of what Mark Luce, International Business Development Director at S.A.B. Miller, calls 'Malicious Compliance' – people who agree to go along with implementing the vision, but simply in order to demonstrate that it cannot and does not work. We will see an incidence of this in the OK Soda story in Chapter 12.

The point about creating a genuine conversion to Champions in the people around one, rather than simply Bystanders, is that the strength of one's vision – and indeed the degree with which one believes it – may not of itself be sufficiently persuasive. We need to make sure that we have taken them through not just the vision but the *journey* we have been on to get there, and that the ideas that bring the vision to life are always travelling with the vision itself, to stimulate the emotional energy as well as the conceptual understanding. We will need to remember that the people at the top of a company usually aren't the target market, and we will need to help them remember that too.

For all these reasons we need to be absolutely sure that once we have developed our brand vision we do not get lured into 'an elevator pitch' or ten-minute summary, even for the CEO. And that we do not allow any of the team to talk about the strategy until we have the ideas to go with it. These will be covered in more detail in Chapter 14 ('Writing the Articles').

One officer who visited the USS *Benfold* said to Abrashoff that it felt like he recruited his people every day. 'The truth,' said Abrashoff, 'is that the recruitment never stops.'

Personal Example

Ultimately, much in binding those around you depends on personal example. Anders Dahlvig, the first CEO of IKEA after the founder, remarked that it is very easy to get people to do something as the CEO – they will put at the top of their agenda what they think is at the top of your agenda.

David Nelms, the CEO of Discover Card, encourages Innovation as one of the key values of the company. In a cross-functional ideation session at which he was present, the group were tackling the issue of how to overcome a key problem that Discover faced, namely that because it was not accepted as widely as Mastercard or Visa, many Discover Card customers were taking one of the Big Two cards out of their wallet first. So the ideation session addressed the question: 'How do we get the card taken out of the wallet first?' And the solution two out of the three ideation breakout groups came back with was not to have it in the wallet in the first place – have it somewhere more convenient than the wallet: in your pocket, on a key ring.

Now we have all sat in ideation sessions with large organizations like financial service companies, and had great ideas. But in the majority of cases they die the Death of a Thousand Apparently Insuperable Internal Hurdles – people telling you why it cannot be done, and can they now return to what they were doing before, which always seemed to make perfect sense to them. It took several years for the Discover Card key chain card to come from idea to reality, and the principal reasons that it survived that long, long road (over and above the nature of the cross-functional team, which we discussed above) were simple and primarily threefold:

(i) Nelms was personally and continually involved on the project. Sometimes he was in meetings twice a week, sometimes once every two months. But he was personally and continually involved for however long it was going to take:

> Developing the Discover 2GO® Card took a long time and many efforts . . . But I wanted to remain personally involved. In a project that's trying to do something important, don't rely on a chain of command: you have to have senior management time and commitment, or it won't work.

(ii) Every time someone told him there was an Apparently Insuperable Hurdle, he told the cross-functional team they would do whatever it would take to solve it. And they had a lot of very difficult problems to overcome: in order to understand how to store the necessary information on a reduced magnetic strip, for example, they had to bring in and work with a physicist – most of the work that had been done on data storage had been done so long ago, that they almost needed to start again from scratch. Then they had to create a case to protect the magnetic strip and account number – the issues went on and on, because they were in effect completely reinventing the physical credit card. But there was always a solution, as long as there was that senior management commitment to the team finding it.

(iii)   He built an excitement and emotional energy in the team. When they began to prototype the first version of the innovation (which at that stage was an unprotected card on a key ring), he got enough copies of the prototype done for each of the team and their spouses to use for themselves in their everyday life. They themselves experienced what it was like to use it in everyday life – and were excited and re-energized by the huge interest and positive intrigue it was greeted with from the clerks in the stores they began trying it in. In a sense what Discover was prototyping here was the brand idea, then, rather than just the product concept – because they wanted to prototype the feeling the consumer would have (the emotional reward), as well as what form the product would take.

But what if you are not the CEO? You still need to continually lead by example, even if you get a little dented yourself in the process. Scott Lutz used the dog tag metaphor in a different way to describe the need to continually put yourself in the firing line:

> The thing about being a Denter is that you have to recognize you are going to get dented back. But look at that dog tag. A dog tag when it is flat, without any markings, is actually not very strong. It gets stronger, more rigid, the more you dent it. So in a way, you get stronger the more you put yourself out there.

We will discuss further in the next chapter how one deals with such internal and external exposure.

Becoming a Storymaker, Not Just a Storyteller

Much has been said about storytelling in business – but less, curiously, about story*making*. Yet what fostering a Challenger culture really needs us to be is storymakers.

Southwest Airlines is a company where all the Executives have to exhibit four times a year the brand value of 'Positively Outrageous Service' in field visits in front of their staff. I was on a ranch in Texas with Joyce Rogge, the SVP Marketing for Southwest, and she had just come back from doing one of her four visits. So I asked her what she had done.

She told me that Southwest sponsored Shamu the Killer Whale in SeaWorld, and she had taken with her a number of Shamu the Killer Whale inflatable baseball caps as prizes. Arriving at the gate where she had chosen to spend the day, she took the microphone from the gate staff and put on one of the inflatable caps. 'Ladies and Gentlemen', she says to the Southwest passengers waiting for their flight, 'while we are waiting, let's play a little game. I am going to offer one of these magnificent prizes (and she points to the Shamu the Killer Whale inflatable baseball cap on her head) to the person who can show me the largest hole in their sock.' She sets up a judging panel, and those that wish to compete take off their footwear, and hop on up to the front to display their wares in front of the judges.

After the winner is announced and receives their magnificent trophy, Rogge takes the mike again. 'Ah, but the fun is not over yet, ladies and gentlemen,' she says; 'I have another of these magnificent prizes, and this one is going to be for . . . the person who has the most credit cards in their wallet.'

And so it goes on. The point, Rogge says, is that when you have 36,000 staff, you can have all the training videos you want, but unless they see the senior management of the company really delivering what the company is about themselves, they are not really going to commit to it themselves. What Southwest is doing here is asking its Executives not to be storytellers but storymakers. They are not sitting round a campfire telling others stories of Herb and the kinds of things Herb does; they are in effect making stories of their own, that others will tell about them, that demonstrate that the brand is serious about its sense of Positively Outrageous Service, and thereby binding everyone in the company to delivering it.

A Different Kind of Contract

This chapter is called 'Binding: A Different Kind of Contract', because we are looking to create a much stronger emotional commitment (in our team and the broader organization) to what it will take to genuinely deliver the brand opportunity. Up to now we have been using the concept of a contract here figuratively, but let us finish the chapter by looking at a more literal expression of a contract between a team embarked on a common challenge – one that is curiously similar to a set of Articles.

Here's the context for this particular contract. In 1962 Avis is running at an annual loss of $3.2 m; it has not made a profit for 12 years. It has just been bought by a bank (Lazard Frères), and being a bank they are not happy with owning a venture that continues to lose money. The team running Avis have to find a new way of doing things, one that will take share from the brand leader, Hertz, which outspends them 5:1.

The new president, Robert Townsend, first tackled some key operational practicalities (arranging better financing, buying a new fleet, improving services, and so on) and then turned his attention to the advertising. He discussed what they would have to do with Bill Bernbach, the legendary head of DDB NY, in order to create advertising five times the impact of Hertz's advertising. On the basis of these conversations, and recognizing that, as the Marines say, 'hope is not a method', Townsend himself wrote the 'Avis Rent a Car Advertising Philosophy'. It had seven points (see Figure 6.3).

Townsend then had these principles framed and put in the office of everyone who worked on the account, at Avis and DDB, as a template for the way they were to develop and decide on every piece of advertising that was made. As I say, this was in theory just about advertising, though we should note that before each ad ran, Townsend put a copy of it in the pay packet of each Avis employee, so it effectively helped continually fuel the agenda for how they were to think and behave.[3]

There is much to admire here: an explicit recognition of each other's expertise and an explicit refusal to countenance compromise, for example. And I wonder how many clients today stick to Principle #4, and how many agencies stick – genuinely – to #5.

The results? In 1963 Avis made its first profit for 13 years – $1.2 m. In 1964 the profits more than doubled to $2.9 m. And both sides in due course became icons.

The point about this is that we all have contracts between agencies and clients. And they are to do with the apparently important things like fees (revenue). What this contract is about is something different,

---

Avis Rent A Car
Advertising Philosophy

1. Avis will never know as much about advertising as DDB, and DDB will never know as much about the rent a car business as Avis.

2. The purpose of the advertising is to persuade the frequent business renter (whether on a business trip, a vacation trip, or renting an extra car at home) to try Avis.

3. A serious attempt will be made to create advertising with five times the effectiveness (see #2 above) of the competition's advertising.

4. To this end, Avis will approve or disapprove, not try to improve, ads which are submitted.
Any changes suggested by Avis must be grounded on a material operation defect (a wrong uniform, for example).

5. To this end, DDB will only submit for approval those ads which they as an agency recommend. They will not 'see what Avis thinks of that one'.

6. Media selection should be the primary responsibility of DDB.
However, DDB is expected to take the initiative to get guidance from Avis in weighting of markets or special situations, particularly in those areas where cold numbers do not indicate the real picture.
Media judgements are open to discussion. Conviction should prevail.
Compromises should be avoided.

7. All ads will be Fordable, and the agency will secure approval in writing from Ford on each ad.

Figure 6.3   **Avis Rent a Car Advertising Philosophy**

which is mutual profitability – whether the agency gets the right work approved first time makes all the difference in the profitability on the account for them (going round and round in the creative system is very expensive), and whether the client gets work they need first time is fundamental not just to their business success but also to their relationship with their agency and getting the best out of them. And for Avis and DDB, thinking about a contract that represented a different kind of binding – one about the quality rather than the quantity of the brand's communications – served subsequently to make them both not simply financial successes but business icons.

Summary

Binding represents a different kind of recruitment and a different kind of contract. *Individually*, it represents a recruitment when people have already joined the company. This will probably involve some different ways of thinking about who are 'the right kind of people' (a preference for temperament and personal qualities over experience), and being very clear about what it is going to take to enlist champions in one's superiors. *Collectively*, it represents a new kind of contract, a form of the Articles, if you like: a contract between a group that they are going to behave and think in a certain way to drive the success of the brand journey they have embarked on. A singularity of vision and purpose, even if you need a group of people involved.

The Excuse for the Navy

Binding thus contributes to stripping away the Fifth and Sixth Excuses for the Navy. The Fifth, which was about 'leaving me very exposed', is something Binding is clearly designed to reduce – though it will not take away the need to lead by example, and indeed lean into exposure internally and externally at critical points, as we shall see in the next chapter.

And we continue, of course, to chew on the Sixth, and whether or not one needs a founder.

Exercises

The Covenant

Write a covenant for your brand ambition. Write it, as Lexus did, as a building sequence:

- the scale of the challenge facing you;

- your credentials for facing up to that challenge;
- your Intent – what exactly success will consist in;
- the three key ways in which you will succeed;
- the state of mind it will take of everyone involved in the brand to drive success.

Make it one, rather than five sides of paper. Make it simple and powerful. Now decide what you are going to do with it.

Southwest Airlines

Imagine that four times a year everyone on the brand team has to demonstrate to those around them, through something they do, the values of the brand. What would each of them do?

Are they doing it at the moment? Why don't we start? And why don't we make it one of the things we are bonused on?

7

Leaning: A Different Kind of Commitment

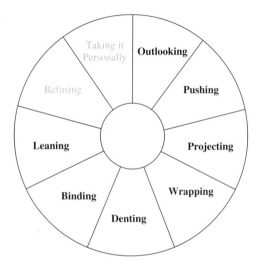

Figure 7.1 **Leaning**

Howies is a biking and skateboardwear brand in Wales. In 2003 they received an unexpected package from the United States. Inside the package was a letter from an organization called 'Legal Strategies Group' – the legal counsel for Levi's.

The letter stated that it was their view that the grey Howies tabs on the back of Howies jeans were 'confusingly similar' to Levi's own famous red tabs – and that their use of these tabs created a 'substantial likelihood' of customer confusion as to the source of Howies jeans, and indeed the relationship between them and Levi's. The letter went on to say that Levi's legal counsel regarded this as an infringement, demanded that they stop producing jeans with these tabs within ten days, and that Howies let Levi's counsel know the total number of jeans with such

Howies tabs produced to date, so that they could work out whether or not to seek 'monetary damages', and the amount of such damages to pursue if they did so.

So let's imagine we are running this little company in Wales, what do we do? On the one hand, we might feel that these suggestions are a little odd – our tabs say Howies, not Levi's, they are positioned on the other rear pocket of the jean, and of an entirely different colour. On the other hand, one of the world's largest clothing brands, with presumably some of the world's most experienced lawyers tucked firmly under its wing, is coming right at us. What would our response to this be? Pull in our horns? Cease and desist?

David Hieatt is one of the founders of Howies. The following is a note sent by Hieatt to Olivia Knight, the researcher on this book, the weekend after the Levi's letter arrived:

From: David Hieatt
Sent: 06 May 2003 10:56
To: Olivia
Subject: RE: david and the goliath
Hey Liv
How are ya.
The Levi's thing is great. And, boy, are we milking it.
Today, we are introducing spelling lessons and colour blind tests for all customers of our jeans. (Levi's seemed to think there was confusion in the market place.) We are also sending out free Howies tabs to all Levi's wearers. And we are putting a patch over our tabs, which is quite funny. They are being sewn on by blindfold. (We didn't want to implicate the machinists.)
All fun
David

Reproduced by permission of David Hieatt

Rather than flinching from it, Hieatt actually leans into the exposure: he looks to generate additional publicity for his brand by (in his words) milking the threatened suit rather than running from it – by taking particular pains to ensure that no customer is confused at point of purchase, as Levi's fear they might. He produced two tests for retailers to give anyone trying to buy a pair of Howies jeans when they carried them up to the counter. The first was the colourblind test he referred to in the email – a piece of card on which a large square block of Levi's red stood next to a similar block of Howies grey, with the words 'red' and 'grey' in each box to ensure absolute clarity. Once customers had proved their ability to differentiate between the two colours, they were then offered a spelling test to ensure they knew the difference between the written word 'Howies' from the written word 'Levi's'. The spelling test looked like this (Figure 7.2):

Spelling Test

1. Corporation
2. Greed
3. Machiavelli
4. Oppression
5. Imperialism

Figure 7.2 **Howies 'Spelling Test'**
Reproduced by permission of Howies

Once the customers had passed both these tests, they were allowed to buy the jeans, but offered the following tab to put over them:

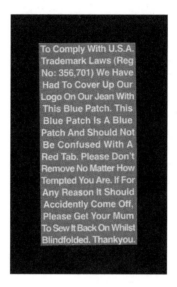

To Comply With U.S.A. Trademark Laws (Reg No: 356,701) We Have Had To Cover Up Our Logo On Our Jean With This Blue Patch. This Blue Patch Is A Blue Patch And Should Not Be Confused With A Red Tab. Please Don't Remove No Matter How Tempted You Are. If For Any Reason It Should Accidently Come Off, Please Get Your Mum To Sew It Back On Whilst Blindfolded. Thankyou.

Figure 7.3   **Howies 'Blue Patch'**
Reproduced by permission of Howies

Hieatt then released the story to the press, who lapped it up. Immediately following the publicity in May, catalogue requests increased 300%; by December, Howies' sales had done the same.

So what this chapter is about is how one deals with exposure – and in particular recognizing that there does come a point where you have to put yourself out there. You have to deliberately put yourself in a position where you are exposed – and to some degree lean into that, and embrace it, rather than try to flinch from or minimize it. The Howies example above is an external one, but there will also be an internal exposure to lean into. While doing things differently may be necessary, success is not predictable or inevitable, and certainly not foreseen by those around you. You will be living in an exposed place, sometimes for quite extended periods of time, when you have stuck your neck out and it is far from clear whether the results will kill off any scepticism within the organization you may be encountering.

External Exposure

The voracious and consistent manufacture of PR, which is one of the characteristics of a Challenger (at least to initiate and champion it), leads, of course, to walking a fine line between fame and notoriety. PR is different from editorial – in putting an idea in play, one does not know how the press is going to respond to it, but one has to be prepared to put it in play just the same.

The Wasatch Brewery in the USA produced a couple of years ago a new variant called Polygamy Porter – marketed with the ingenious tagline 'Polygamy Porter: Why have just one?' This would be merely mildly entertaining as a brand concept were it not for the context (context, after all, being everything): the brewery is sited in Utah, the home of the Mormons and therefore a place where, on the whole, alcohol consumption is frowned upon and polygamy is an expression of a religious belief.

The new line ran into potential trouble when the billboard company refused to run the posters advertising the new beer. But Wasatch kept at it: they looked for another less cautious outdoor company, and rang the journalists; local TV was joined by international media, including the BBC, *The Economist* and Associated Press. Sales of the beer more than doubled to almost 2,000 cases in two months, and they sold $55,000 of merchandising – mostly T-shirts – in one month on the website alone.

Wasatch had, as they say in heist movies, 'previous' on this. In 1998 they had already done their best to rub up against the US Olympics Committee, who had scheduled Salt Lake City as the location for the 2002 Winter Games (and signed up Anheuser-Busch as the official Olympic sponsor) by having the sales manager drive around in a Chevy Blazer plastered with the sign 'The Unofficial Beer of the 2002 Winter Games'. The Salt Lake Organizing Committee contacted Greg Schirf, the founder of Wasatch, with a cease and desist order, and Schirf promptly contacted the local TV station to say that they were being picked on by the SLOC. The result: 'We were the lead on local television for a week straight.'[1]

Schirf and Wasatch decided there was further mileage to be played out of this. While they dropped the explicit 'Winter Games' claim, they added a new product to their line-up called 'Unofficial' Amber Ale, in the middle of whose label was the number 2002, crossed out.

The SLOC continued to threaten legal action – and then the bribes scandal broke. Wasatch rubbed their hands together and produced T-shirts shouting 'Beer Not Bribes'. Once more, the media covered it. Sales – well, you get the idea.

Soft Shell, Hard Centre

Wasatch were not leaning into exposure like this just because they were fun-loving people who like to bring a smile to everyone's faces. They began doing it as a strategic solution, because the business was facing considerable pressures; in particular they had built a larger brewery in the mid-1990s, but increased competition from local microbrew-eries meant they weren't hitting the numbers they needed to make it work. So Schirf and Wasatch decided to provoke – to dramatically increase word of mouth and saliency through sailing close to the cultural wind in order to create standout and desirability for their products. Keg sales doubled over the 'Beer Not Bribes' time. Beer revenues as a whole grew 32% from 2000 to 2001. The controversy around Polygamy Porter grew not simply sales of the brand itself, but drew Wasatch to the attention of interested distributors in three neighbouring States.[2]

As ever, Soft Shell, Hard Centre: we are fostering different behaviours as a Challenger because we are interested in the better commercial return from the brand behaving in this way.

Looking for the Other Surface

Externally, this kind of exposure rarely comes knocking – you have to go out and look for it, or even create it yourself. When Yorkie used sampling, they offered free samples of the product on the streets – but only to men (hey, 'It's Not For Girls', after all). In order to get some real attention here, they deliberately chose as sampling points left-wing boroughs like Lambeth and Liverpool, to increase the chance of the promotion causing a little flurry and getting media attention. They put one sampling point outside the offices of Liverpool Council, which is famously left-wing. Sure enough, a female council worker came down the steps before too long and asked for a sample. She was refused, on the grounds that these were not for girls; outraged, she spun on her heel, went back in to the council and told them what had just happened to her. The council banned the promotion, Yorkie's PR company phoned the national newspapers, the newspapers covered the story the next morning.

If I make it sound inevitable, I do not mean to. Nothing in PR is predictable – that is the nature of such exposure. And sometimes one can lean into a certain kind of exposure, only to find it appearing from an entirely unexpected quarter. So when Yoo-hoo sponsored OzzFest, they expected some backlash from the Bible Belt US and accepted they might well risk some distribution loss. In fact, the fallout was relatively small, the most serious of which was C-stores in San Antonio, who wouldn't participate in a linked promotion because Ozzy Osbourne had once relieved himself on the Alamo.

Within the Company: Internal Exposure

Living in exposed places internally is also part of being a Pirate. Simply selling the vision to one's senior management can require a certain degree of courage – especially if you know you are recommending something other than what they want to hear.

We saw in Chapter 5 on Denting Yoshio Ishizaka going into his meeting with the most senior management group of Toyota, who were expecting a proposal on a single flagship product for their existing brand, and instead trying to persuade them to launch a new brand with two new models. He was, he says, 'very nervous' – and it must have taken a great deal of courage to push this through. Here he is at a Lexus Dealer Conference telling the story of how he felt about that meeting:

> And, after many . . . executive meetings, a consensus was reached and we went back to TMC [Toyota in Japan] to present our plan.
>
> Just before Yuki and I left for Japan, Bob pulled me aside for some last minute advice. I remember he looked at me and said: 'Yoshi, don't screw this up.'

Thanks, Bob.

The meeting was early in 1987. Entering the large TMC boardroom, well, you can imagine I was a little nervous. In fact, you have a phrase in English that says it better – I was sweating bullets! We were facing 20 top TMC directors and other executives with a plan that was radically different than what they were anticipating.

And then, Yuki whispered to me ... 'Yoshi, go ahead, I'm right behind you.' But he was SO quiet throughout the meeting.

Ishizaka makes his proposal into what is potentially quite a hostile audience (see Chapter 5 for the rest of the story), and waits for the response:

I was sure my career was on the line.

Then it was time for the chairman, Mr. Eiji Toyoda, to speak. We held our breath. He looked at us and then slowly around the room and, after what seemed like an eternity, said, 'Let TMS do as they are planning.'

Grinning like two schoolboys who had just passed the hardest exam of their lives, Mr. Togo [the man he refers to above as Yuki] and I reaffirmed our commitment and promised to make the utmost effort.

We were relieved, but as we flew back to Los Angeles we both thought: Can we pull this off?[3]

I love the emotional honesty of this piece. Because this is really how great brands are won or lost. What Ishizaka has done in this meeting, with the support of Yuki Togo, is set in motion the birth of Lexus. But he describes it, 17 years later, with none of the mythologizing one might be tempted to use. He describes it instead as the very human moment it was, as all meetings actually are: one of personal courage, and keeping one's nerve, and sticking one's neck out. And then the doubt following the elation: 'Can we pull this off?' The emotional rollercoaster of giving birth to a Challenger, within a large company or outside it, beginning all over again.

Loneliness and the Long Haul

If you are on your own, trying to do something new, in a way the category hasn't done it before, can be an enormous test of one's faith in oneself.

Charlotte Semler of Myla, three years in:

> One of the hardest things is that you are constantly doing stuff you haven't got a bastard clue how to do. It makes you feel incompetent and it makes you feel neurotic, and if you do that for three years where every decision you make is actually critical, it's pretty tough on you.

Richard Reed, of innocent, about the consequences of taking nine months to find someone who would make the product the way they wanted it:

> The seed money didn't kick in until about the April. So we had about eight months of trying to make it work without any money. It was just getting worse and worse. We were down to eating breakfast cereal three times a day. That was a very, very bleak period.

The reassurances as you face such personal difficulties are not always forthcoming, but you have to find the strength of character to push ahead anyway. Take the relaunch of Hovis: Paula Moss needed a certain strength of resolve. Not getting the reassurance from some of the other functions around her at work, she looked for reassurance from her husband, who was also a marketer. It backfired:

> I remember taking the packaging home and being really proud of it because, you know, it got the origination right and we were nervous about whether we could actually deliver on a poly bag what we'd actually sort of seen in the art work, and I put all the new packs along our shelf in the kitchen, waiting for him to come home to be so impressed with them . . . and he came in and he said, 'Oh my God, what have you done?'
> That was a real shock to me . . .

Nor was research, initially, to offer much more comfort. It was important that she had results – the brand was the largest in their portfolio, and both the MD and the Chairman had given support conditional on her doing 'due diligence' in research:

> I was mindful of the brand that we were working with, and that it was really pushing quite hard, and I knew how hard I wanted to push – but, obviously, I didn't want to fall over the edge. So it was really important

that we were confident. I mean, I felt if we could have real confidence in the solution then we would sell it more effectively and we'd have the numbers to back it up.

But in this case the researcher did come back and say, 'Well, they really don't like it, and it's really quite risky.' The first debrief was actually quite damning . . .

These results were just ten days before they had to press the button on packaging. So she got the team together very fast, so as not to let them get too down or distant from the idea, and then looked at why it wasn't working. They found it was to do with the brand identification and quality cues – they had moved too far in terms of some of the core equities of the way the brand presented itself. They modified the packaging a little, writing the name in the five gold letters it had always had, and recognizing that the historical 'wheat sheaves' were in fact an important part of cueing quality to consumers. And then put it through exactly the same research and researcher again.

This time it worked.

Exposure Can Give a Denter Energy and Strength

But in a curious and almost perverse way, this sense of having to live on your own in an exposed place leads to a kind of energy and strength. As we mentioned earlier, Scott Lutz of 8th Continent commented that one of the things about being a Denter in a large organization is that you are going to get dented back. One might think this is a disadvantage, but in fact Lutz's view was that the hardest thing about being a Denter is the moment *before* you yourself have been dented – because this is often the well from where you yourself start to take some of your determination and energy. In the same context Glen Senk of Anthropologie quotes a friend: 'The iron that passes through the fire comes out the hardest.'

On an entirely different level, Lance Armstrong's fightback from cancer is something he draws on to give him strength during setbacks in his sport: in an interview in 2003 he was asked whether surviving cancer was something he thought about in moments of difficulty on the Tour de France. He replied:

> You better believe it helps . . . Being down is good for me. I know I've
> been even lower and I can draw on those experiences to rescue myself. I
> think my team understands that too.[4]

To an obviously lesser degree the same was true for some of the serial Denters and Challengers we spoke to – it was leaning into exposure the first time that gave them the strength and determination to endure it the second, and third, and fourth. There is no substitute for simply doing it.

How Do You Live in an Exposed Place?

So you cannot avoid exposure, and you need to *lean* into it rather than flinch from it. But how do Challengers manage this difficult emotional state?

At one level, everyone finds their own ways. In *Easy Riders, Raging Bulls*, Peter Biskind tells the story of Steven Spielberg making *Jaws*. It is hard to imagine the movie now as anything but the extraordinarily successful and influential blockbuster it became (nor its director as anything but the supremely confident director he seems to be), but during the filming many of the team, including the cast, began openly to believe that it would be a flop. In interviews with *Time*, its stars were both frank: Robert Shaw said that he thought the novel on which it was based was 'a piece of shit' and Richard Dreyfuss predicted it would be 'the turkey of the year'; the crew for their part began supportively to refer to the film as 'Flaws'. The mechanical shark kept going wrong – or sinking. A 55-day shoot spiralled into 159. The budget ballooned by 300%. Who's to say at this point that they were all wrong? Spielberg lost his confidence, and in fact reached such a low that he brought a pillow from home and began sleeping with a stick of celery inside it, because he found the smell comforting and he needed that comfort to help relax him and steady him for the next day of shooting. A stick of celery.[5]

For those of you hoping for something more nutritious than celery to get you through the first 12 to 18 months, when you have committed yourself and have yet to have back the results that say whether you were right or wrong, an entire chapter in the second half of the book is devoted to That Difficult First Year, and how Challengers seem to cope in that sustained period of potential loneliness and stress.

But let's just note at this point that there seem to be three different things you need to get yourself through it, over and above sleeping with fresh vegetables. The first is tenacity; the interviewees all used slightly different words for it, but all meant the same thing. Charlotte Semler at Myla talked about the 11-month wait for funding for their idea – 11 months of going to meeting after dispiriting meeting and being rejected. What kept them going, she says, was 'Bloody-mindedness, stubbornness and pride.' If we really are looking to create a new way of seeing a brand or a category, it is unlikely to be a sprint – you need to have the character, tenacity and resolution to be in it for the long haul.

The second thing you need to get yourself through such exposure, particularly in large organizations, is to hunt as part of a pack: get all your disciplines together. This is Bob Gill describing how the team survived senior scepticism at P&G:

> There is hidden power in getting all the different groups together. Usually R&D is fighting manufacturing, fighting sales, fighting finance, fighting marketing. Usually the five different functions are all going off in their own direction, dysfunctionally. And so I put them all together, made them all in the same team, and that really scared management to a certain extent – that they [the five disciplines] talked in one voice. And I'd tell the R&D director, 'Your job is to make sure your director supports us.'
>
> And when you had the power across the four or five different functions [R&D, marketing, finance, manufacturing and sales], all saying the same thing, which the company hadn't seen that much of, that usually gave you a lot of leeway right there.

And the third is a brand and brand vision you believe in. To go back to Dave Hieatt's observation from Chapter 5: Beware the person who believes what they are doing.

Summary

Leaning into exposure represents a different kind of involvement or commitment. It accepts that to do the best thing for this brand is going to involve some risk – and for someone looking for a rock solid career path through an organization, that may be an uncomfortable thing to contemplate. But if you want to be a Challenger, it's something that has to be accepted, and indeed leant into.

The Excuse for the Navy

The Fifth Excuse for the Navy is 'But that leaves me very exposed.' And how we respond to this is different from all the other excuses of the Navy, which are to deny their truth or necessity. Our response to this particular one is: 'Yes, it will leave us very exposed. And probably for what seems like a long, long time.' So the question we need to deal with is not: 'So how do I avoid that?' It is: 'So how do I manage that?' They are obviously very different questions. We will cover this further in Chapter 15 ('That Difficult First Year').

8

Refusing: A Different Kind of Passion

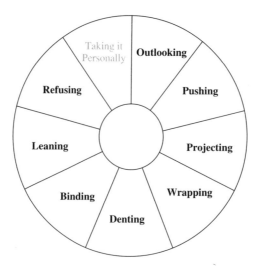

Figure 8.1 **Refusing**

Men stumble over the truth from time to time but most pick themselves up and hurry off as if nothing had happened.
Winston Churchill

In 2002, historians revealed they had deciphered the meaning of 'KBO', Winston Churchill's cryptic sign-off to his weekly messages to Harry Truman during the Second World War. These three letters had been the source of puzzlement for Churchill completists for 50 years; presumably Truman knew what they meant, and one would hope Churchill knew what they meant . . . but what *did* they mean?

The puzzle was solved through the reminiscence of the then 22-year-old stenographer to whom it had fallen to transcribe each conversation. Nonplussed, she had asked her commanding officer what the three letters meant, when he told her not to keep transcribing them. He told her: they stood for 'Keep Buggering On'.

A Different Kind of Passion

There is a lot of talk about passion these days within marketing and business – and it is critical, of course. But it is usually interpreted as a passion *for* something. In a real sense, though, what you *refuse* to accept defines you as an individual as much as what you are passionate about.

Take the early days of M.A.C. cosmetics as an example. M.A.C.'s first big distributor in the USA was to be Nordstrom – a wonderful opportunity for the brand to spread its wings. But M.A.C. had a very clear sense that it wanted its own people to be in the store representing the brand, and it revelled in the fact that its people weren't like other kinds of people selling cosmetics in stores at the time. The fact that they were dressed in black, while the rest of the business was in white was the least of it. This is John Dempsey, the CEO of M.A.C., talking about the two founders (Frank Toskan and Frank Angelo) in their discussions with Nordstrom:

> I think it wasn't without its challenges that Nordstrom became our distributor. In terms of the people we had to work behind the counter in those days, we had drag queens and nose rings and everything, and basically Frank and Frank said to Nordstrom 'If you want to take us, you have to take us as we are.'
>
> The founders of the company understood that because they were casting a show, there was a deliberate expectation there. First and foremost you had to be able to do the job, but there was a deliberate attempt to visually demonstrate the philosophy of the company. When you saw somebody there behind the M.A.C. counter, you said, 'This is not the same as everybody else ...'

Central to one's ability to refuse is obviously a very strong sense of what the brand should be in the first place – in spite of what anyone else tells you. Lorenzo Fluxá was a part of a family tradition of shoemakers – his grandfather hand made shoes in his own workshop on the island of Majorca. In 1975, when setting out to start his own company, Fluxá liked the name 'Camper', which is taken from a Catalan word meaning 'peasant', and seemed to him to capture the simple virtues of the shoe brand and company he was looking for. However, he found himself talked into some research by the young bucks on the mainland in Barcelona, apparently more expert in marketing than himself. They generated four other names (including 'Groovy') and put all five into research.

'Camper' did not fare well. In fact, the name 'Groovy' came first, and 'Camper' came a distant fourth. The experts were clear.

> So the name Camper was eliminated. But I say, 'I don't know'.
>
> I was young at that time: I decided to say, 'Nah, nah, my heart says it has to be Camper.'

If we work in large organizations we have a perception that things are somehow easier for founders of their own companies, because they don't have the internal battles we do. This may be true, but what is easy to forget is the scale and nature of their external battles – sometimes even with the consumer, who simply doesn't understand your idea. When in the early days of Diesel, Renzo Rosso was pioneering heavily distressed denim, including items with holes in as an aged effect, consumers would send him the jeans back again, saying that while they loved the jeans, these were faulty and had a hole in, so could they have a refund.

Sometimes these battles are with the trade. Some stockists on mainland Spain in 1975 refused to stock Camper's unisex shoes, saying that they would not be part of something so 'dirty' as unisex clothing; equally, we shall see later the persistence of Howies in getting into the influential bicycle stores that we noted in Chapter 5 is paralleled in Merrill Fernando's year-long battle to get Dilmah stocked in what is now his most successful market, Australia. Being a Pirate is not necessarily easier in your own company; the challenges just change their shape and nature.

We have attacked a number of the Excuses for the Navy so far, and now we are coming to Excuse Number 4. And it is this: 'Ah, but I have a category that all this does not apply to.' Or rather, more specifically: 'But my category is not one that rewards brand building.' So all we can do (the implication is) is just go on doing the same old stuff, and pretending things are going to get better.

And we are going to see that the key to overcoming it is a refusal to accept this. A refusal to Keep Buggering On. (I can see the placard now: 'Just say no to KBO'. Try chanting it – it has a nice rhythmic quality.)

There are numerous examples of constructive refusal. Imagine if US designer discount store Target had accepted the internal view (which many in the company apparently held) that price was the only way to take on Wal-Mart? What if Dilmah had yielded to the Sri Lankan Government pressure not to break out of being a bulk supplier, and not to become a brand?

But we said this was a book about personal qualities, and the ability of an individual to influence a culture. So let us look in more detail at two cases of people refusing to accept there was no opportunity to build a brand in an apparently branding-unfriendly category – one in an supposedly price-driven and increasingly commoditized market (bread) seemingly locked in a downward spiral, and the other in a distress-driven B2B market in the USA.

Hovis – Breaking the Price Spiral

Paula Moss of British Bakeries was a refuser. It seems strange to label someone who is essentially positive in this apparently negative way, but Refusing was the first essential (and enormously constructive) part of what she did.

Hovis is one of the largest and most famous bread brands in the UK, a tired jewel at the time within the British Bakeries crown. Paula Moss came into the job from Sharwoods, a UK spice brand owned by the same parent, whose essence and marketing had revolved around the notion of 'passion', a value close to her heart. Walking into the Bread Division, however, the physical environment and apparent culture seemed immediately more functional, grey and conservative.

Her predecessor as Hovis's Marketing Director knew about Moss's previous work with Sharwoods, and her role in it as a passionate brand person. As predecessors do, she tried to break it to Moss in a friendly way as to the change she was going to have to make to succeed in this new job. 'Don't try any of that branding stuff here,' she said to Moss. 'This market is all about two loaves for 99p: that's how you drive brand share in bread.' And 'Oh', she added, in case Moss was still debating the idea of having a go at some branding nonsense in spite of this seasoned advice, 'Two for 99p is all the Sales Director is interested in, anyway.'[1] This was not a category or company, in effect, that rewarded an attempt to build a brand.

But it was clear to Moss that there was a fundamental challenge on Hovis that had been ducked up to now, and wasn't going to be solved by offering two loaves for 99p; in fact, such price promotion was simply going to exacerbate it. And the challenge was this: Hovis, a once strong and much loved brand, had traded off its former glories for a dangerously long time. Now number two in the white bread sector to rival Kingsmill, Hovis had been allowed to slide in salience and consumer perception for so long that there was a danger that it was just going to slip away.

So here's the thing. The brand is sliding, the market is resisting brand building, and all your counterpart in Sales wants is two for 99p. What are you going to do? It doesn't help your corner, of course, that as low involvement markets go, this one is right up there. In changing the nature of the relationship with something as basic and everyday as a bread brand you need to get real – the bread fixture itself is the last ordeal in the grocery store ('the last run of the gauntlet' to use consumers' own words), and not a place for the tired grocery mum, only loosely in control of her two toxic children at this point, to embark on the casual browsing and scanning of new information. Consumers spend on average only 3 seconds at the bread fixture: how do you set about changing a relationship in a habit-driven, low interest, price-led market in just 3 seconds?

Moss's view was that the brand needed 'a kick'. And she genuinely meant a kick rather than a tweak; in 3 seconds a tweak was not going to solve anything. She first refused to accept that the imperative of price promotion was or had to be the internal view. And in fact when she explored further, it turned out that the supposed real internal barriers were *perceptual* as much as real: in reality, her boss had spent the last couple of years sorting out operational issues, and had now created a platform on which the brand issues could be readdressed. So there was in fact internal support for trying to break out of the price promotion addiction, including the Sales Director.

So Moss set up an internal project called 'Winning in White', central to which would be making consumers take a point of view about the brand, rather than simply take it for granted. In doing so, she wanted to build the brand to the point where not simply did it become brand leader in white bread (the largest segment of the market) but did so profitably – that is, without engaging in price-led promotion any more. In effect, therefore, she would be passing on a price rise at the same time.

Along with the ambition to give the brand a 'kick' came a refusal to allow the business partners she was working with to treat the brand's historical equities with too much respect. She realized that one of the issues with a brand that had a long-standing relationship with the consumer was an overly great respect from the people involved in positioning and communicating it, so she explicitly briefed the advertising agencies pitching for the business *not to respect the brand too much*. Tweaking, as we saw above, was no longer an option.

Even so, the mindset of the organization internally had not yet been changed – when the packaging designers Williams Murray Hamm came back with their recommendations, the marketing people below her screened out the most 'radical' route – not on the grounds that they didn't like it, but on the grounds 'that would never get past Paula'.

This packaging route was unlike anything else in the category – and not much like anything else in food, although it was full of food values. The idea was simply to make the packaging the kinds of food you ate with bread – from baked beans, to cucumber to fried eggs (Figures 8.2 and 8.3). The colours of the food would be associated with the colour cues of different types of Hovis from the previous packaging (principally to denote thickness of cut), but apart from that would be a radical re-presentation of the brand, and a considerable departure from the packaging the brand had had before.

Convinced that it was what the brand needed, the design company pushed to present it to Moss. She liked it; the route was indeed a radical change, although she wasn't sure how it would be received internally. Yet to her surprise when she presented the packs to the commercial team they seemed comfortable with it (though only, as she discovered later, because they thought it would never happen).

There were, however, two significant stumbling blocks on the road. First, the Trade were more polarized in their response: some were support-ive, some overtly questioning. Second, they researched the packaging

Figure 8.2   **Hovis Old Packaging Pre-launch**
Reproduced by permission of British Bakeries Ltd

Figure 8.3   **Hovis New Packaging**
Reproduced by permission of British Bakeries Ltd

and it was not the unequivocal hit they were hoping for – they had, it seemed, gone too far. With time now short till the launch, she and her team looked at some key cues from the old packaging again, and put the revisions back into research. A couple of weeks before they had to press the button, she was sitting in a meeting with the Sales Director, discussing the uncertainties. 'Sod it, let's do it,' he said.[2] And they did.

On the day of the launch, they all went out to the Trade wearing beans suits and beans dresses (Figure 8.4) – even the MD (this was not left to the 'wacky marketing people' – the brand visibly had a cross-functional group over-committing to this).

The launch was to have two key parts to it: the new packaging, and a new advertising campaign which in its own way was as different as the packaging – a cartoon of two small boys practising saying rude words like 'pooh', 'bra' and 'bogies', followed by the suggestion that one should 'Get something good inside' with Hovis.

The first two weeks following the re-launch were anxious ones. The Hovis team had invited letters from consumers about reactions to the new packaging, and letters duly came. Moss read the letters that arrived every day. She read each one and put them into two piles on her desk

Figure 8.4 **Hovis 'Bean Suits'**
Reproduced by permission of British Bakeries Ltd

in front of her – for and against. She measured the respective height of each pile with her hands. Some letters were good, and some were bad. Some of the bad ones were very bad indeed – one, for instance, suggested the company would have been better off using the money they had spent on their packaging as the marketing department's redundancy pay.

And for two weeks the share steadily fell. They were, Moss says, 'The longest two weeks of my life.' But her MD, Peter Baker, did not leave her to endure them on her own. Recognizing what she was going through, he made time every day to come into her office and reassure her that she had taken the right decision, and that they had to hold their nerve.

And after two weeks, the share started to climb again. In the year that followed Hovis White became number one ahead of Kingsmill in white bread, and in fact for a while was the fastest-growing food brand in the UK. But, more importantly, from a commercial point of view it changed the price-trading spiral it had fallen into. Although its primary competitor Kingsmill came back at Hovis by putting themselves on permanent promotion, Hovis resisted matching them. The relaunch increased profitability on Hovis by 32%.

So it is possible to reverse the downward spiral, to get the needle out of the arm – as long as you refuse to accept the inevitability of commoditization, and excessive respect for the brand, and tweaking.

Geek Squad – Refusing to Accept the Category is Different

For the second example of refusing, let us take the B2B category of IT support. This is a business that most of us have a relationship with, but reluctantly. And, for those of us that use an outsourced service here, it is not a business where you would have said branding was paramount – one's only concerns are essentially about a rational combination of competence and cost. This is, after all, in effect about an insurance policy or distress purchase, and the personnel in the business tend to be people with brains the size of small galaxies, but low social skills; and the business (perhaps as a consequence) has a high staff turnover.

Robert Stephens is the CEO of an IT Support Brand based in Minneapolis called Geek Squad. In setting up his business Stephens realized that all the really good people didn't want to stay in the business; there was a pool of good talent doing a horrible job. There would always be a tipping point at which they got frustrated and would leave; this dominoed into the employer getting frustrated in turn, and the customer losing any continuity into the bargain.

Stephens refused to accept that this had to be the way the business operated. The key, he will tell you, is to recognize that there is a difference between nerds and geeks. Previously it had been assumed that IT was a job for nerds; Stephens believed it was a job for geeks. What's the difference between the two? A nerd doesn't know he's a nerd, but a geek knows he's a geek. Geeks are asocial, and he wanted to have a place where they could stay and they could belong.

So what he created was a brand that would allow them to feel special. A brand whose deliberate theatre would celebrate their geekiness and yet give them a stage that would bring a sense of status and pride to what they were doing.

The brand name and concept are 'Geek Squad'. It works like this. First, he calls every one of his geeks 'Agents'. Agent Derrick. Agent Murphy. Agent Ryan. They have a uniform that he took from watching Ed Harris and his team in the movie *Apollo 13* – black trousers, white short-sleeved shirts, black ties. He uses clip-on ties (on the grounds that any self-respecting geek couldn't tie a decent knot themselves), and they always carry a sparc, in case they get cold pizza all down the front of them – an occupational danger of working in IT.

Each carries a die-cast metal badge in a leather wallet, bearing the legend 'Geek Squad'; these are made by the same manufacturers that make police badges, and cost $80 each. At the beginning of each job they announce themselves to the customer by showing their badge – 'Good morning, Geek Squad'. Members of the squad ride around in Geekmobiles. They are familiar with the idea of a Geekmobile from the beginning of their life in Geek Squad, because they have had their interviews in Geekmobile 1 – a huge stretch limo which pulls up on a designated street corner at a designated time to pick them up so that Stephens can see whether they are cut of the right cloth to make it into the squad.

So here we have a strong brand. With high staff retention and motivation. A culture brand, wrapped to the point of being its own country. And yet it is in a market that we would have historically said was low interest, and doomed to high turnover and low motivation. Stephens's sense of theatre, and understanding of the personal as well as professional motivations of the people who work in the business, have combined to create an environment that builds a stronger bond between the customer and company, and the company and the individual. Breaking another, apparently inevitable spiral – one he refused to accept.

Sinead O'Connor once remarked, 'Theatre is the revenge of the shy'; for the Geek Squad it may or may not be revenge, but it has certainly been the glue of the Geeks.

Conclusions

Lena Simonsson-Berge, IKEA's Retail Manager for North America, talks of how there are two ghosts that haunt established organizations – she calls them 'Stuck' and 'Static'. Here is an illustration of these that she drew on a napkin in a meeting (Figure 8.5).

Figure 8.5   'Stuck' and 'Static'
Reproduced by permission of Lena Simonsson-Berge

The two are clearly very different. In areas in which an organization is 'static', most people know what needs to be done, but the brand or the project lacks the priority of a unified team with an energetic sense of direction to drive it.

'Stuck' organizations, on the other hand, really do need a Pirate Inside. These organizations have a way of seeing the market, or a way of doing things that is consistently failing to deliver what the brand needs, but which persists because, well, it's the way they have been doing things. And so it's the way they keep doing things, even though it fails to deliver.

And the first step in changing that piece of 'stuckness' is Refusing. Refusing to accept that the category has to be that way, or the trade relationships have to be that way, or the consumer relationship has to be that way. The best way to think of Refusing, in fact, is not as something negative but as something positive: a different kind of passion. And indeed to recognize that *what we refuse to accept will define our success just as much as knowing what we are passionate for.*

So let's refuse a little more. Let's refuse the Fifth Excuse for the Navy – refuse to believe our category is in some way different. Refuse to duck the challenge.

Refuse to just KBO.

9

Taking it Personally: A Different Kind of Professionalism

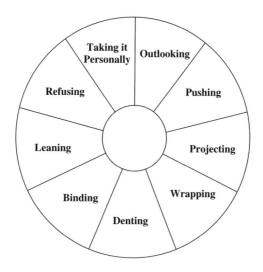

Figure 9.1 **Taking it Personally**

Today I see ladies in America wearing mink coats with trainers. They make me want to cry.
Manolo Blahnik[1]

Y ou have to be able to take it personally, of course. To care, one way or the other. Historically we have regarded professionalism as a compliment: to say 'they're a real professional' is a great tribute. Yet if we look at all the people we are discussing in the book, the relationship they have with their brands, their jobs, their challenges and what they demand of them is not a professional one, with all the distance that suggests, but a personal one. And 'Taking it personally' is one of the key factors that makes the difference.

Have Your Own Reason for Doing It

Why should you want to take it personally at all? Well, you often get into a particular category for your own reasons. Perhaps because you are founding your own business: Barry Sternlicht, the founder of the W Hotel chain, said, 'My goal with W was to cure all my pet peeves about hotels.'[2] Yes, he called it W because all the values he was missing in contemporary hotels seemed to start with the letter W (Witty, Warm, Welcoming, Whimsical, Wild, Wired). But a key part of the founding vision for the hotel was also about being as comfortable as you would be at home. You would feel embarrassed, for instance, being in the lobby of the Ritz Carlton in flip flops and wet hair – so Sternlicht wanted a place that was stylish, but where you could do just that and feel entirely at ease.

Sometimes you get into a particular company because it is your personal view on the way the world ought to be – and that there are enough people out there who share your view to make a business out of it. Luke Lewis, who started the Lost Highway record label under the aegis of Universal, did so because he faced a personal crisis. His work with Shania Twain on 'Come on over' had helped her into the top ten best-selling albums of all time. But in the period immediately following that success, Lewis realized that he was losing his personal connection with the country music business – which was increasingly targeted specifically on 35–55-year-old women:

> I'm not one, so the music suddenly was not particularly gratifying on a personal level, do you know what I mean? It wasn't meant to appeal to me. I'm a boomer, and I grew up with singer/songwriters being probably the mainstay of my tastes throughout my life, and suddenly the format that I'm working in is sort of not driven by music that's targeted at anybody that's my age, or has my tastes, and so I was thinking that I couldn't be as good at this as I might have been in the past, because I'd lost my passion for the product.

Lewis, in fact, had been at school with Gram Parsons, the legendary singer-songwriter and one-time member of The Byrds and The Flying Burrito Brothers, and realized that while he felt that he had lost his passion for mass marketing to female 'Middle Youth', the empathy for Parsons and what he represented in music as a singer-songwriter remained. Lewis wanted to find a way to let artists make albums the way they wanted to make them: without the pressure for a single, or huge volume sales. He knew this would have to mean a different model of how one broke and promoted an album – one that did not rely on radio play and videos on MTV to break it.

> I had had, over the years, this dream of someday finding an opportunity to have a label where I could actually make music that suited my own tastes, because I believe I'm fairly common and that there's a huge music-buying audience out there that are, if not from my demographic, share my tastes. So that I might be able to sign artists and make music that I was passionate about personally, and that it could find an audience out there to sustain a business, which in the middle of a corporate environment is sort of like a wet dream.
>
> So I put together a business plan that let the powers that be inside the corporate environment here know that it wasn't a hobby, and that I could – without counting on radio air play [this is critical to the Lost Highway model] – sign artists, and make records and make money, or at the very least break even. And if we happen to make a record or have an artist that made a record that *did* find some radio air play, that would be incremental to the business plan and there would be an upside.
>
> Little did I know at the time that the upside would come from something that would fit the model exactly . . .

Namely, the platinum success of the *O Brother, Where Art Thou?* soundtrack.

Manolo Blahnik finds mixing sneakers with mink makes him want to cry – it is, in his eyes, a lamentable affront to lovers of crushed velvet and crystal stilettos everywhere. Merrill Fernando of Dilmah calls teabags 'a ruthless desecration of all the beauty and romance of tea'. Founders have strong personal feelings about aspects of their category, that influence the way they approach it.

But you don't have to be a founder to take what you are doing personally in this way. For some, like Paula Moss, a high degree of personal commitment is simply a necessary part of delivering against the challenge you are facing: 'I believe you can make things work, if you put enough passion and energy into what is right. It depends on how much personal commitment you put into it yourself.'

Others within larger companies, we will see, adopt the values of the brand so clearly in the at-work persona of themselves and their brand that they really are embodying the brand in the way they push internally as well as the way they think internally, even if they are selling something as apparently innocuous as chocolate milk. Others again take it personally because they believe that what they are doing is an exciting and important new way of thinking that the parent needs to learn from – as the OK Soda team did within Coca-Cola (see Chapter 12).

Now we will not feel this way about every brand or brand opportunity we could work on. But the reason it is important that we find a brand or opportunity that we do feel that way about is because it influences so considerably the standards we and the team bring to what we are doing, our preparedness to fight for what we believe in, and the propensity to get things done, rather than just talk about them. Let's briefly dig into each of these in turn.

Have Your Own Standards

If you do take it personally, then you have your own standards. Richard Reed of innocent tells the story of how, a year or so into the brand's life, he is finally contemplating the pleasures of some kind of social life again, in the form of an evening clubbing with his friends. His girlfriend is away, he can get home as late as he likes – a great evening is on the cards. As he is on the verge of going out, he gets a call from someone who knows the founders and the company to say that they have just been driving down the motorway into London and seen a large pile of innocent leaflets by the side of the road, blowing all over the road and into the neighbouring field. Reed has to weigh up whether to go out and have fun, or to go and sort out the problem with the leaflets. He spends his Saturday night at the edge of the motorway – he doesn't want the brand to be seen like that, or to be something that litters the environment.

Fighting for What You Believe

If you take it personally, and if you develop your own standards, you fight harder for what you believe is right for the brand. Theresa Fatino's first job was at Ralph Lauren. She was struck by how they could spend three meetings debating which shade of blue they would use for a line of clothing. She took that learning on with her into her job as Design Director at W Hotels:

> My lasting impression from my experience [at Ralph Lauren] is that details are ever, ever so important. I remember once we had three meetings about the colour blue of a particular fabric that was apparently 'just not right' and yet I couldn't tell the difference. My boss was having these very heated conversations with our licensees and she would not back down on the exact quality of blue that she was looking for. This made a real impression on me – you just can't back down when it comes to what's right for the brand, even if everyone else thinks you're nuts. What's really important is staying true to your vision for the brand and in all of my experiences since then, I have been many, many times the only person in the room who wants it white when everybody else wants it black. I'm saying 'No, it's gotta be white, it's gotta be white' – and eventually it ends up being white.

You Make It Happen

If you take it personally, you have a higher propensity to just make what needs to happen, happen and happen faster. And one recognizes here that needing senior approval can sometimes simply bog one down. If we look at two different individuals in two hugely different organizations, we can see two interesting strategies emerging here – both of which, in effect, represent an individual personally committed to moving initiatives as fast as possible through the system.

The first strategy is UNODIR. Commander Abrashoff believed that 'you don't get anywhere by blindsiding your boss'. But, equally, he didn't want to have to wait for formal approval for everything he did. So he never asked permission for any of the revisions in procedures he implemented – he communicated his intent to his superior officer, followed by the letters UNODIR, a standard Navy acronym for 'Unless Otherwise Directed'. He didn't want to blindside them, but he wanted them to have to do something *active* to stop him. 'I'd say: "This is what we intend to do, and you have to get up out of your chair and tell me 'No' if you don't want me to do it."' And he was banking on the fact that usually they wouldn't.

Theresa Fatino, on the other hand, just does stuff without asking. The W is unlike more traditional luxury hotels such as the Ritz Carlton, in that it places a high emphasis on constant innovation – so that even regular guests are engaged by something new and fresh every time they come. Fatino can only do this by *not* seeking permission every time, and accepting this will count against her in the eyes of her superiors, but feeling that the results for the brand will outweigh the internal issues this raises for her:

I had a conference call with the CEO last week and he said: 'Theresa, why is it that you can always get things done?' And the answer is partly because I have a very productive group, but also because I run a very high risk – I don't run everything by him, I just do it. And I told him this. I said, 'It's because I just do it – and if you don't like it, then I run the risk of getting fired, or whatever, but it's worth it.'

I think risk is rewarded, intellectual risks and smart risks are rewarded and embraced, because six years later I'm still here. When we get reviewed, one of my dings [i.e. rebukes] against me is always, 'Theresa, you never get counsel' or 'You never seek us to get approval' and I say to them, 'If I did, I would never get anything done.' And so I'm saying this to the President and the CEO, and they look at me and they say: 'OK, yes, you're right, you're right.' So here we are every year, every review: 'Theresa, you've got to show us more.' And every year I don't, and every year we get things done.

Now of course, the cultural context in the Navy is different from that of the W; the nature of the admirals is rather different, and the consequences of making mistakes are rather different. But the point is that each of these two individuals in their own way is recognizing that going through a traditional approval system with their superiors will not allow the necessary initiatives to move ahead at the speed they need to move ahead. And each is finding a way to push as fast as they can through the system without actually getting themselves fired.

So exactly how we choose to do this depends on our culture and the consequences of the initiative. But if we are taking it personally, we will find a way to do it at our speed, rather than the natural speed of the company.

Putting Some Skin in the Game

Finally, 'Taking it personally' means, a bit like Manolo's Blahnik's minks, that you have to put some of your own skin in the game.

We talk a lot of 'skin in the game' as a metaphor; it is hard to resist, though, looking at someone who is taking the idea a little more literally. I should warn you that what follows on the next couple of pages will be a little graphic for some tastes – if you are feeling hungry, and are a carnivore, you would be better eating lunch before reading this next section than after it. But that is exactly this Challenger's point: she wants to provoke and challenge our constant and complacent looking-the-other-way.

The person is Ingrid Newkirk, who is the founder of People for the Ethical Treatment of Animals (PETA). In drawing up her last will and testament, she has directed that, after her death, parts of her body be put on display or sent to those responsible for abusing animals. The following are some of the individual directions within that will:

- That the 'meat' of my body, or a portion thereof, be used for a human barbecue, to remind the world that the meat of a corpse is all flesh, regardless of whether it comes from a human being or another animal, and that flesh foods are not needed.

- That in remembrance of the elephant feet umbrella stands and tiger rugs I saw, when a child, offered for sale by merchants at Connaught Place in Delhi, my feet be removed and umbrella stands or other ornamentation be made from them, as a reminder of the depravity of killing innocent animals, such as elephants, in order that we might use their body parts for household items and decorations.
- That my pointing finger be delivered to Kenneth Feld, owner of Ringling Brothers Barnum and Bailey Circus or to a circus museum, to stand as the 'Greatest Accusation on Earth' on behalf of the countless elephants, lions, tigers, bears and other animals who have been kidnapped from their families and removed from their homelands in India, Thailand, Africa and South America, and deprived of all that is natural and pleasant to them, abused and forced into involuntary servitude for the sake of cheap entertainment.
- That my liver be vacuum-packed and shipped, in whole or part, to France, to there be used in a public appeal to persuade shoppers not to support the vile practice of force-feeding geese and ducks for foie gras.
- That one of my ears be removed, mounted and sent to the Canadian Parliament to assist them in hearing, for the first time perhaps, the screams of the seals, bears, raccoons, foxes and mink bludgeoned, trapped and sometimes skinned alive for their pelts; that the other ear be removed, preserved and displayed outside the Deonar abattoir in Mumbai to remind all who do business there that the screams of the cattle who are slaughtered within its walls are heard around the world.
- That a little part of my heart be buried near the racetrack at Hockenheim, preferably near the Ferrari pits, where Michael Schumacher raced in and won the German Grand Prix.[3]

You may not have read to the end – and if you haven't, I would draw attention to the last of her directions, about Hockenheim. This is, for me at least, the moment at which she has me. Just as we are starting to think she is not merely passionate but perhaps a little unhinged, she shows us that she has a softer side, and other passions too. It is a detail that changes one's reaction to the whole piece, because it shows you an object of her love, as well as the objects of her anger – and reminds you that she is just a human being who is very angry and taking it very, very personally.

There is a story about one of the three politicians other than Nixon later implicated in Watergate. The story goes that this man had a party piece which would involve putting his hand over a naked candle flame and simply holding it there, even when the flame appeared to be beginning to singe and sear the flesh. 'What's the trick?' someone once asked him. 'The trick,' he replied, 'is not minding.'

In a sense we are the exact opposite of the amoral politician. For us, the trick *is* minding. When it stops being personal, it becomes less likely to happen.

But Can You Really Take it Personally in Large Multi-brand Organizations?

It is natural that founders have a personal engagement with the brand they found; the founder of *Time* Magazine, Henry Luce, in fact rather charmingly put 'Time' as next of kin on his passport. But this sense of personal engagement can, and should, carry through into those of us working within large organizations, that are not our own. And we will come to discuss a number of such examples later in the book, but it is worth briefly looking here at why it sometimes *doesn't* happen. The most common reason is perhaps that people are not always proud of what they are doing. Simon Clift, the President of Marketing for Unilever's Home and Personal Care division, talked about the fact that sometimes college graduates, with Summa Cum Laude or Double Firsts recognizing their brilliance, join a detergent company like Lever Brothers and at some level find themselves embarrassed by what they are now doing, working on a soap powder or a body shampoo. So they take solace either in the more Important Job of General Management, or The Art of Process Administration. Jobs that genuinely merit a keen brain and years of educating the mind.

But the hell with that. You have to be able to align yourself emotionally to the task facing the brand. Because you care about the brand and what it stands for – whether championing decent food, or educating people on the power of a healthy mouth, or encouraging a move towards taking control of one's wellness. Or because you get enormous emotional energy from the nature of the challenge, such as around a tired icon that everyone else was afraid to touch. Or because you feel that what you are doing will impact the larger organization.

You may not own the brand, and you may not be the target audience – or at least, rarely. But unless you can take the brand personally it probably will not get the fight and spirit from you that its challenge needs to succeed.

10

Brand-centricity

Great brands are built by people. Not processes, or research programmes, or pieces of architectures such as pyramids, or bullseyes, or keys, or onions. Not through skill bases or training programmes. They are built by people.

And by people here we do not mean consumers. We mean the people who have the responsibility for shaping and deciding the future of those brands. People like you and me. Who are consumers, of course, but also people with a responsibility for the ideas and decisions and spends and risks that decide whether a brand will go up or down. Who recognize that, in a sense, getting the strategy or brand vision right is the least of it. And who use their personal qualities and ways of seeing the world to drive the implications of the strategy forward, even if it means running up against the old or established ways of doing things, and the people who are still doing them that way.

But it is important to remind ourselves that there is a centre, a brief to all these qualities and behaviours, because it might be construed by the reader moving through this book at some speed, that I am simply advocating cutting loose emotionally. 'Refusing', 'Pushing', 'Denting': all these are characteristics of people we have worked with at some points in our lives, and pretty poisonous and difficult experiences at times they were too. Gloria Steinem remarked that, 'Nice girls don't make history' – are we simply giving people the licence to be assholes? We have worked with people like this before, and the prospect of doing so again has all the charm and appeal of a daily suppository.

There are two parts to the answer to this. The first is that, yes, by people we are indeed talking about individuals and types of individuals as well as teams. Perhaps there is 'no I in team', but there are individuals within a team, and those individuals play certain and different key roles, and need to bring certain and different key characteristics to the table if they are working on a Challenger brand. And these people may well at times make those around them uncomfortable. Denters, for instance, are not necessarily people who will perform well in 360-degree evaluations, because not everyone around them will want to be moved on at the pace the Denter is trying to move them on. And such evaluations can be a chance to voice that reluctance to move – it is not for nothing that in the US Army 360-degree evaluations are apparently known as 'SYB', which stands for 'Screw Your Buddy'.

But the second, pivotal point to be made here is that these qualities must *all be exerted in the service of something other than the individual's own whims and ego*. We are not advocating these because we want people to be free to pursue their own personal ambitions unimpeded, nor are we advocating intrapreneurship per se; they are instead doing it in the interests of the brand (the brand, not the company), and specifically the business need or opportunity of the brand and the strategic vision that will drive the realization of that need or opportunity.

So the final step for the first two parts of the book, diagrammatically speaking, is to put the opportunity and vision for the brand at the centre of this set of personal behaviours and qualities (Figure 10.1).

Ensure that we as individuals are brand-centric as Challengers, rather than ego-centric.

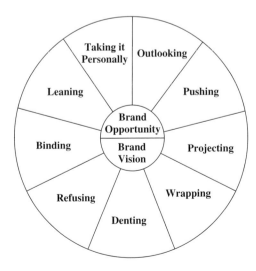

Figure 10.1   **Brand-centricity and Pirate Behaviours**

Welcome to Behemoth, Inc

I am an optimist in the sense that I believe that individuals are noble and
honourable, and some of them are really smart. I have a very optimistic
view of individuals. As individuals, people are inherently good. I have a
somewhat more pessimistic view of people in groups.

Steve Jobs[1]

There is of course another possible kind of centre to such behaviours
and qualities, particularly if one is in a large multi-brand organization,
namely the company, rather than the brand. Putting what is right for the
company at the heart of one's actions, and the corporate way of doing
things, rather than what is right for the brand.

So having explored the idea of brand-centricity in individuals through
the first two parts of the book, Part III is going to explore the idea of
brand-centricity within teams, within companies, and in particular
multi-brand companies. Specifically, we are going to explore the idea
of brand-centric subcultures within a larger organization, with a set of
values and practices aligned around the vision for a particular brand,
rather than the historic values and practices of the parent company.
And in doing so, we are going to look for grounds for being optimistic
about people in groups.

This will bring us to the Sixth Excuse for the Navy – and the one
that on the face of it is the most justifiable. It is this:

> It is hard for me to be a genuine Challenger because I am not in a single
> brand company with a charismatic founder at the helm. I am in a big
> multi-brand company with a conservative culture, and I am just another
> marketing director or manager.

In other words, what does it take to be a Pirate, a brand-centric
Challenger if you are already *in* the Navy? And in particular, what does
it take to be a Pirate in the Navy without getting hanged?

Let us first start by unpacking the reasons that are sometimes offered
as to why it is harder to be a Challenger within a large company, so that

we can get a good look at them. They probably run something like this:

> I understand how single brand companies can establish brand-centric
> Challenger cultures. As a single brand company they are able to take
> some fundamental decisions about what they want their brand to stand
> for, and then project that to the consumer externally on the one hand,
> and live that culture internally on the other. They are, after all, only one
> brand, so it becomes easy to live that sense of the brand inside as well.
> And that in turn makes it easy for the individual – for all individuals
> involved in the brand – to adopt any or all of the values we have been
> talking about so far, because everyone else throughout the organization
> understands those values too, and is behaving the same way. And if
> anyone falters, they have a charismatic and belligerent founder still at
> the heart of the organization to make sure everyone understands and
> lives the brand, day and night.

'But', this argument continues:

> That is not the situation I am in. I am not in a single brand company. I
> work in a large, multi-brand company called Behemoth, Inc. My company
> is not known historically for being entrepreneurial, and indeed might be
> called at times conservative (with a small c). It has a corporate culture,
> with clear guidelines, consisting in apparently prescribed ways of doing
> things that are based on a benchmarking of internal practices within
> ourselves and the rest of our category. It has a watchful shareholder, our
> responsibility to whom is frequently mentioned as a brake on ventures
> that appear to depart from the well-trodden paths. And in this situation
> the parent culture interacts with the individual brand culture. Impedes
> it, even. It limits not simply *my* ability to behave in this way, but limits
> the ability of any brand to step outside the commonly prescribed ways of
> doing things for all the other brands in its portfolio.
>
> So this is the big question – after all, there's got to be more people
> like me, in these kinds of companies, than there are like those senior
> founders and entrepreneurs in single brand Challengers. How does all
> this work in my kind of company? In a Kraft or a Unilever or a P&G or
> a Pfizer or a Johnson & Johnson? In Behemoth, Inc?

Although many of the examples have alluded to brands in such companies in passing, perhaps the key issue facing this book is to look at

how the model works in this kind of multi-brand situation – in a big company, without a charismatic founder, with many brands to think about. In short, if we are in this environment, does anything about this emerging model change?

Before we move on to Part III, which will start to answer this question, let us first slay one potential misconception about what kind of subcultures we are and are not really talking about here. Because there tends to be an assumption when one talks about a company creating a different way of going to market for a particular initiative that what has precipitated this is a bunch of middle-aged marketers recognizing that they are about to go after a youth market, and setting up an offsite skunkworks full of primary colours and skateboards for the launch of a small new counterculture brand aimed at Gen ∞, or whatever the latest *appellation du jour* happens to be.

I think this particular association is also an excuse – it is an excuse for giving too much rope to certain kinds of projects, if they fit that bill, and not giving any to others that fall outside it. But Brand-centric subcultures are not all the same, and the brands we are going to be looking at as examples do not all fall into this easy cliché. Altoids is hardly new – it is a mint brand that has been around since 1780. The audience for Lost Highway's breakthrough bluegrass album O *Brother, Where Art Thou?* was hardly youth – the initial marketing push was on NPR. Axe is hardly small – it is Unilever's largest men's grooming brand.

The overall commonality in the brands we will be looking at, then, is not the easy categorization of 'small, new, countercultural youth brands'. The commonality is in fact a much purer one: that these brands and the people behind them needed to go to market externally in ways that were not characteristic of the parent company as a whole – that in some cases were perhaps even counter to the corporate culture of the company, or the global template – because they were single-mindedly focused on making a success of a particular opportunity for their brand, and that is what success in this case demanded. In some instances these external marketing differences were also reflected in an internal culture that grew up around the nature of the brand, that in turn influenced not just how they acted within the brand team, but also how they behaved in relation to the other brands and resources within Behemoth, Inc.

I should also note that not all of the examples share all of the commonalities we shall define. But we are looking for the patterns rather than the universalities, and yeasty examples that will inspire our own creativity – and it is from these that we will draw the concepts and the 'provocations' to derive our own Articles, and our own ability to create a genuinely brand-centric team and brand-centric culture, even if we are part of Behemoth, Inc.

How to Be a Pirate in the Navy, Without Getting Hanged

Part III will look specifically at Pirates who find themselves already in the Navy, that is to say, Challengers who find themselves within a large, multi-brand organization. It will look at what we can learn from successes and failures in such situations, and the benefits, when they do work, not just for the brand but also for the parent organization.

Chapter 11   Red Pill, Blue Pill: Learning from Success

This chapter looks at the four preconditions for success for a Challenger brand within a large multi-brand organization. These are: a commonly understood brand or business requirement to find a fresh way of going to market; a different approach to how one puts the core team together; the establishment of a broad understanding of the cohesive new brand model; and the ability to market the brand imperative in commercial language.

Chapter 12   Why Brand-Centred Subcultures Fail: Learning From Failure

While the previous chapter learned from success, this chapter looks at the learnings of failure – the five principal reasons that brand-centred subcultures fail. These reasons for failure are: the preconditions for success not being met;

a lack of belief from your business partners that you are genuinely trying to do something different; unreasonable expectations from the parent; the brand failing to deliver the financial return its status requires; and a change in the way that the parent and child see the symbiosis between the two.

Chapter 13   Biting the Other Generals: The Wider Benefits Successful Subcultures Bring

This chapter looks at the beneficial influences of successful Challengers on other brands within Behemoth, Inc's portfolio. It argues that there are five such influences, ranging from the systemwide spreading of new perspectives and practices, to the individual impetus and inspiration it can create in other team leaders to take risks in pushing their own marketing and communication ideas further.

11

Red Pill, Blue Pill: Learning from Success

Of course we are Spanish. But first we are Majorcan.
Lorenzo Fluxá, Camper

Buenos Aires. A darkened room, full of thirtysomethings in casual dress. Your first day as a member of the Global Team on Axe, Unilever's largest male grooming brand.

Someone presses the video remote. A movie starts to play, a movie you have seen. Whatshisname, that great African American actor, is sitting across a table from Keanu Reeves. Black leather seems to be the dress of the day. *The Matrix*, that's it, now you recognize it: *The Matrix*. Laurence Fishburne is sitting across from Keanu Reeves and he has two different coloured pills that he is holding out in his hand. One pill is red and the other is blue.

Morpheus (Fishburne) spells out to Neo (Reeves) the choice represented by these two pills. If he takes the blue pill, he returns, in effect, to his previous life of safety and predictability. If he takes the red pill, on the other hand, his will be a life of discovery, adventure, uncertainty and risk.

Red pill or blue pill. Which does he want to take?

The man beside the TV turns off the film. His name is Neil Munn, and he is the Global Brand Director on Axe. 'Welcome to the Axe team', he says. 'Now there is one important thing you need to understand in working on this brand. Unilever takes the blue pill; but on Axe, we take the red pill.'

A recent article in the *Harvard Business Review*[1] argued that the successful acquisition of a brand by a parent company relies on the ability of the acquired brand culture to 'match' that of the parent company culture. However, what we shall discuss in this chapter is in effect the inverse of this: we will look at brands that have decided that the best way to succeed is to 'take a different pill' from that of their parent, and what it took to make such a subculture possible and sustainable.

As an overall context, let's look at the flow of a brand development process as defined in most marketing organizations. Roughly speaking, it goes:

Insight – Strategy – Brand Expression – Innovation – Implementation

What is interesting, though, in looking at Challengers within large companies, and the factors that make such subcultures successful, is that three of the four key stages that tend to determine success occur *before this traditional flow even begins*. These are:

- A commonly understood requirement to do something different from the current approach based on a clear Brand Need or Business Imperative.
- A clear understanding of the necessary nature of the people, sponsorship and team.
- A Common Understanding of the New Model (and the new Brand Neighbourhood) and what it entails in terms of working practices.
- Noisy Bilinguality – the ability to speak the language of both the brand subculture and the parent company simultaneously.

We will explore these four one by one.

A Clear Brand Need or Business Imperative to Do Things Differently

The initial incentive for establishing a Challenger brand subculture has almost always been a recognition that there is an opportunity or need for this brand that cannot be realized by approaching marketing in the same way as either other brands in the parent's portfolio, or indeed the way the brand has been marketing itself up to now.

Sometimes this is because there is a different kind of business imperative. For example, what gave the team on Pringles the initial licence to push hard for their own way of doing things was having a factory in Jackson, Mississippi, built to manufacture their product that was losing money. This is clearly an unacceptable situation for any company, and their parent, P&G, was not about to take a lenient view. They had tried marketing it the way they knew how to sell soap powder – now a new team determined to approach it in a new way.

With Yoo-hoo, the nature of their distribution drove the change in focus, and the change in marketing culture that subsequently flowed from that. They had previously been marketing on a 'warm and fuzzy vitamins and minerals' platform to Moms and kids. But Kristin Krumpe, the Marketing Director, knew that the target (and therefore the way they marketed) had to change:

> One of the things that we were seeing every time we would get research back was that the brand had completely lost touch with that teen young male consumer – and so much of our business is convenience store business. I mean, the brand is primarily a single serve, 'drink it down the street' type of product. And, you know, we'd had no business really talking to young children and mums as the primary target audience. So it was a complete 180-degree shift as to who we wanted to talk to. And their feelings about the brand at that time were that this was a very old brand.

Sometimes it is because of a brand need. Kraft picked up Altoids in the US almost by accident. They had apparently bought the Jacobs Suchard business primarily for the chocolate brands in Europe, and along with the crown jewels of cocoa came a strange, square metal box of mints costing four times as much as the US market leader. Kraft knew that they could not market with this kind of price disparity the same way they marketed cheese slices – they would have to find a new way of going to market to make it succeed.

Sometimes the issue is not one of brand need but a brand opportunity that can only be realized by casting a brand in a new way, as with 8th Continent. The soy milk market was large and growing, and was one that General Mills and DuPont both wanted to be in.

And sometimes both need and opportunity are combined – in effect, because there is an internal mindset about the brand that needs to be overturned in order to release the brand's real potential for growth. Though still very profitable, the Tango brand had been static for a number of years when Tony Hillier took up the position of Marketing Director. Hillier saw there was an opportunity to drive it much harder but as Tango's parent Britvic was also the distributor for Pepsi, Hillier realized that in order to drive this change Tango would have to break out of a mental marketing lens that was heavily influenced by Pepsi – their primary brand as licensee – and the way the two cola giants successfully defined marketing in the soft drinks arena. The constriction that bound them was in effect one of an internal way of thinking that they had created themselves: they would have to approach marketing the brand in a very different way to release the brand's greater potential.

So the first precondition for success is to recognize a business or brand need or opportunity that requires the brand to behave and go to market, both internally and externally, in a different way than has been done in the past. These people are thus not Vanity Pirates, but Necessary Pirates.

A Clear Understanding of the Necessary Nature of the People, Sponsorship and Team

Any powerful drama or narrative is driven by the nature of the characters involved. These narratives and brand stories are no different.

The Individuals

Now while none of these brands, lying as they do within a larger company with at least one other brand as well, has had a single person in the sense of a founder driving them, at the heart of each of them was a team whose *collective* qualities in many ways made up what a founder brings. The individual components of most of these teams were as follows.

A Denter

We talked in detail in Chapter 5 about Denters, and at the heart of each of these Challenger subcultures has been such a Denter – someone who, you will remember, 'wants to put a dent in the world'. While none of us wants to be just another grain in the Great Risotto of Life, we noted that Denters have a number of very particular characteristics that are important here, besides their desire to make their mark.

First, they are people who regard themselves *as employed by the brand rather than the company*. This is an interesting and important distinction that many of them make. Remember Bob Gill's remark about seeing the company essentially as a financial resource – their real loyalty is to the brand, because this is a better way of realizing the commercial opportunity on the brand (and therefore the return to the shareholder) than doing it in a more 'corporate' way.

They are *not driven by careerism in and of itself*: they are not doing this job for the one that it will get them afterwards. This is obviously important in terms of one's relationship to a parent company. They are totally committed to doing whatever it takes to make this one succeed – even if in doing so they rub up against people who might seem to be important for their long-term relationship within the company. As such, many made it clear that they were not overly concerned about whether they would still be in the company in 10 years time, if the company pushed against them for this. While they would not necessarily choose to leave, they were very confident that they could find a job elsewhere.

They have a *preparedness to embrace tension, rather than accept dilution*. We saw that while they are not people who seek tension, they neither mind it nor retreat from it when they encounter it. The tension that Denters have to deal with comes in two kinds of situations – where they have to go up against a particular function or person to deliver what the brand needs delivered and where they have to resist people who want to dilute the expression of the brand in some way, even if those are more senior people. (As we saw in Chapter 5, Denters do not easily accept the answer 'No'.)

Denters within large organizations retain their ability to go the way they feel their brand demands, largely thanks to the fact that they are on a *personal mission to drive the brand vision forward*. Crucially, they make sure they have the superior knowledge to support this vision when questioned. Kristin Krumpe says:

It helps a lot, being able to sort of, talk circles around people when it comes to Yoo-hoo. There is an intimidation factor, and I completely appreciate that and I use it when I need to.

In spite of their preparedness to embrace tension, Denters are not isolationists – when they find themselves in large multi-brand organizations they make sure they understand the rules, structure and hierarchy, they just don't necessarily always play by those rules. To be effective, Denters cannot be wild isolationist mavericks. It is not in their interest to run deliberately and constantly counter to the organization and its hierarchy because the fact is they have to take at least a piece of the organization with them when creating the space that will ultimately allow the brand to go on doing things differently, until success generates permission of its own. This is Bob Gill of Pringles on finding a different way to play the system:

> If you're trying to make a decision with your team, the first thing is to get your team to decide what it's going to do and then how you're going to sell it up through the hierarchy. I tried to develop a relationship for a long time with the Chairman – not the one that tried to fire me, but the other one. Recruiting is a big deal at P&G, so I got on his recruiting team. I was the head of his recruiting team for the school, because that's a big thing, so I'd spend a week every year running around with him recruiting, but the real purpose was to make sure he was aligned to our programme. So any and all the guys on the team had to do similar things with their bosses to make sure they were aligned.

None of this is to suggest, obviously, that all is always peaceful. Certainly, if one looks at examples of vigorous brand renewal within large companies, however the story has been rewritten now, the success in bringing the ideas to market in their undiluted forms was as much to do with the conviction with which the team fought for the idea against the constraints of the corporate requirements, and indeed the views of very senior figures within the company, as it was the power of the idea itself.

An Idea Hamster

An Idea Hamster is someone who is a constant source of ideas for the brand – ideas to do with communications, or ways of bringing the brand to life. Sometimes this role is taken by a member of the agency or other creative partner who is an integral part of the team. Churning ideas constantly through the brand team; communication ideas, PR ideas, internal cultural ideas – anything that Wraps the brand, gives it saliency, gives it a greater chance of delivering the brand opportunity. These people are not necessarily very good at getting things done, but then that is not their role on the team. Theirs is simply to make sure the ideas are constantly flowing through, certainly for launch, but also sustaining momentum in the years that follow.

Sometimes an imaginative approach has to be taken to create this function if a single Idea Hamster does not already exist within your team. This involves tapping into the ideas of a much broader group of people by showing them that if they offer such ideas, they genuinely will come to life. Commander Abrashoff, in taking command of the USS Benfold, called each of the ship's ratings into his cabin in turn and asked them three very simple questions – how they felt about working on the ship, what is the one thing they would like to fix, and what they would do about it.

He had the microphone for the ship's PA system sitting in front of him on his desk as he conducted each interview. If an individual came up with an idea he liked, he picked up the mike and immediately announced to the entire ship who he had in his cabin, what their idea was, that he liked it, and that it would be implemented forthwith – effectively reducing the amount of time between suggestion and implementation in some cases to about 20 seconds. After he did this a few times, Abrashoff observed, the number and quality of the ideas started to rise significantly.

We should note that the presence of a member of an advertising agency is not in and of itself the presence of an Idea Hamster: a script on demand every six months does not an Idea Hamster make. Some agencies (of any kind) are enthusiastic and constant generators of ideas – as long as they think you are going to do something with them – and others are not. You need to choose your partners, and perhaps even the team in the agency, accordingly – who has worked on other Challengers, and understands what you are going to need here?

Implementation Rhinos

The third kind of person or function one needs on the core team is someone who makes stuff happen. Roger Kirman of Unilever was at the centre of a team that doubled Close Up's share in Brazil from 7% to 14% in four years. A key factor in this dramatic performance was the increased rate of innovation introduction into the market – from one every two years to one every eight months. And what made this possible was a certain member of his team, who simply took innovations happening elsewhere in the world, brought them to the team for development, and then got them launched, five in four years. One failed (a floss, that in retrospect had been wrong for the brand), but that didn't stop them – he and they just kept going. One of the people I interviewed put many organizations' perspective on such individuals very well:

> What many large organizations like my own know how to prize is articulacy – if you can talk about your brand for 45 minutes without hesitation, deviation or interruption, you will go far. What these big organizations are less good at understanding the value of is the people who arguably really matter, which is the less articulate doers.

'Less articulate' in this context was not intended in any way by the speaker to be a put down – it is simply a way of drawing attention to people whose primary talent is *delivery*, rather than standing on podiums in front of Venn diagrams expressing a new model of Brand Architecture. The Implementation Rhino is absolutely critical, and is the great (and often) unsung hero of any organization.[2]

Smokejumper

Denters who find themselves in large multi-brand organizations clearly cannot flourish in isolation. They need protection and air cover because, if they are doing their job properly, they are going to rub some people in the organization up the wrong way. This may be because they are unblocking a blocker, or going outside or around the usual system, or because they are choosing to ignore some corporate way of doing things.

So Denters need a sponsor. And they need a very particular kind of sponsor to ensure that this abrasion will not be problematic – and in particular not the benign but absent sponsorship of the *éminence grise* who has lunch with one every eighteen months or so, and enquires genially how it is going. A different kind of sponsor, a Smokejumper.

Firefighting in dense woodland is a difficult task once the blaze has caught. Smokejumpers are people who fly low over forests in North America and, once they see a plume of smoke rising from out of the trees that indicates the beginning of a more dangerous blaze (if left unmanaged), parachute in on their own and cut a firebreak around it to limit its potential effect. That is, they proactively look to stop it before it causes a bigger problem – while it is still warning smoke, rather than an actual fire.

Let us play out why we are talking about Smokejumpers rather than sponsors here. A sponsor denotes a benevolent, but in practice frequently absent eye, able to be called upon in case of difficulty. But the reason we are replacing the term sponsor with Smokejumper here is because the people the Denter and his team need to support them in creating a brand subculture must play a very different role from the traditional sponsor. The Smokejumper must be:

- Very high up – they must have the authority to be able to stop early signs of smoke turning into fires.
- Actively watching – because they know putting this project or this person in play may (and perhaps should) create heat.
- Focussing on where they may need to take *preventative* action (rather than only remedial work).
- Ready to intervene before a potential problem becomes a real problem.
- Prepared to then get the hell out and leave the people on the ground to continue doing what they do best.
- Able to return to an active watchful role.

The point is that being a sponsor is not just a title ... one has to be prepared to *do* stuff. Let us look at a couple of examples of such smokejumping, and the role it played.

Two weeks into the Hovis relaunch we discussed in Chapter 8, there was a sales conference. Sales had been falling for the two weeks since the new packaging and advertising had appeared, and the price promotions had been withdrawn, and although the brand was starting to show some signs of stabilization, many of the senior managers who were about to attend the conference had been voicing their disquiet. Paula Moss, the

Marketing Director, was very worried how this disquiet might impact the marketing group sitting at the conference.

Her boss, the Managing Director, Peter Baker, had come into her office every day since the relaunch and reassured her that the decision had been the right one. And at the beginning of the conference, without telling her what he was going to do, he stepped in again:

> After about two weeks, there was a big senior managers' conference. A lot of the senior managers around the business were losing confidence because they'd seen the volume drop off and from previous highs where we had been on heavy promotions and stuff to the 10% loss – and in some bakeries it was more substantial because some lines were more down than others. So they were getting really, really, negative about it. And he stood up in front of the whole group of these senior managers within the business and said: 'We did our homework, we know what we're doing, it's the right thing to do, and we have every faith in it. There are signs of recovery already, and I do not want one piece of negativity undermining our position on this. We took the decision jointly, and we stand behind it. We will make it work – and your job in this is to make the product worthy of the premium that we're putting through. It's an unprecedented move and we need to be behind it, not chucking bricks at it.'
>
> And the whole room was just silent. And I didn't know he was going to do it, but I must admit I never felt so well supported.

As it turned out, that was the time when the brand turned the corner: the conference over, the sales started to rise again.

Pot Noodle is another interesting example, where the Smokejumper actually changed the reporting lines of the Denter involved – whereas everyone else in (what was then) CPC reported to the Commercial Director, Woods reported straight to the MD. This upset the Commercial Director, but the Managing Director took the view that this was a snack brand, and had to play by different rules from the rest of the organization, whose portfolio (such as Hellmann's and Knorr) had a different user and usage.

> So we launched this mad campaign where this Welsh bloke was running around with his mate John and a camcorder. It was badly shot on video,

the lighting was bad, you could not understand the dialogue, and the images were appalling. It was at the time when *Men Behaving Badly* was on a roll so it was ahead of that kind of 'lads' thing.

So we start running this campaign, and it bombed out in all the CPC tests: the scripts haven't been passed by Legal, there is not enough mention of the brand, and there isn't the logo in the corner.

We only got around these CPC 'mandatories', because I did not have to go to the existing marketing structure; I had Ian Ramsay's [the Managing Director's] support. I told them that it was no surprise that it had failed the CPC tests, and it just went to prove that they did not understand snacks marketing. I just said, 'This is part of what makes this brand different.'

The campaign proved tremendously successful: in the first 18 months sales rose over 20%, with excellent margins to boot. But it would never have happened, even with Woods' undoubted relish in playing the role as a Denter, unless his Managing Director had proactively taken Woods and his brand out of the normal approval system, foreseeing what would happen if he and it were allowed to stay within – the MD acted as Smokejumper, rather than just a sponsor.

As an example of the visible signal to the rest of the organization, consider the development and launch of Lexus, the new luxury brand within Toyota, in the USA. They over-committed in product, certainly (they produced over 400 prototypes of the LS 400 in Japan, because they were so committed to getting it right), but they also sent a very clear signal about the seriousness attached to the project through the overt sponsorship of the project in the United States. The Chairman of Toyota in Japan sent over his son to be the Japanese co-ordinator on the project. Co-ordinators within Japanese companies in the USA (or anywhere outside Japan) have an important role on a project. They may or may not contribute directly in terms of input or ideas, but they are the eyes and ears of the parent organization in Japan, the link with the HQ, and thus have a critical influence on the outcome. By sending his son, the Chairman indicated how high the success of the initiative lay on his personal agenda – he was, effectively, the very visible sponsor of the project, and would receive briefings on it throughout the development process.

In this case, Dave Illingworth points out, there were two critical points where the Chairman's son made a very valuable contribution – enlisting Nakamichi, who had never done a sound system for a car before, to design the sound system for the LS 400, and getting the engineering help the US team felt they needed on the second model, the ES 250.

The role of the Smokejumper is not always to support a process or an initiative – it is often the brand culture itself that needs vigilance. Simon Clift, Unilever's President of Marketing on Home and Personal Care, describes a key part of his job as to protect the necessary brand culture within the corporate organization. He talks about one of the male Axe brand managers in Argentina, who runs up against the local President because of the way he dresses – the former sports, says Clift, shoulder-length hair and 'just a little' make-up. But Clift's view is that part of his job is to protect not just the strategic integrity of the brands under his domain, but the culture of the teams charged with delivering those brand visions. And thus, he concludes: 'My job is to defend the hair length of the brand manager in Argentina.' It's a joke, of course; but he isn't smiling.

While the Smokejumper should be able to have a wide-ranging influence, it is crucial to note here that it is not the Smokejumper's role to determine the brand strategy. There is an interesting relationship here between Smokejumper and Denter, which sometimes needs to be hammered out between the two of them at an early stage in the process. There can only be one Marketing Director, and the Smokejumper has to respect that he or she is providing the air cover, but not determining the strategy on the ground.

Let's stay with Simon Clift to illustrate this. Axe as a brand is very close to Clift's heart, because he was the Marketing Director when the brand made its initial breakthrough in communications in 1996. His General Manager at the time was a man called Helmut Ganzer, a long-standing Unilever player, with a different view about advertising from Clift. When Clift first presented the new Axe work to his superior, Ganzer's response was unequivocal: 'Simon, I hate it – but you are the Marketing Director.' Ganzer didn't like the work – but he had given the Denter the job, and did not try to do it for him. The work ran, and the renewed success of Axe began with it.

The actor Will Smith had an Air Force father. He relates how his father was very clear about decision-making: 'My father always used to say "I'm in charge. If two people are in charge, everybody dies."[3] We can only have one Marketing Director, or the brand subculture dies. Once the Smokejumper has prevented an obstacle interfering with the team's ability to do what is right for the brand, they need to leave the team to it again.

The Nature of the Resulting Team

So we have seen that the core team needs to consist of four types of people: Denters, Idea Hamster and Implementation Rhinos, supported by a Smokejumper. The next commonality that successful brand sub-cultures share then is the *consistency* of this core team – keeping this team together long enough to make the necessary difference.

It is hard to avoid the view that many companies misuse the concept of team – they talk as if having four people in a room at any one time with clearly defined roles constitutes a team. They will invest in team-building courses and understanding people types and HR people – but when it comes down to it, they are not in reality committed to teams collectively solving deep brand problems, because the unity of the team is being constantly undone by the revolving door that is career management in such large multi-brand companies. A revolving door where the average period a person spends in a particular job is 18 months, and where the make-up of the team is constantly changing as people arrive and move on – and where the team as a whole, therefore, is never the same for more than five months at a time.

Besides the obvious problems of this constant change in and of itself (briefing and re-briefing the new people to get them up to speed, and so on), the change is usually accompanied by a very particular perception within that new individual of how they are going to add value to the brand in terms of marketing: in that time frame they can refine the wording on the proposition, produce a new ad and tweak the pack – and then they can move on. Box ticked, brand improved, job done. On to the next.

But one of the striking things about the teams that work on Challenger subcultures is that the core group of (say) three or four stays together for a relatively long period of time. And when I say long time, I am only talking two or three years – but enough to really drive a brand's identity beyond the obvious implications for advertising and packaging, and to stop the continual reinvention by tweaking that is a substitute for really moving the brand on.

Cross-Functional Teams and Hunting as a Pack

I don't know who it was that first observed that Brand was not a department. That Marketing was a department, but Brand wasn't, because Brand is the responsibility of everyone. But in the same way being a Challenger brand and having a Challenger culture is not solely a marketing function or responsibility: it has to involve everyone across all the key disciplines.

This is not simply a philosophical view about branding – there is a very *practical* point to this. For Pringles, cross-functional alignment was important to drive the project forward in the face of questioning from above. It makes it harder for someone around or above you to say that you are wrong if every discipline is aligned, if every discipline strongly feels and argues that this is the right way forward for the brand. It gives one much more confidence to hunt as a pack.

Indeed, to some degree this cross-functional, brand-centric team almost comes to represent a company within a company. Some of these Challenger subcultures deliberately set up mini business units within the larger company, including an accountant, the factory manager, the supply-chain representative, the sales and trade marketing people, and the marketing team. Meetings would be deliberately alternated between the marketing department and the factory, in some cases, to signal that this was genuinely more than a 'marketing plus selected invitees' initiative, but a brand-centred business unit within the larger company, in effect.

The Team Replicates the Founder

Is the typology for individual roles that we have put forward here too simplistic? Well, while I am aware that there are a number of highly sophisticated models of people typologies, I have felt, in talking to Challenger individuals and exploring their subcultures, that in reality the model for a successful Challenger team is very simple – it is the combination of the four individual roles we have been discussing so far in this chapter. And I would suggest that one of the reasons is that the combined power that the Denter, Idea Hamster, Implementation Rhino and Smokejumper create in a subculture team is in effect what a rounded founder has the ability to do themselves.

What such a rounded founder would offer is usually a union of the following five things:

- Seeing the category in a different way – from which they have a vision for a brand with a different place to stand.
- Ideas – if they are not natural originators, then they are like PacMen in restlessly searching for and adopting ideas for driving the business forward. (Richard Branson is an example of this – he is a great feeder off other people's ideas.)
- Doing – they make it happen. They have to, or the business would die.
- Denting – they want their brand – and usually themselves – to be famous, to make an impact on the market, the consumer and the competition. And they accept that they have to push (indeed, they want to push) in order to make that happen.
- Being fireproof – they cannot be fired. All that can happen is that the brand fails because they have failed in one of the previous four requirements above. In which case, they tend to start again with a new opportunity and new brand.

And collectively this is what the four are able to do as well. So in attempting to 'Replicate the Founder' it is crucial that each member of the team plays in position. A single individual in someone else's company – unlike a founder within their own company – can't play every role: each individual has to recognize who they are, the role they are best suited to play, and what other kinds of people, therefore, they need to have around them.

And, indeed, even in single brand companies, much though the publicity would give you the impression the brand starts and ends with the founder and their vision, this is in reality often far from true. Colleen Barrett, the President and COO of Southwest Airlines, argues in fact that it never is *just* about the founder – it is at least as much about the people underneath and around them.

In the case of the emerging vision for jetBlue, for example, the founder and CEO, David Neeleman (who had come from Southwest) wanted to make the airline's proposition one that was just about low prices. But the three people he had hired from Virgin wanted to make it about something more – and for the first year this created a certain tension between this small group and the rest of the people starting the airline, founder included. Gareth Edmondson-Jones, the VP of corporate communications:

> David felt bargain hunters were our calling ... we were saying 'We should set our sights higher'. The first year felt subversive because we were saying 'This is about bringing the humanity back to air travel', and everyone else was saying 'Aren't we just low fares?' And we were like 'No! If you pick on price, you'll be destroyed.' It took a while, but finally everyone agreed we had to think and talk product, too.[4]

The argument didn't stop there. His colleague, the Marketing VP, also went into bat about the details: while the founder had been considering the now famous leather seats already, he had envisaged them as being dark in colour. Amy Curtis-McIntyre fought for the paler grey that the airline eventually went with, because, in her words, 'I just said we should let our people be the colour and the life.'[5]

In the same way key parts of the original vision for Orange came from below Hans Snook, even though he subsequently eloquently championed it, and came to embody it in the eyes of the organization and the press. So also within Diesel, although Renzo Rosso is an extrovert and sometimes boisterous founder, he will seek out the opinion of the quiet Wilbert Das in a board meeting because, even though he may not like what he says, he knows he needs that counterbalance to his own thinking.

In a sense, then, these kinds of roles are often reversed between a Challenger that is also a single brand company and one which occurs within a large multi-brand organization. In a single brand company the most senior person, the founder, is usually the visionary, but they still need someone else below them, or another group, to push back against them; few are genuinely the autocrats the media portrays them as. In a subculture within a multi-brand organization, on the other hand, the

Denter is the precipitator, the pusher, and the backboard or counterpoint is the person above – the Smokejumper.

External Catalysts Early

Let us finish this section on Challenger teams by looking at how and when external catalysts such as agencies and design partners tend to be used in creating such Challengers.

There is sometimes a temptation to brief the key business partners only when you know what you want to say to them. This seems obvious enough, at one level. That's part of what our job is, after all, isn't it? And of course some companies such as Diageo have deliberately taken back the strategic planning process from their agency partners in recent years, and developed more rigorous internal templates in order to raise the quality of their internal strategic thinking.

Most of these subcultures we are looking at, though, have involved business partners, particularly design and identity companies, from a very early stage – and used them, in effect, as an integral part of the team to help *define* the new brief, not simply respond to it.

Why? After all, this appears to break with the rigorous, disciplined, linear approach that many of our companies seem to guard and favour. But there are two key reasons why it can be so much more valuable to do it this way.

The first value they add lies in the questions these outside partners ask of us – particularly if they are not overly respectful and not the so-called 'Internationally Preferred Supplier', and if they have the confidence, or even arrogance, to challenge us ('arrogance with substance' is not necessarily a bad quality to have in one's agency). Because they have not worked on the brand or perhaps even on the category before, they do not know what 'the right questions' are, so they tend to ask different, and in many ways more interesting and provocative questions. Natural Outlookers, they bring the kind of healthy Intelligent Naivety to the process that just might start off a whole new way of thinking about the opportunity in the category and for the brand.

The second great value that a creative team in particular with this kind of expertise brings is the possibility of an early visualization of the Identity while the 'clay is still soft', so to speak. The value of this – if they are any good, and we have asked them to push us rather than play safe – cannot be underestimated (it is important to be clear here at this early stage that we are *not* asking them for final packaging recommendations, for instance: we are asking them to bring the identity to life through packaging).

This prototyping allows the whole team to do the following:

- To see what it would mean to adopt this positioning.
- To feel an emotional excitement as well as an intellectual understanding and commitment by seeing the ideas that reflect the potential vision.
- To feel the confidence that knowing everyone is absolutely aligned can engender. This confidence can be a lasting and important part of helping the restaging of our brand become a reality rather than a frustrated proposal. Helping you through That Difficult First Year (see Chapter 15).

A Common Understanding of the New Model (and the new Brand Neighbourhood) and What it Entails in Terms of Working Practices

The two key preconditions for success we have considered so far look at the identification of a brand need, and the putting together of a team using specific types of people rather than skill levels. The third precondition for success is about managing the concern in the parent that what one is doing in departing from the customary way of operating is in some way irresponsible wildness, and specifically disarming this concern by establishing a very clear understanding that this is a different, *equally robust but more appropriate* model to the identified need or opportunity for our brand.

So this is not about unleashing 'The Beast of Chaos' within an otherwise fairly process-centred organization. This is about deliberately moving from one strategic/cultural model to a different strategic/cultural model. With processes, but just with different kinds of processes. With various kinds of rigour, but just different kinds of rigour. And making sure that everyone within both the team and the parent understand and recognize that.

What kinds of impact do these new kinds of model have? In looking at those brands that have found their own set of 'rules' within larger organizations, we can see that principles long fundamental to that organization have found themselves changed by the brand's need to create a new kind of relationship in a different kind of way. Take copy-testing within P&G, for example, a long-term standardized system throughout the organization. The first time P&G changed their copy-testing methodology was when Pringles produced their MTV-style advertising aimed at teens. They couldn't use the traditional way to test copy because, well, there wasn't any copy in it. And it is hard to test for persuasion if the ad doesn't try to persuade anyone of anything.

Even internal fundamentals like quality control may fall outside the systems of the corporate culture. Lindsey Owen-Jones, L'Oréal's CEO, noted that certain products from Kiehl's, one of L'Oréal's growing brands, fail some of L'Oréal's basic quality control evaluations: 'it leaves a mess in the basin' and the label on the tube 'occasionally doesn't stay on' – but 'it just happens to leave your skin smoother than anything else I've used'.[6] And while this kind of quality would be unacceptable for another L'Oréal brand such as, say, Recital, it is something L'Oréal is prepared to tolerate on Kiehl's because this brand has a different kind of a relationship with a different kind of consumer (almost that of a microbrew, perhaps). The opportunity for the brand demands a different way of thinking about something as fundamental as quality control.

Now in a sense this is a different kind of example because it is an acquisition. But it is interesting to see that the owner of Kiehl's – a small, cultish cosmetics brand originating in New York – has continued to market it in a fundamentally different way to the parent's history: without promotions or print advertising, simply low key store openings in selected US and European cities.

A Cohesive Alternative Model in Every Regard – Axe Within Unilever

But these are simply examples of how rules or best practices were changed in a particular area. For a more comprehensive overview of what moving to a new model means, let us look in more detail at Unilever's Axe.

Changing the Brand Neighbourhood

The initial impetus to rethink the marketing model came from Simon Clift attending focus groups and realizing that although Axe in theory performed competently compared to other deo-fragrance advertising, actually that comparison was at best irrelevant (and at worst dangerous in the complacency it permitted), because the core target didn't have a strong relationship with any of those brands. What the Axe team did, therefore, was to ask themselves: what if we were to take it out of that brand neighbourhood, and make it compete in a neighbourhood of brands they did have a strong relationship with, like (at the time) Levi's and Nike?

And what they did specifically was to look at the model from one of these other brands in this other neighbourhood and work through what it would mean to apply that to Axe: the Levi's model.

Changing the Way of Thinking about the Target

The advertising agency they used, BBH, had not simply worked on Levi's for years but made it an icon of youth culture in the UK. And one of the first observations the agency made in applying the Levi's model to Axe was that specifying a broad target (say 14–40-year-old males) was not helpful, because demographically these people were so different. Instead they proposed the idea of targeting an 18-year-old, because every male wants to be 18. Target, in effect, an aspirational age rather than reflect a necessary demographic. Target narrow, but catch wide.

Changing the Communications Model

The second profound change explored was in the communication model. For years, Axe had used an advertising equity called 'Double

Drop' – an idea in which during each commercial the product gets dropped twice: once accidentally by Our Hero, and once accidentally by The Woman He Encounters, because she is so marvellously struck by the scent of Axe on him (a touch of Paganini, perhaps). What the agency convinced them of was that for this target market it was more important to focus on what one wanted the consumer to take out of the advertising than on structuring what went into it. So the Double Drop device, and indeed the notion of 'advertising equities', which Unilever in general was very persistent in looking for and preserving at the time, were abandoned on this brand in favour of communication that worked on the target market's terms, rather than Unilever's.

Use of PR

Within this new communication model, what they learnt from a jeans brand was the importance of PR not to simply reach a relatively elusive audience, but also to create a different kind of conversation around the brand. If you want to generate editorial in the pages of *Maxim* or *FHM*, for instance, you have to play to the currencies of those magazines. And 'more efficient deo delivery systems' are not one of those currencies. Instead, the brand team deliberately cast a porn star in an upcoming commercial because they knew that this would get picked up by the 'lads mags' – which it duly did. Not what you would expect from a sometimes cautious Anglo-Dutch company specializing in 'the housewife's shopping basket', but absolutely brilliant at delivering against the needs of this brand and its specific need and opportunity against this target.

Use of Research

The Axe team are very clear about how they will and will not use research in developing brand communication for this audience. Although Unilever has its own universally used methodology for pretesting commercials called PreView, on Axe the team will not spend money on quantitatively pretesting any of their ads before production, because the production qualities for the kind of advertising they are doing to this visually sophisticated 18-year-old audience are so vital to the way the commercial will be received that one can only test when the film has actually been produced.

It would be wrong, though, to interpret this as a disdain for research. They use research either side of this point in the process with rigour and creativity. So they will research commercials after they are made and have been in market to see what lessons can be learnt and reapplied for the next stage. And they put a great deal of emphasis on upstream understanding of their target for the brand team. Because the mating game is a difficult subject to get teenage boys to talk honestly about (either individually or in front of their peers), they will find new ways to get to insight.

So for instance, prior to the US launch in 2003, they hired a comedy club, and brought a bunch of male and female teens in to watch stand-up comedians doing routines all about the mating game. The brand team sat on one side, the teens on the other. The comics would do their stuff and every 15 minutes or so they would take a break, and the brand team would talk to the teens. Why had they found that particular observation hilarious? But hadn't laughed at that other one, which seemed just as true? A little near the knuckle, perhaps? Oh, OK. And why is that? And then back to the routines.

The result is a strong visceral understanding of what motivates the target – what they think and don't think, what they like and don't like, which allows them to trust their judgement about variables like advertising scripts, and commit to them confidently and early.

Location of 'Rigour'

Unilever has a very clear 'Path to Growth'; it has financial targets and an accountability, as all public companies do, to the shareholder. It thus understandably puts a lot of stock in rigour in its processes and development. Neil Munn, the Global Brand Director on Axe, has therefore been very specific about publicly articulating in what very specific ways rigour is and isn't being applied on Axe. Before we look at that definition, let's understand why he places such importance on this:

We have articulated what rigour is for the people who don't really get Axe; those who aren't comfortable with it, who haven't enjoyed, or touched its success. The sceptics who are thinking it sounds like it might be a bit of a fly-by-night brand, where everyone sits round saying 'What shall we do next? Yeah, that sounds good, we'll go and do that.' Sceptics who may be thinking that we're not checking stuff, that we're not being rigorous, when in fact we are – we're being very rigorous *upstream* in terms of understanding the consumers. Almost anal about it.

So I'm just trying to identify where we need to be different. Not for the sake of being different, but to try and give our ground a bit more focused advantage. Most of Unilever's rigour is downstream. It's checking advertising and double-checking it and getting the research company to do more analysis on the findings and so on. But most of Axe's rigour needs to be *upstream*, understanding the consumers, what makes them tick. How they live their lives. Then we need to go and create communication which we believe turns a light on in their heads. And the quantitative research company can't tell us that; they can help us in terms of comprehension, but they can't tell us whether a piece of advertising is going to create excitement and talkability.

Here is Munn's formal definition of what makes Axe rigour different:

AXE RIGOUR

- In many ways, there is no team more intense, more committed to consumer learning, more responsive to cultural and societal change than the Axe global team.
- Axe people must be students of the key but constantly changing themes of masculinity and seduction – never feeling comfortable with their knowledge base, always sensors to change.
- This rigour and focus 'upstream' then builds the confidence and empowerment to make key brand/communication decisions 'downstream' without abdicating responsibility to the consumer, or even to Millward Brown.
- In this way people should not believe that Axe is purely a 'gut feel' brand, one where the work is directed by a group of mavericks. The Axe brand is stewarded with flair and fun, but always underpinned by a rigour and robustness that is unique and ongoing.

The Attitude Towards Risk

Truman Capote observed that the bad part about living outside the law was that one no longer had the protection of it. So how does one take risk on a brand that is a huge cash generator for the parent company? Axe is an enormous brand for Unilever – worth somewhere in the region of $800 million; you don't want to mess with that kind of revenue generator. Yet Clift knew that he had to change the model. So in looking to break through on Axe he actually made two different commercials using two different agencies. Only when the new approach using the new agency proved more successful did he formally bring the new agency onto the brand alongside the incumbent.

'In retrospect, I should have just gone ahead and done it anyway,' Clift says. But he observes that the penalties for failing *within* the system are not that severe – you are using the agency you are supposed to, doing things the way they have always been done: if it doesn't work, well, then, they can hardly blame you. The risk attached to failure if one tries to change it by going outside the system, on the other hand, is usually much higher. And in fact what large multi-brand organizations are historically less good at doing is *sharing*, rather than assigning the consequences of failure. Compare Diesel here, for instance. This is a company with a turnover of $700 million, which effectively tries to reinvent itself – in its product range but also in its communications – twice a year. High risk, in many ways. Yet they are prepared to apparently increase that risk by using very inexperienced people – indeed, if they like an idea they will give an entire part of the line to someone who has just come out of art school. But who picks up the tab if it goes wrong? At Diesel, if something fails, and they have all approved it, then no one gets blamed. When we pushed him on this, the Creative Director expressed complete bafflement that it might be otherwise.

If one puts all these individual components of the way Axe thinks and behaves together, it is clear that not only is the Axe model a different model from the one it historically used (or indeed the one used by most other brands within Unilever's portfolio), but it is also very evident that in its own way this represents a model that is just as rigorous as the old one. But in *its own way*: a way that is more appropriate for the brand in order to realize its opportunity with its consumer, and deliver a better financial return to the shareholder. And central to realizing that opportunity is not simply a different tolerance for risk, but a different encouragement by one's leaders to lean into it. Getting your team to genuinely believe this is as much about little signals as fine words, of course. Leaving the meeting in Buenos Aires we opened on, Munn took his team member to the place in the city every leading-edge 18-year-old guy had their hair cut, and each had to choose one of the three most popular styles of the moment. One involved blonde highlights, one a red streak – two visible marks that you are part of the Republic of Axe.

Axe is now Unilever's fastest-growing global brand, with a 24% volume increase in 2003.

Noisy Bilinguality

The fourth precondition for success is the way the team and team leader interact with the broader organization, as the subculture creates the success that will give it licence to endure. This interaction often combines a consistent internal marketing of the brand, and the parading of its differences from the other brands around it, with the understanding that this constant delineation of how and why we are different needs to be able to be couched in the language of commercial return, as well as brand conception and ideas. In terms of internal marketing, let's go back to Pot Noodle:

> We did things that marketing people had never done before in that organization. Before we even turned up, we mailed everyone in the company a letter telling them all about Pot Noodle, what a great brand it was and sending them all samples. Really marketed it to the workforce of the co-company that was acquiring it. Then we wandered around the halls dressed as Ned Noodle ... this giant size Pot Noodle costume ... we gave out samples, we gave out mugs ... We absolutely blitzed the company in the first year that we were there ... They weren't allowed to forget where the money was coming from, they weren't allowed to forget what a wacky brand this was, because all the time it was like you were fighting for your right to exist, with the best form of defence being attack. We were always on the front foot, going out there and overcommitting more sales force time than we needed, hammering it

home to the accountants and the lawyers. 'Yes, I know that you really don't like it, but look at the results' ... There was a big marketing task to be done internally to the organization, and that really helped.

But this internal noisiness has to be bilingual to be accepted. Tom Brown of Yoo-hoo:

> You have to be able to speak both languages. You have to be able to stand up in front of management and look at the business strategy as much as the brand strategy, and speak to the kinds of issues that go beyond just the culture of Yoo-hoo. I think that's the key.

So Neil Munn talks about the importance of taking the Red Pill in terms of connecting with their target market, but he also talks about the fact that since they have embraced this greater propensity to take risk, their annual growth rates have tripled in each region.

And, of course, financial success is the currency of being allowed to go on behaving this way; of continuing to be one's own subculture. So: Soft Shell, Hard Centre. You need to be bilingual: talk in the right language at the right time, and often both together.

Summary

This was a long chapter, so let's briefly look at the key points again. It said that successful Challengers or brand subcultures within larger organizations are indeed possible, but there are four key preconditions for success they need to understand:

- The prior establishment of an understanding that there is a clear brand or business need to develop a different model.
- Thinking much more carefully about the kinds of people one needs in the core team – a Denter, Idea Hamster, Implementation Rhino and Smokejumper – and giving them the length of tenure on the

brand that makes success possible. Surrounding this group with a cross-functional unit that is fully aligned.

- A clearly understood articulation of what the new model is, and why it is, in its own way, cohesive and rigorous – but just more suitable for the job at hand.
- You need to be bilingual – able to talk the language of your own brand subculture and the commercial language of your corporate parent.

12

Why Brand-centred Subcultures Fail: Learning from Failure

I t is relatively easy to see when and how such Brand subcultures work. But success is an easier thing to research than failure. People are refreshingly honest about success – but it is much harder to find candour about the lack of it. However, we can look at a couple of well publicized examples, as well as some (OK Soda, for instance) where the protagonists were prepared to talk about what had not worked, and what they and the organization had learnt from it.

Why Brand Subcultures Fail

Overall, there seem to be five key reasons why Brand Republics/subcultures fail:

1. The preconditions for success are not met.
2. Your business partners do not believe you are really trying to do something different.
3. Unreasonable expectations from the parent (or specific groups within it, such as the sales people) about the speed or nature of success of the child being allowed to detrimentally influence the nature of the brand model.
4. Soft shell, soft centre – the brand doesn't deliver the financial return that justifies its continued subculture status.
5. The parent and child see (or come to see) the nature and value of the symbiosis between them in a different way.

Let us look at each of these in turn.

The Preconditions for Success Are Not Met

Clearly we have set up a number of preconditions for success, but rather than attempt to take them all one by one, let us look at Aston Martin as an example of a brand that began to create the beginnings of an intriguing subculture (certainly externally), but was overruled by someone within the parent organization – and lacked the Smokejumper to protect them.

Aston Martin is a luxury car that is now part of Ford's Premier Automotive Group (PAG). A car marque known historically for its associations with James Bond, an association which it has recently successfully rekindled through film product placement, in 2001 it decided to produce a range of merchandise to develop its image with existing and potential customers. At one level this was apparently seeing and wishing to emulate the success Ferrari had had with merchandising in the past few years in branded clothing and luggage, but at another level one would imagine that the goods were to help further define and promote the brand's sense of individuality and culture. The new collection of branded Aston Martin goods was to include clothes and accessories, principal among whose themes were handcuffs and leather. The sterling silver handcuffs had found their way onto belts, key rings and cufflinks, and the leather, intriguingly, into men's underwear – including perforated leather boxing shorts (whatever those are) and denim suede boxers.

Now one looks at this list and one cannot but be intrigued. This is clearly provocative, very different from the range one would expect from any other luxury car (Mercedes, for example), and yet particularly appropriate for Aston Martin because it is rooted in what we know about Ian Fleming's hero, and his portrayal of a certain kind of hedonistic (even cruel) masculinity that enjoys pushing the limits. A promising and distinctive expression for the further development of a highly individual subculture, we might think. And they thought so too. So they mailed out catalogues of the collection to 3,800 customers.

Unfortunately, one of the recipients of the catalogues was Edsel Ford, a non-executive director of the parent of Aston Martin, Detroit's Ford, and in fact a cousin of Bill Ford, the current chairman and grandson of the founder. Edsel Ford, a committed churchgoer, and a man who takes a strong line on family values, found that the perforated leather boxer shorts and handcuff belt not only were not to his own personal taste, but not something he wanted to be part of anyone else's taste either, and demanded key merchandise within the catalogue be withdrawn.

The result was that the merchandise was overhauled, replaced with branded briefcases and pens, and the catalogue was reprinted. In commenting on the overturning of the development, an executive who was part of the project said that the decision highlighted very real cultural differences between Ford and the luxury brands within its PAG division:

> On the one hand you have a go-ahead, multi-brand, international company and on the other a very blue-collar, conservative carmaker from Michigan. This shows the Michigan side has won out.[1]

Now at one level one has some sympathy with Mr Edsel Ford. The principles he is fighting for are not relative ones about types of research methodology, or the amount of fat used in every portion. They are absolutes: religious and moral beliefs admitting no relative ground. These things are wrong, in his view, in any country.

But on the other hand Ford has huge ambitions for the brands within its Premier Automotive Group – as its average profit per vehicle sold within Ford dropped from $1,955 in the 1990s to a *loss* of $190 per vehicle in 2002, so it understandably looked to its premium marques to represent a considerable share of the future: one-third of corporate profits, in fact, by 2005. And if one has that kind of ambition one should recognize the need for a brand to create its own culture, and indeed be applauding a brand trying to get people to pay a little attention to it through the building and creation of that subculture. There should have been a Smokejumper who said 'No – this is the way this brand needs to be built to deliver to the shareholder.' And that Aston Martin is not Ford: the values of Ford and the Ford family are good and right for Ford, and long may they stand, but they should not be the values of Aston Martin – or indeed any of the other luxury brands Ford owns. The parent has to allow the subculture to grow in the way that is right for that brand.

The Great Steak and Fries Co-conspiracy

The second problem comes where you need a different kind (or level) of communications idea from your primary business partner and they don't believe you are actually going to buy what you are apparently asking for. Having witnessed the real impact of this problem a number of times (including a number of occasions when the business partner was right to doubt it), and because it was a source of great personal frustration to me when I worked in an advertising agency, indulge me in spending a little time unpacking the psychology on both sides.

I used to work in a large agency in the USA, which had a car client. The agency did very creative work for many of its other clients, and it did car advertising for its car client. One day the CEO of the car company decided he was going to do something about the difference between the two. He set up a meeting with the CEO of the agency, Bob Kuperman, and in the meeting asked Kuperman why it was that the agency was producing this highly noticeable, 'good' work on other accounts and not on his.

'Well, it's like this,' Kuperman said:

> Imagine you are running a restaurant, and a guy comes in one day and asks to look at the menu. Well, you've got all sorts of different kinds of stuff on your menu, so you hand it to him and leave him to look at it, and then you come back and ask him what he'd like. And you have got the whole gamut of what you can do on that menu, from fancy stuff to steak to Spam Fritters. And the guy looks at it for a while and he orders the steak and fries.
>
> So then the next day the guy comes in again, and you show him the menu again, and he orders the same thing. And he does exactly the same the next day, and the next day, and the day after that: steak and fries, steak and fries, steak and fries, day after day. And you know what? About this regular and important customer of yours? After a while you stop showing him the menu any more – as soon as you see him coming up to the restaurant door, you just throw another steak on the grill.

I always liked this analogy – it is very true. And I am going to expand on the story a bit to explore the point, for which I hope both parties will forgive me. Because the interesting moment occurs when one day the guy looks up and says that today he'd like something different. Today, he'd like to try some Fancy French Cooking. Today he'll have the Nightingales' Tongues in Filo Pastry.

What do you, the restaurant proprietor, do?

Well, you are probably surprised, but act delighted, and scurry off into the kitchen, and bring him back something under a *feuilleté* of filo pastry smothered in a delicious creamy sauce. And his reaction is just what you were expecting. First, can you take the garlic out? He is sure other people like it, but it isn't really for him. And the sauce – can he have that on the side? And not too much of it, please; he really just likes his meat pretty straight. And is it possible to have the dish with beef? Medium rare? And a bit more of it – these nightingales' tongues don't seem to be very substantial. And no pastry – he knows he shouldn't with this kind of dish, but some fried potatoes, if that was possible? Thank you.

All very polite. And all simply confirming to both sides that, while an interesting and no doubt worthwhile process to have gone through, what the client was really looking for all the time was steak and fries, whatever they pretended they were ordering.

Now what happens from an agency point of view is this – if you offer a broad menu to different kinds of diners (as most of the top 20 agencies do), you tend to have two kinds of cooks working in your kitchen. You have creatively brilliant but emotionally taut French Pastry Chefs, who tend to refuse to change anything, and you have got easygoing steak cooks, who are used to having their order sent back until it is just the way the client wants it.

And when diners who usually order steak and fries start asking for Nightingales' Tongues in Filo Pastry, you – the restaurant proprietor – have a problem. If you really start giving these briefs to the creatively brilliant but emotionally taut pastry chefs, if you make them start cooking for a customer who you are pretty sure won't eat it when it is really put in front of them, and you know the chefs will take it badly when their masterpiece is sent back for extensive modifications – well, you get worried that these pastry chefs will just start getting dispirited, and throw up their hands, and run off to start their own patisserie round the corner. And you don't want them to do that. People who can do really innovative things with pastry are hard to find.

So what you actually do is this: you take the order for Nightingales' Tongues, but you put the steak people onto it. You pretend, and the client allows themselves to be persuaded, that they do the fancy pastry stuff as well. And in fact they don't really do pastry, but then they don't believe the diner really likes pastry anyway, so they produce something that looks like the kind of pastry they think the diner will buy, because it is really just steak with a little dough and parsley on top. To you and me it still looks like a T-Bone but, when pushed, the proprietor and cooks both staunchly defend it on the grounds that the nightingales are coming up very large this year. And both parties can pretend they have been a little more adventurous in their eating now, although in reality nothing has really changed.

The point is that neither side really changes *because the agency doesn't believe the client wants to change*; and much of the time they don't. This is the reason it is a co-conspiracy. Both sides pretend to each other. The Client pretends to look at the menu and contemplate other dishes. The Agency pretends to cook up those dishes. In fact, neither side really believes they are getting a request for, or a serving of, anything much more than a bit of béarnaise sauce on the usual steak and fries. And even if this time you as the customer *are* serious, the restaurant proprietor, by and large, will still do what they have successfully done every time you or someone from your company has asked for pastry before – give the order to the steak cook until the momentary departure from the norm blows over. They just don't believe you are serious – or, even if you are, that your organization will ever allow you to run what you are apparently asking for.

Consequently, many of these breakthroughs have come, sadly, through people breaking with their immediate pasts and changing agencies/clients. And one way to avoid the Great Steak and Fries Co-conspiracy is certainly to do this: to go to a restaurant that doesn't necessarily accept your order in the first place, and go into that restaurant and that relationship believing that to be challenged is a fundamentally good, healthy and productive thing.[2] This certainly was the case on Skoda – Chris Hawken had to fire the incumbent to get the challenging thinking he needed. So too Axe – when Simon Clift told the agency who used to work on Axe that he was bringing another agency onto the business as well, and would be running their work in the UK and possibly Europe, they told him they hadn't believed until that moment that he was really serious.

But you shouldn't have to fire the agency to get them to believe that this time you really do want and need something more. Jim Carroll of the advertising agency Bartle Bogle Hegarty (BBH) tells of a client who wanted to be sure that BBH would produce the best quality work they could on his piece of business. So he asked to be able to speak to the entire creative department in person. The agency collected their creative department together, and the client spoke of why they needed breakthrough, and what it was going to take to get that.

In other words, the first thing we may need to do, like this client, is create some kind of internal symbol of re-evaluation in terms of our relationship with our primary ideas partner or partners. Be creative about it: putting them under review won't necessarily get the best work out of them; a spooked agency doesn't always productively challenge the client.

The second thing you may want to consider is drawing up an entirely new kind of contract with your agency – the kind Avis drew up with DDB (see Chapter 6).

Unreasonable Expectations from the Parent

The third reason for the failure of a brand subculture is where the parent (or specific groups within the company) has, or comes to have, unrealistic expectations of what success will look like, and how soon it will come.

Here we are going to look at the case of OK Soda, a brand launched by Coca-Cola in 1994, and a deliberate attempt to set up a brand that lived by a completely different model to the Big Red One.

It came about like this. In early 1993 Doug Ivester was promoted to Worldwide President of Coca-Cola. A numbers man, he didn't feel comfortable with marketing, but didn't get on with his Global CMO, so he brought back Sergio Zyman, initially on a freelance basis, to sharpen his marketing expertise.[3]

One of the key issues that Ivester faced was an unhappy bottler group, who felt Coke was moribund: not innovative, and allowing other new entrants to eat into their volume. So in the spring of 1993 Ivester asked Zyman to take on a special project to create new brands to launch against the teen market in answer to this challenge. The existing CMO was still in place, so this would have to be done in absolute secrecy – they would have the meetings on the project at Ivester's house at the weekends, and he would personally be involved. Zyman could take one person of his choice from within the marketing department, but that person would again have to operate in secrecy. Even after the CMO left and Zyman was appointed in his stead in July, the secrecy was maintained, to circumnavigate the 'moribund' system within Coke.

Zyman chose Brian Lanahan, whom he had originally recruited during his earlier spell at Coke in 1986, and who was on the point of leaving. They then asked three agencies to pitch for the business, in effect needing the winning agency to act as their research and marketing functions for them, because of the leanness of the team and the secrecy in which they were having to operate. The brief to themselves, and thus to the agencies, was to 'challenge the whole category' – challenge the whole way soft drinks were marketed to teens, and come up with a radical new brand in doing so; they would figure out the product as they went along. As such, the process was to be the exact reverse of the way Coke usually did things, which was to come up with the product first, and only then work out how to brand and sell it.

The team found when they started their consumer work that soft drinks were an easy target; there had been so much hype by manufacturers that there was plenty of room for creative subversion of the existing 'conventions'. And an interesting brand idea began to emerge in the process. In briefing the agency team, the planner, Mark Barden, stressed the magnitude of the resource that Coca-Cola had to make this succeed. Coca-Cola, he said, by way of dramatizing this, is the second most recognized word in the English language. What's the first? asked the copywriter on the team. 'OK,' Barden replied. Well, that's your new brand name, then, the writer replied. The team laughed at the time, but the name stuck – and OK Soda it became.

The thinking behind every aspect of the brand was hugely inventive, and did indeed look to change most of the rules of soft drink marketing at the time. In fact, while Coke made much of the continuity of its classic iconography and ownership of red, OK Soda was going to be all about change – there would be four different graphic pack designs in market at any one time, one of which was to have the brand's tongue-in-cheek manifesto on it. The brand essence itself would be about balancing the cynicism of Gen X-ers (as they had just been called) about the world, with their own personal sense that they would be, well, OK. The product would mimic what the target market called a 'Suicide' – the practice of taking your Big Gulp cup in your local 7/11 and filling it up by holding it for 10 seconds under each of the sodas on offer one after the other, so that what you ended up with was your own combination of Sprite, Coke, Mello Yello and Cherry Coke mixed together. The product, an amber colour based on a beer (Killian's Red), scored well in blind tests and, initially planned to be uncarbonated, was developed in six weeks.

The launch was planned for two key markets – they wanted to seed the new brand with teens and let it grow at its own pace. To help this, it was to be planted in single serve containers in 'discovery channels': i.e. the kind of distribution that would allow early adopters to try it for themselves and spread the word. Focus groups told them teens loved the brand and their ideas for it; they were almost ready to go.

And then they tried to bring it back into the Coca-Cola organization to manage the practicalities of the launch. The meetings of three or four at Zyman's house stopped, and were replaced by enormous rooms of up to 30 in the office in Atlanta. And two cross-winds ripped across the project.

The first cross-wind was the top of the organization getting excited about the potential for this new brand for teens. Very excited. And in their excitement they 'Coked' it: almost unconsciously decided to make it successful in the way they made Coke successful – by Thinking Big. Why seed it in two markets? Let's make it eight. Why use discovery channels when we can buy the end aisles in grocery stores? The bottlers understood the desire to be flat, but they needed carbonation to hit their production efficiencies: so carbonated it now was. In 2-litre bottles, of course. Oh, and PR fixed up an interview for Brian Lanahan with *Time* magazine to talk about the forthcoming launch. The whole brand model found itself suddenly fundamentally distorted.

The second cross-wind was the blast of ill will which greeted the project and the small team on it from those departments and individuals below Ivester and Zyman who had been excluded from the process up to now. The feelings were best characterized by the Head of Advertising leaning over to Lanahan at one of these enormous internal meetings just before launch, and saying quietly, from his reading of the other individuals in the room, 'I hope you realize that everyone around this table is wishing you every failure.'

The OK Soda launch failed almost immediately – generating what Lanahan calls wrily 'virtual consumption'. The brand did indeed create the enormous interest the groups had predicted: at one point one million kids a day were calling the 1800IFEELOK toll-free line to take the personality test, or leave voicemails about their experiences drinking OK; some high schools even banned it because their pupils were skipping class to participate with the brand in this kind of way. Yet while trial was massive, repeat purchase was minimal; the product was not a success (and perhaps was too close to a conventional soda to match the very different promise of the launch communications), and the momentum withered very fast. It was shortly after launch that the Head of Research at Coca-Cola began, unknown to Lanahan, a secret quantitative project to demonstrate that not only was the brand a failure, but was also damaging Coke. OK Soda was withdrawn.

Looking back on it nine years later, Lanahan drew five conclusions from the failure:

- The brief was to 'turn the soft drink category upside down'. Yet the OK Soda team tried to overturn everything in too short a time. The product in particular was something they rushed through in six weeks; they should have taken six months and got it right. Product is such a fundamental, one cannot treat the process of getting it right as instinctively as the brand development.
- They should have defined success more clearly with all the stakeholders at the outset of the process. The brand sold a million cases in its test markets – a huge failure for Coke based on the Coke model and the scale of the fanfare with which it had been launched. But if they had defined what a 'seed and grow' success would look like for all, perhaps a million cases might have been viewed as a promising start.
- They should have brought the other disciplines on board earlier in the process. That is to say, they should either have stayed outside the whole system throughout the launch, or played within it earlier than they did – to create multi-disciplinary ownership. They needed to hunt as a pack.
- They should have kept the launch at the pace their sense of the brand originally demanded. It became a brand operating by another brand's launch model; the integrity of the vision was diluted by all the concessions they had to make to the excitement of senior management.

- Finally, Lanahan wishes in hindsight, 'that I'd held the line a bit more. Hadn't let them change so much of the initial vision'. That he'd Refused more, at the right time.

In short, there were a number of reasons for failure, but central among them was that the parent couldn't really reconcile itself to the implications of a different launch model – by wanting too much, too soon, it overturned key parts of the brand development process and launch model, and the brand failed as a result.

Soft Shell, Soft Centre – It Doesn't Deliver the Return that Justifies its Continued Subculture Status

The failure of Boss Woman demonstrates that there is no point in creating a different model, even with a highly differentiated culture, if it doesn't lead to a greater financial return (and a further useful reminder here, after OK Soda's experience with product development, that some principles of marketing have to remain constant).

In principle, much of what Werner Baldessarini did in taking Boss into womenswear made sense – and indeed was to be apparently applauded as someone genuinely trying to think like a Challenger. His first step was to distance the sub-brand from the parent by siting it far from the conservative town of Metzingen in Germany, the headquarters of Boss menswear, and in fact to move away from masculine concepts such as office blocks as the cradle for the feminine side of Boss. He bought a villa in Italy, near Milan; the staff of 120 enjoyed an interior with antiques, and lunches on the terrace: this was to be a different kind of working environment, perhaps one more attuned to feminine qualities and aesthetics. The creation and production functions were to be as different in their own way: as creative director he brought in a previously unknown German designer, and production was to be distributed across a large number of self-employed seamstresses in the area.

Now in many ways, as I said, they are appearing to be doing much that is right; one could interpret all of this to suggest that it showed a number of signs of good Challenger thinking:

- They 'Break with the Immediate Past' – move to a new country, and away from the parent organization. And a country that perhaps some might view as having a stronger sense of the feminine and the aesthetic, more appropriate for a woman's brand.
- They create a wholly fresh and stimulating environment – a villa, rather than an office block, and one full of beautiful things.
- They try to put some intelligent naivety into what they were doing by taking a chance on a new designer.
- They attempt to create a new kind of brand culture (the lunch on the terrace, the antiques around them and so on).
- They go outside the traditional Boss supply chain in using local seamstresses, perhaps to create a higher degree of craftsmanship and personal finish.

So, at one level, you would have said all this was very promising: a deliberate attempt to create their own less masculine, Germanic subculture.

And yet they just ignored the imperative of 'Soft Shell, Hard Centre'. Managing the network of local seamstresses created huge problems of logistics, significantly increasing overheads and contributing to the clothes requiring a 50% price premium which obviously impacted sales. This was not helped by the designer and the brand culture failing to come through with designs that people wanted to buy – described as 'more haute couture than city office'.[4] The clothes didn't even conform to standard sizing.

In 2001 Boss Woman lost roughly $12 m – losses which were estimated to rise by 25% the following year;[5] the operation has now been moved back to Germany. So in reality, while the brand elements were provocatively different, and more appropriate to a female brand, the underlying business model was flawed. And so the whole initiative failed to generate the return necessary to allow it to continue as a subculture, and was subsumed back into the parent organization.

The Parent and Child See the Nature of the Symbiosis Between Them in a Different Way

The fifth reason the brand subcultures seem to fail is where the parent and child come to see the nature of the symbiosis of them in a different way.

Perhaps it is harsh to call Saturn a failure: in 2003 the brand sold over 230,000 cars,[6] though it had still to make a net profit. Yet given the extraordinary initial impact of the brand on the consumer, both on the car category and, for a while, in the relationship it embodied between GM and the UAW as a new way of working – a relationship that would at last make US cars competitive in production costs with the Japanese – one has to ask oneself why all Saturn's momentum seemed to dry up five years or so into its life. Where were the new models that would keep it up to date? Where were the new ideas that would repeat the success of the Homecoming Reunion? Saturn today is regarded as at best a limited success – but its success was apparently limited not by the intrinsic appeal of the brand, but by the changing relationship that success brought it with its two parents, GM and the UAW, and how those parents chose to respond to that success.

At birth Saturn was a wonderful example of a subculture. Its chairman, Skip LeFavre, said at its inception:

> Saturn is more than a car. It's an idea. It's a whole new way of doing things, of working with our customers and one another. It's more of a cultural revolution than a product revolution.[7]

Within two years, Saturn was an important leader for GM in both image and sales. Topping the rankings of US cars in JD Power's Customer Satisfaction Index was complemented by its leading the entire US car market in terms of new car sales per retailer – the first time this had been true of a domestic marque in 15 years.

By any measure, this was a fabulous success story. And much of the engine for that success was the cultural revolution LeFavre had spoken of, at the heart of which lay a new kind of working agreement between GM and the United Auto Workers Union (UAW), which historically had been locked in a somewhat macho adversarial relationship. This agreement between the two broke new ground in a number of ways, including:

- No time clocks for workers, no prescribed break times, no direct monitoring by supervisors.
- Bonuses dependent on defect rates achieved by the whole company.

- In joining the company, people gave up seniority, so that everyone started in the same level.
- Elimination of complex work classifications and pay scales – to be replaced by two job definitions covering all union employees.[8]

And yet, as Saturn hit years four and five of its life, it emerged that neither of the parents seemed to want the new child to succeed, because for their individual reasons they didn't want this new model to spread into other parts of their respective organizations. For the Union's part, the National Union President announced in 1994 that he wished to renegotiate the agreement for Saturn with GM to something more in line with historic union practices – against the wishes of the local Union president. And, in the end, he effectively pushed such a revision through and reversed many of the breakthrough areas.

For GM's part, many of the other divisions had historically been unhappy that the initial capital outlay on setting up Saturn and its plant had taken away their ability to modernize their own plants. In 1995 it was announced that, due to budget cuts, new models originally allocated to Saturn would go to other divisions. And during a record sales month for Saturn, the team were told that there would be no funds for investment behind a right-hand drive export model for the brand – though there would, it seemed, for the Chevy Cavalier and Pontiac Sunfire. Jack O'Toole, an UAW member who was part of the initial Saturn team, wrote in 1996 of 'predators' within GM who were threatened by the success of Saturn and its new way of working:

> The ferocious anxiety felt by our 'miraculous' success had been metamorphosed into a very covert but doggedly determined strategy by these same predators to try to discredit every single accomplishment we achieved, to keep the spotlight from turning on them and their blatant inadequacies in the very same areas.[9]

Of course, it is hard to see into an organization as large and complex as GM and know what really happened; when relationships start to break down, every decision can turn into a Rorschach test for paranoia. But perhaps it is indicative that as early as 1985, GM had been hesitant about committing to the idea that they were going to learn anything from the experiment – in the analysis on which this section is based Doris Mitsch, its author, concludes: 'I think it's telling that, as early as 1985, in the manuscript of a speech I found, a key phrase was crossed out, with the word 'OMIT' scrawled in the margin:

> Saturn's challenge is clear ... Market vehicles developed and manufactured in the United States that are leaders in quality, cost and satisfaction through the integration of people, technology and business systems, ~~and to transfer knowledge, technology and experience to General Motors.~~[10]

If the parent thinks it will be impossible to transfer any new knowledge, and the subculture's success (and investment behind it) will only lead to politicking and counterproductive jealousy, then the financial success of the brand itself can become not enough – unless there is a very determined Smokejumper behind it.

And in GM's case, allowing the brand to wither and the model to change seems more than a shame, because American car companies still remain considerably less profitable than Japanese ones in the USA – the intent and business strategy had surely always been absolutely right.

What Is and Isn't Failure?

There is of course a danger of Clintonesque semantic quibblings here about the meanings of words we know we understand perfectly well. Is 8th Continent, for instance, a success or a failure? A qualified success, perhaps: at the time of writing it had about a fifth of the soy milk market, though it is a growing market. Not what the muscle of General Mills might have hoped for in volume terms perhaps, but a respectable enough share and a valuable piece of learning for both the individuals involved and the parent organization, one would hope.

But sometimes even failure has benefits to the organization, if it is prepared to learn from them. Consider the failure of OK Soda, and its influence on Coke: while the brand failed, a number of its learnings lived on. At a more abstract level, the three most senior people involved in the project, the President of the company, the CMO and the Head of the largest bottler got closer to both their target market (and indeed the process of creating breakthrough communications) than they had in years – or ever, in Ivester's case. At a more specific level, the insight that 'teens rejected the hype of soda marketing' resurfaced within the same company the very next year to great success on a different, established brand, with the 'Obey your thirst' campaign for Sprite. (Which brings us onto the next chapter – and the effects of subcultures on the broader organization.)

A Sixth Reason

There is a sixth reason why such ventures fail, but since it lies outside multi-brand companies, I include it as almost a footnote: it is when the subculture isn't centred on a different brand, but another expression or model of the same brand.

In 1999 Nike launched the World Shoe – a Nike-branded, low cost, low price shoe to compete in Asian markets, and especially China. Costing a fraction of Nike's usual prices, and less than a third as much to make, it nevertheless incorporated elements of Nike's original 'waffle' technology on the sole on the one hand, and innovative elements the consumer responded well to on the other: they were sold in a drawstring bag instead of a shoebox, for instance, that could act as a backpack after purchase.

There are a number of reasons why Nike withdrew support for the World Shoe. One was that it was unable to adapt its high margin business model to a market where low price imitators demanded that one move to a low margin/high volume model to succeed. But the other principal reason that is given is that key figures at Nike were uncomfortable with selling low price Nikes – the World Shoe's price point seemed to be at odds with everything that the brand had stood for and the emotional premium it had built over such a long period of time. It may have been a subculture demanding its own model, but because *it was the same brand* as the parent culture, the internal resistance was, in some ways rightly, too difficult to overcome. To make it work, perhaps Nike would have needed to find some way of creating a sub-branded diffusion range.

Summary

The easy summary is that creating a brand-centred subculture is much easier if you don't have to take on a Union. But the rest of the apparent reasons why such brand-centred subcultures fail seems to fit the model we have developed already – they fail because they do not meet the preconditions for success, or ignore the realities of the necessary business model and results within the new brand/cultural exoskeleton.

What the failures also show, however, is that although in looking at Denters we noted the cheerful talk of tension and the energy they can give, if they turn against the brand team those tensions and politics can be very destructive. It is critical that one has an adequately united and multi-faceted team to be self-sufficient, and strong enough to withstand the scepticism that will come their way.

Finally, looking at cases such as these is a sobering reminder of course that even with a clear vision, great talent, inspiring thinking and a united team, such Necessary Pirates can and do fail. Success is far from inevitable, and in embarking on such a project we need to understand the implications of failure as well as the importance of success. We will return to both of these in the final chapter.

13

Biting the Other Generals: The Wider Benefits Successful Subcultures Bring

irates are not confined to the Navy, of course. You can be a Pirate in the Army, and have plenty of people lining up to hang you just the same. Consider the case of General James Wolfe.

From 1756 to 1763 the British and the French were engaged in what became known as the Seven Years War – a fierce battle for control over what is now Canada. Leadership of the British Army, though it could be anachronistic and inflexible in other theatres of war around and after this time, in this particular arena was rather different, largely through the brilliantly unconventional strategic vision of a 32-year-old General called James Wolfe.

King George III took a keen interest in Wolfe, because while the rest of his high command showed every sign of being well on track to losing their particular colonies for him, Wolfe seemed to be doing a startlingly good job of hanging onto his. But Wolfe's unconventionality and temperament did not endear him to some of his less imaginative political lords and masters back in London, some of whom, knowing of His Majesty's partiality for Wolfe, tried to undermine the general by complaining to the king that Wolfe was 'mad'.

But the king, to their surprise, would have none of it. 'Oh, he is mad is he?' George famously remarked, with some feeling: 'Then I would he would bite some other of my generals.' (The point being that the madness of rabies, rather more prevalent then than it is now in Western countries, was transmitted through biting another victim.)

And while the primary reason, of course, for encouraging or setting up a Brand subculture is for the success in and on that particular piece of business, there is also another key value within a multi-brand environment, namely, the influence on the other brands, and people behind those brands, around us. The transmission of some of the subculture's apparent 'madness' in trying to do things differently. Biting the other generals.

The Kinds of 'Madness' One Seeks to Spread

There are four kinds of effects on the rest of the organization that one seeks to create with Brand subcultures, over and above making the brand more successful in its own right:

- the spreading of new perspectives, behaviours, standards and practices;
- the impetus and inspiration in other team leaders to take risks to push further their own marketing and communication ideas;
- one's ability to bring out the Peroni in a napkin;
- a more intangible spreading of energy and belief.

We will look at these one at a time.

The Spreading of New Perspectives, Behaviours, Standards and Practices

Some Challengers within a large company are keenly aware that besides realizing an important opportunity for themselves, they are also doing something that will influence the way the parent thinks and behaves: Ken Kutaragi knew from the beginning his company-within-a-company would influence Sony profoundly:

> I told Ohga-san when we set up Sony Computer Entertainment in 1993 that someday our business would become a big business and influence our corporate betters in the same way that children influence their parents. It's natural, the way of nature.[1]

We saw in Chapter 5 that Commander Michael Abrashoff of the USS *Benfold* had been partially motivated by the desire to become the best leader in his field: the Navy responded to his success in the *Benfold* by paying more attention to the areas he had seen as key in turning the ship around. Commanding officers are now held accountable for retention rates, and a number of the programmes Abrashoff instituted, from new ways of painting the ship to training his men, have now been implemented Navy-wide.

Pringles had a number of broader effects on P&G. First, the category it represented, Food and Beverage, which had never featured prominently in the Annual Report, began to appear as something of a star in the presentation of the company to Wall Street. Then the way that P&G had developed the copy-testing methodology for Pringles (to include more emphasis on whether the consumer liked the advertising, as well as the recall of the key strategic communication), was taken through into the way the company evaluated all advertising. The cross-functional working relationship between the brand team and the Jackson plant was also something that Gill felt senior management watched and noted for the future.

In the case of Pot Noodle, initially the 'rump' of CPC in the eyes of many when it was acquired (Woods had felt), their 'brand team' concept, incorporating the factory manager and so on, was liked so much by CPC as a catalyst for success that the approach was adopted by the other more 'conservative' brands within the company to stimulate a unified push for growth within each team.

The Impetus and Inspiration in Other Team Leaders to Take Risks and to Push Further Their Own Marketing and Communication Ideas

In terms of spreading the beneficial 'madness' of doing things in a new way, a key value is the encouragement for other 'generals' leading other brand teams to push their own teams to think more adventurously.

The new advertising from Axe inspired a number of the brand managers within Unilever around Europe. One of them, Frank Weijers, who worked on Domestos, Unilever's European bleach brand, was inspired – as much as four years after the original Axe work broke – to begin producing innovative communications of his own. His first piece of advertising showed a young man waking up in a flat after a party, or maybe several months of happy excess. The man stumbles in to the trashed main room and looks at his turntable. It is going round, trying to play a pizza, which someone has put on it instead of vinyl. He turns it off, and picks his way over to a formica surface. While cooking himself a couple of eggs he takes out a Domestos wipe and cleans a spectacular collection of gunk from the (eventually) white surface. His eggs done, he then flips them straight onto the surface, cuts one with a knife and fork, and begins eating his breakfast straight off the formica. Weijers recalls the effect the Axe work had on his realization that cleaning advertising had been locked in unreal clichés for too long:

> Seeing the success of Axe stimulated me to break out of the category conventions in advertising for Domestos. Just as Axe didn't show a traditional 'hunk' as protagonist (the convention for most male fragrance advertising), why did we always have to show a housewife? And why are all the homes in Household Cleaner advertising so pristine and unreal? Is that really the only kind of communication our target would respond to as traditional wisdom suggested or were we [Unilever and other manufacturers] more conventional, conservative and risk-averse than our audience?
>
> The film we made broke many conventions. And we employed a production company who'd never done a household cleaning ad (or indeed, any mundane, everyday product) but who had real vision for the film. We trusted our instincts and went with that vision – even down to the pizza on the turntable.
>
> Was it easy? No! But the main barriers were internal, our own fear of taking a risk, moving outside category norms. But it was worth it. And the results proved that our consumers can be more open to new ideas than we are ourselves.

Besides Abrashoff's overall influence on the Navy, there were other key officers who adopted some of his policies directly on their own ships – his second-in-command, for example, took command of his own destroyer, and through implementing many of the *Benfold* practices achieved an equal success.

> My people are going out and doing this stuff and getting great results, and the Admiral would send captains over to our ship, to find out what we're doing; they'd take it back, and a year later their ships were some of the best in their squadron.
>
> So, did we change the whole 400,000 person organization [the US Navy]? The answer is no. But are we changing how 50, 75 or 100,000 people think? Sure.

The success of the bluegrass soundtrack for *O Brother, Where Art Thou?* also influenced some of the long-standing artists in Nashville, which had up to that point been moving away from its roots to the glitzier packaging of Garth Brooks and Shania Twain. Commented *Forbes* magazine afterwards, with apparent enthusiasm: 'The revival has swept along Dolly Parton, who recently reinvigorated her stalled career by recording two bluegrass albums of her own, one of which won a Grammy.'[2] It is people who create strong brands. And creating a potent subculture near them within the parent is one way of inspiring them to push further on their own brands.

Finally, it is interesting to note the beneficial effect of a different kind of Pirate – Pirate Radio. Although disliked by the authorities, Pirate Radio stations in fact frequently prove an essential new source of both music and talent (in the UK, Radio 1's 'Dreem Teem' were lured from the Pirate radio station Blackbeard). It's interesting that while Pirate stations are not set up for commercial reasons, they commercially benefit the music industry – bringing new music, ideas and talent, whatever. They help drive the whole industry forward.[3]

Peronis, Napkins and Saucers

Interviewing Challengers is, of course, one of the great pleasures of business life. And sharing and building on an emerging hypothesis does not always happen in the formal environment of an office: as always, the most interesting conversations tend to happen nowhere near a desk or meeting room at all.

On this particular occasion I am sitting in a pizza restaurant with Iain Hamilton, a Glaswegian Denter at Kimberly-Clark. It is getting towards the end of the meal and the table is less than tidy – there are a couple of empty bottles of Peroni beer on the table alongside the coffee cups and napkins. We are discussing the issue of how one can affect the propensity to take risk and be prepared to challenge the status quo in one's organization; we use what is at our disposal from the debris of the meal to develop the point of view as we go along.

We agree that organizations have basically three kinds of people:

1. *Peronis*. These are the natural Denters. There are relatively few of them in any organization, and indeed the business world. If we are lucky, there is at least one in each department, and probably one near the top of the organization. They are people who, if they do not have the ability to follow their heart within the organization, will become frustrated and leave to start their own venture.

2. *Saucers*. At the other end of the scale are the Saucers – these are the people who are not interested in rocking the boat. They are the 'steady hands on the tiller' whose ability and strength lie in doing (sometimes very well) things the way they have always been done. There will be certain kinds of brand and certain kinds of situation where these people will be really important, but at the same time if they are allowed to set the tone for the culture of the organization, nothing will ever change or progress. Saucers are primarily interested in career security and pensions – they will be very loyal to the company and remain there for a long time.

3. *Napkins*. In between the Peronis and the Saucers lie (as Hamilton puts one more piece into the middle of the table) the Napkins. These are the people who could go either way. On the one hand, they have the appetite and ability to play by a different, more Challenger set of rules, but on the other will take their cue from what they see as the dominant culture of the company. If they see the culture rewarding and promoting Peronis, and Peroni-type behaviour, they will bring more of that out in themselves. If they see careerist Saucers rising inexorably to the top of the department or organization each time, they will suppress any Peroni instincts, and be slightly bolder Saucers.

Essentially, the two of us agree, the success of spreading fresher, Challenger thinking in a large multi-brand culture does not depend on simply buying in more Peronis: there are a limited amount of these in the world – you can't simply go all out to recruit more of them. Instead, success in spreading such thinking and approaches depends on what happens to the Napkins. Do they see a successful Challenger microculture in a brand close to them as just a flash in the pan – something that represents a brief flirtation on a brand that is of low status, or was going to die anyway? In that case, the influence of that brand will remain confined to the brand itself. Conversely, if the Napkins see that Challenger microculture near them as an indication that there is a genuine movement (and desire) in the company to open up new ways of thinking about its brands and how they go to market, then they will be more inclined to become the Peronis the company needs them to be. Unilever took Simon Clift, the successful Marketing Director on Axe, and made him, at the age of 42, the President of Marketing for their Home and Personal Care Division – a clear sign to Napkins in that division that this kind of behaviour and thinking was something they needed more of to succeed.

A More Intangible Spreading of Energy and Belief

There can also be a more intangible and general release of energy within the organization from a cross-function team that has both this powerful sense of itself and why it is different, and is expressing that in different ways.

In terms of biting the other generals, the vibrant Yoo-hoo subculture was not attractive to the rest of the Pernod Ricard brand groups (the brand's owners before it was sold): 'They couldn't stand us. I mean, we were noisy and messy and bright and colourful, and all those things that the liquor, wines and spirits business was not' (see p. 275). But then perhaps Yoo-hoo were targeting a group of teens that the drinks companies would not want (or be allowed) to target, so the opportunity of transfer was limited. But the Snapple Group which acquired Yoo-hoo welcomed Kristin Krumpe and her team for *exactly that same energy*:

> When we moved over to Snapple, immediately senior management here said, 'We want you to put up your stuff, we really want to capture this

positive energy that you guys are bringing here. We really think that you are going to be able to infuse our organization with a lot of that.'

They welcomed the noise, and the 'mosh pit' (see p. 275), and the internal iconography the team brought with them, because they wanted to create more of that around them. Snapple, originally the little alternative beverage culture, is presumably in danger of becoming a culture that dominates the other brands in the portfolio. And the management realizes it needs to encourage more individuality in its internal cultures, as well as external communications for each brand, in order for the company as a whole to thrive in the ways it needs.

But what this example also highlights, as we will come to see in the final chapter, is that spreading the learnings and influence from such a subculture only works if it is the right time for both parties: the individual and the organization. Not all of the larger organizations may feel it is the right time yet, but enough of senior management need to in order to give the Brand subculture the space and support it needs to work.

Finally, with such energy often comes two kinds of renewed belief. The first is a renewed belief that other brands can be turned around or punch above their weight (as happened with some of the brands around Hovis after it was successful within British Bakeries). And the second is a renewed personal belief in, and excitement about the company one is a part of, and a renewed faith that there is an opportunity for one as an individual there, rather than simply as a corporate soldier. Both kinds of belief are strong builders of loyalty and commitment.

Perceived Culture vs. Real Culture

We need to make a distinction, of course, between the *perceived* barriers within a culture and the *real* barriers. On the one hand, mid-level managers often feel they are restricted by the corporate way of doing things, even though they have not had direct pushback in a given area themselves; on the other, senior managers feel they are all too rarely pushed, and too infrequently have to say 'no' to a request. So within each culture one needs to determine which aspects of the 'constraining corporate culture' are really restricting the possibilities of a brand and brand team, and which exist only in their minds.

It is very easy for both sides to deceive themselves here. The difficulty, of course, is that people take their cues from doings, rather than sayings. The so-called 'Iceberg theory' of human contact suggests that a large amount of how we form our impressions about someone is at a non-verbal, subconscious level (their posture, the look in their eye or the expression on their mouth, the way they move their shoulders, and so on), and that this has a far more profound and immediate impact on our view of them than what they say. In the same way, both these sides of the same view about real or perceived corporate culture are true. The senior manager doesn't *say* 'No' a lot. But the cues the middle manager is reading are not 'saying' cues. They are the deeper, below-the-water cues, that are thrown out in meetings or during conversations with others (how they interpret why Harry has been promoted and Milo has not, for instance). Conversely, senior managers feel aggrieved that such conversations too easily become theoretical – and that the reality of a great idea once seen and embraced creates a lot of freedom to do things in a fresh way; in their own way they want less 'saying' and more a piece of 'doing' before being asked to facilitate the breakthrough.

This is why creating a success in an adjoining brand, which comes through a new way of thinking about some key aspect of the marketing mix, can be so potent. It is an action, a piece of doing, that punctures the membrane of double-guessing and resistance on both sides.

Summary

We saw that there are four key reasons why a parent should be looking to set up a brand republic for the beneficial effects on the parent, over and above the benefit to the brand itself. They are:

- the spreading of new perspectives, behaviours, standards and practices;
- the impetus and inspiration in other team leaders to take risks to push further their own marketing and communication ideas;
- one's ability to bring out the Peroni in a Napkin;
- a more intangible spreading of energy and belief.

Each of these is of enormous value to the parent organization over and above the success of the original brand in itself, and a powerful reason for thinking about how one promotes and ripples the effects of such brand successes more systematically.

We noted, though, two provisos. The first was that the beneficial effects only spread more broadly if the rest of the company – or some of the rest of the company – is ready to learn. And the second is that along with the visible promotion of success comes how failure when taking risk is seen to be managed by the company; as well as 'forces of inspiration', there are also 'forces of dampening'. We shall come on to look at this a little more in the final chapter.

PART **IV**

Writing the Articles

Part IV will be about 'Writing the Articles' of Intelligent Piracy in our own organization. It will offer an overview of how to precipitate these ways of thinking and behaving in your brand and within your organization to increase the likelihood of them taking seed, and becoming part of a genuine Challenger culture. This part of the book will also offer some sense of what may be in store for you emotionally, and how to prepare yourself for that.

Chapter 14   Writing the Articles in Our Own Organization

This chapter pulls together a number of the learning points from the book so far into an overview for a Challenger wanting to foster a Challenger culture within their own organization. While putting forward a practical sequence of actions, it is also designed to prompt the behaviours and qualities we need to evidence at each stage, as discussed in the first two parts of the book.

Chapter 15   That Difficult First Year: Emotional Preparation

This chapter discusses the emotional preparation for the long days at sea during 'That Difficult First Year' – the time when a Challenger team have had to commit to their vision, sometimes in the face of open scepticism, without yet having the results to be sure that they are on the right course. It looks at the kinds of setbacks Challengers have faced in this period, and where they have found the strength to overcome them.

14

Writing the Articles in Our Own Organization

Steve dreamed up the pirate metaphor, first springing it on his small Mac team at a retreat in the September of 1982. 'It's more fun to be a pirate than to join the Navy' Steve would say. It was Steve Caps, a software ace drafted in from Lisa, and Susan Kare, the Mac's graphic designer, who had sewn together the black skull-and-crossbones flag that would become the group's symbol. It was a funny way to convey the fact that this was no traditional development team. This group shunned corporate orthodoxy and the conventions of society.

John Sculley[1]

So far we have, to use the Brazilian expression, been 'talking to our buttons'. What if we want a little less conversation, and a little more action? What would it mean to actually try to write the Articles for our brand, and catalyse an appropriate subculture within our organization? The brand of corporate piracy that John Sculley sketches in the quote above sounds wonderfully full-frontal – what does it mean to shun the conventions of society, exactly? And is this what we are advocating for ourselves?

Quite when Jobs came up with the quote seems to be a matter of debate. *West of Eden: The End of Innocence at Apple Computers*,[2] describes its unveiling at an offsite for the whole Macintosh team in late January 1983 at the tranquil La Playa Hotel in Carmel, a place used to catering to an older, conservative clientele looking for some

Writing the Articles in Your Own Organization

1. Establishing the Preconditions for Success
- Is there a business or brand case? *
- Finding the right people
- A Smokejumper*
- Tackling the Five Tyrannies *
- Recruiting the broader team *

2. The Opportunity and the Vision
- Change the Neighbourhood
- Outlooking
- Visioning
- The Map of Consumer Engagement
- The Articles

3. Giving It Meaning and Support

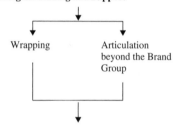

Wrapping

Articulation
beyond the Brand
Group

4. Keeping It Going
- Keeping the beat
- Maintaining recruitment
- Avoiding dilution and the Navy drift *
- Feeding The Beast

* Denotes a stage particularly relevant for Brand Subcultures

Figure 14.1   **Structure of the Chapter**

peace and quiet. That evening after the meeting, some of the Mac team had gone skinny dipping in the hotel pool while the rest of them had dinner, and then the whole group had lit a bonfire on the beach. One can imagine the sense of piratical pleasure and bonding would only have increased when the police later arrived and told them to put the bonfire out – and indeed continued the next day when the hotel management asked them never to come back again. If you are Pirates, it would be somehow disappointing if manifestly Navy establishments started giving you Preferred Guest Memberships.

But what would it actually mean for *us* to try to be Pirates in our own organization? What would it mean for us to try to write our own Articles, drawing on what we have learned so far? This chapter will try to pull some of the many threads together into a single path. It is clearly not the promise of a guaranteed path, but more a collection of questions, learnings and stimulations that may perhaps shade the odds a little in your favour, should you or your organization be Necessary Pirates.

It is a long chapter, and is designed to be used as much as read. I cannot repeat enough that the value to us as Challengers will lie in how we approach each stage, rather than the fact that we approach them in the right sequence. I have therefore flagged at regular intervals the behaviours and qualities we saw in the first two parts of the book which we will need to bring out in ourselves and our teams.

Because it is long, I have expressed the flow of the chapter, and the series of questions, challenges and exercises diagrammatically in Figure 14.1. The flow runs from the top to the bottom; I have asterisked areas that are particularly relevant to brand subcultures within larger multi-brand organizations, but even then they will often also contain some areas of value to single brand companies. It falls into four distinct sequences: Establishing the Preconditions of Success, the Opportunity and the Vision, Giving it Meaning and Support, and Maintaining Momentum.

Establishing the Preconditions for Success

First, is there a real business or brand case for doing things differently? Are you wanting to do this for the right reasons?

Are you a Necessary Pirate? Or a Vanity Pirate? Is There a Business or Brand Case?

There are obviously right and wrong reasons for trying to set up a brand subculture within a larger organization. The right reasons, as we have seen, are to do with a real business need or opportunity. The wrong reasons are often to do with vanity – we want to do something different because we feel we are in some way special or want to rule our own little empires.

Is there a clear business need to do things differently? Do you have targets that are greater than your historic performance over the past three years? Are you making money?

Equally, do you have a clear enough sense of what your brand stands for? How well does the current marketing model the company practises suit the identity you have? Is there a case to be made for pursuing a different model to those above and around you?

Behaviours and Qualities to consider: Refusing.

Finding the Right People. Including Yourself

If there is a case to be made, you need to find the right people for the task, in two senses:

1. The right people for a brand subculture: How do you personally and the rest of the possible team fit into the Denter/Idea Hamster/Implementation Rhino model?
2. The right people for *this* brand subculture: What do you care about? Are you working on the right brand for you?

Think of answering both of these in terms of *knowing* yourself and *being* yourself.

First, 'know thyself', as the Delphic temple pronounced. I myself, for instance, Adam Morgan, am not a Denter; I have all the snarl and swagger of an electric milk float. But what I am is an Idea Hamster. I feed on ideas. They give me energy, scratch my Great Unspoken Itch. So were I personally starting a brand subculture I would need first to find a Denter in the team, to share the centre with me.

Second, is this the right brand for you? That allows you to *be* yourself? Rather than yourself-as-professional-marketing-or-communications-person? Is it and its vision something you care about? That you can feel personally aligned to?

It is curious how often people make a distinction between 'me' and 'marketing me'. The ads they like as people bear no relation to the rubbish they approve as marketers. Marketing, of course, is not the only discipline we find this kind of artificial behaviour in. People beginning as Radio DJs on rock and pop music stations for the first time have a clear preconception of the kinds of things Radio jocks say and the kinds of ways they say them. This on the whole consists of a stream of forced jollity and innuendo, which is false, strikes the listener as false, and does not lead to the strength of listening relationship most current radio stations need in a world of saturated choice. The radio station GWR, in fact, has a course to remedy exactly this tendency which it calls 'Authentic Radio Personality'. Essentially, the course consists of taking a group of new Radio jocks, and helping them to understand that they will connect better with their audience if they stop trying to be someone else and start to allow more of themselves, allowing their own personal culture, view and enthusiasms, to come through. It might also seem to the casual observer that there is a very interesting course to be created called 'Authentic Marketing Personality'; and there ought to be a long waiting list for it.

But we should not be one of those people. Let us not leave ourselves at the door, or allow anyone into the team who we think will do this. Take it personally.

There is another way that the people on the team need to be 'the right people' – make sure your partners are not just right for their assigned role, but also play position. Even if they think they can do a number of things, make sure they understand which role they really need to play, and ensure they have what they feel they need to do it.

Behaviours and Qualities to consider: Taking it personally. Denting.

Risk, Smokejumpers and Losing the Eighth Passenger

Next, you need to find a Smokejumper. You will clearly need to persuade them of a number of things:

- There is a huge need or opportunity.
- This need or opportunity cannot be achieved by thinking about the brand in the way that we have been, or the way that the company defaults to as a matter of best practice.

- Get them to see that this is moving from one model to a better one, for sound commercial reasons.
- Explain the difference between a Smokejumper and a sponsor and what they will need to do.

If you are feeling theatrical, have an empty chair in your initial team meetings, including perhaps that with your Smokejumper – the empty chair of the Eighth Passenger. Discuss and be open about the nature of and reasons for the Eighth Passenger (it may be fear, it may be something else). Agree what you need the Smokejumper to do to remove the empty chair.

Make sure he or she understands that you are still in charge of the marketing decisions. That is not what you need their help for.

Behaviours and Qualities to consider: Denting.

Tackling the Five Tyrannies of the Navy

Then there are five tyrannies of the Navy to be tackled. And for some of these, too, you will need your Smokejumper's aid.

- The tyranny of the career path – you must keep your core team together for at least two years.
- The tyranny of the internationally preferred supplier: make sure you have a mixture of business partners in your team – those that 'know' what the real questions and issues are, and those that have no idea, and so ask different ones.
- The implicit tyranny of thinking that agreement is a more important currency within the team than energy – be prepared to embrace tension. Have a Denter who will do this, and a Smokejumper who can minimize any adverse effect in the way it impacts relationships outside the team.
- The tyranny of thinking 'it is my job to define the communications brief' and only briefing your agencies (and other communications and ideas partners) when you know what you want to say – involve a key group in asking the questions and defining the brief. Include creative people in this. All of you should work through the problem together. Don't allow people with less experience on the team to believe that

somehow what they think has less weight than those with category experience – if anything, we should be listening to them more.

- The tyranny of individuals thinking the way they are going to add value is by playing with the centre, rather than richness at the edges – you need to redefine how people on (or coming onto) the team are going to be adding value once the vision is set. It will not be by interrogating the centre; it will be by adding value to the Wrapping – richness at the edges, in ideas or implementation.

Behaviours and Qualities to consider: Denting. Refusing. Taking it Personally. And an eye on the kinds of partners you will need for Wrapping.

Recruiting the Broader Team Beyond the Core: Make it Clear
They Are Citizens of a New Country

First, those joining the team from another brand should 'interview' for the job. The mere fact that they have been successful elsewhere in the organization, and have certain process management skills and this or that seniority level – all these things are necessary but not sufficient. We need to know if they – if their personal culture – is, or could be right for this brand and what this brand believes.

And to find this out we need some border control. The interview is not just a verbal one. What is our equivalent of the trampoline? Because we'd better have one. Otherwise mere skill in marketing is going to be enough to become a citizen of our country, and in that case, our culture will be evaporating faster than you can say 'Yo ho ho'. We need to operate border control more strictly than that.

Second, you need to make it clear to those that you do recruit that they are citizens of a new country. Think back to Axe's red pill and blue pill, or 8th Continent referring to themselves as 'On the Continent' – how are you going to symbolize to them that this is a different place where different rules apply? Are there any kind of 'Gatorologies' you want to think about – initiations that help reframe their perspective and point of view before coming onto the brand?

Third, in terms of recruiting across the other functions, although you want all the key functions, you do not necessarily want the most senior person – you want the ones who will bring the right qualities to the team.

Fourth, plan for the unexpected – especially in terms of keeping the team together. The regional President of a large multinational in Latin America gave me fairly short shrift on a proposed pilot of such a Brand Subculture when I suggested that people should be staying together in teams for two to three years. His point was that one cannot stop someone leaving the company altogether and joining an equally attractive one at Pepsi, for instance. While one can look for continuity within the team, then, one must plan for the possibility of discontinuity. One should always, in his view, have a minimum three-month transition period, during which period both the incoming and the outgoing person would work side by side.

Behaviours and Qualities to consider: Taking it personally. Denting.

The Opportunity and the Vision

Change the Neighbourhood

Perhaps the most useful place to start thinking about new Insights of Opportunity for your brand – particularly if you are in a multi-brand organization – lies in Changing the Neighbourhood. Although in reality a part of Outlooking, I am going to play this particular idea out in a little more detail here to help kick start the process for the whole team.

The whole concept of Brand Neighbourhoods is fascinating. (For those of you uncomfortable with such a naked display of vanity, I should be clear that this is a piece of thinking originated and first used by the advertising agency Fallon, and its US President, Rob White. I am simply pushing how we use it in a slightly different direction here.) The very simple premise is that there are three kinds of 'Neighbourhoods' we need to think of our brands as living in:

1. The first Brand Neighbourhood is *the competitive set in which we are currently putting it* – that is, surrounded by the brands we usually think of as either competing with or sharing ways of going to market with (these will therefore usually be either the competitive set, or the rest of our own portfolio). This explicitly informs external communications – how and where we advertise, whether we use PR, the role of promotions, and so on.

2. The second Brand Neighbourhood is the set of brands that surround us *within our company*. The effect of this neighbourhood is more implicit. It will have three kinds of effect – one to do with a mindset about how 'we' (that is, the company) go to market, what kinds of risk the culture is up to, and so on. The second kind of effect is a perceived 'pecking order' about which are the glamorous or 'sexy' brands to work on; this is usually to do with the size of the brand, the size of the advertising budget, and the quality of the existing brand or advertising idea. This is also a very influential neighbourhood, whose influence on us we need to explicitly understand, and whose less useful mental frameworks we need to be able to overturn. The last kind of influence is the trickle-down from those kinds of large or prestigious brands – how the way that they do things (from marketing to innovation) becomes unconsciously the model for the way all the other, 'lesser' brands do things as well.

3. But the third Brand Neighbourhood will be a very different sort of Brand Neighbourhood – the neighbourhood of *brands outside our category that we can learn the most from*. Brands that we can learn from because they are the kinds of brands our consumer has the kind of relationship with that we would like to have. Or (and clearly this is related) because they are the brands in categories around us with similar kinds of ambitions and budgets, and who are succeeding in doing more with less – getting a greater traction on the consumer's imagination and pocket than we are, through fresh ways of going to market, inside and out.

So the first act of many subcultures is, in effect, to ask: what are the (confining and irrelevant) rules that we are imposing on ourselves through blindly accepting the first two Neighbourhoods? Often the first act a Challenger does is to recognize that if it is to succeed there is no value in remaining in the Brand Neighbourhoods within which it already finds itself – they are restricting the way it needs to think about the consumer, the brand or the category to break through.

So create a visual Brand Neighbourhood exercise as a trigger for breaking with your immediate past. In a room, allocate three walls, leaving a fourth free.

On one, surround your brand with the other brands in your company.

On the second wall, surround your brand with visual representations of the other brands in the category.

On the third wall, surround your brand with the brands in *any* category you actually think we can learn most from – in particular the ones that your consumer has the greatest emotional affinity with (particularly a *growing* affinity). This is most productively done as a team exercise, where everyone on the broader team is asked to bring one or two examples of brands from outside our category that they think we can learn something from. Make sure that some of these brands are in categories a long way from your own.

On the fourth wall, write up your vision for the brand – the identity and the opportunity; clearly this will be a reference point for how you interpret the other three walls. (Note: The Outlooking and Visioning sections below will also be pushing this further.)

For the first wall, create on a large sheet of paper next to it two columns: in one, write what you have in common with those brands, really, and in the other what makes you different. Discuss which of the differences are important differences, and which are incidental ones. Then write down which of the key practices and ways of doing things you will need to reinterpret or reinvent, reflecting the important differences in order to make your brand a success on its own. (These should not be hugely long – identify the key 3–5 to focus on.)

Example: Altoids, whose communications and media strategy are likened more to those of Absolut than they are to the rest of Kraft.

For the second (category) wall, write down on a large sheet of paper the differences that your vision demands that you will need to create in the consumer's eyes between your brand and the others. What kinds of ways of thinking about the consumer, innovation or the trade are we really just accepting as hand-me-downs from the biggest brand(s) in the category? That we need to be able to fundamentally rethink in order to realize the brand opportunity? There may be none, but I doubt it; it is more likely that there are none *yet* – that you will need to repeat this particular wall when you have your vision and are looking at its implications.

Example: Axe, which in effect redefined its advertising competitive set and changed its communications model as a result.

For the third wall, write down on a large sheet of paper next to it what it is that your brand can learn from each of these other brands – what is it about the way they are presenting themselves to the consumer that creates that stronger affinity? What can we learn from each of these ourselves for the new model we are trying to create? These may seem obvious to us, but it will not be so to the whole team, and we will need to move them with us. Be systematic about it – make sure the team feel emotional ownership of the fresh ideas that come out.

Example: Yoo-hoo. Yoo-hoo looked at the big youth brands on the Warped Tour and learnt not to follow the 'canned sponsorships' that they seemed to be doing – hence their highly customized and interactive site there.

Behaviours and Qualities to consider: Refusing, and the beginnings of Outlooking.
    (Note: This last wall will also act as a form of initial Uncompetitive Review for you.)

Outlooking

Once you have started to think afresh about where you do and don't belong in terms of Neighbourhoods, start thinking about where the real opportunities may lie for your brand in terms of the other dimensions we discussed in Outlooking.
    Set aside a day to use the Outlooking framework from Chapter 1. Preface it with a review of the Reflective Insights you can draw from previous consumer work. Then generate a number of possible Insights of Opportunity, based on what you know about your consumer. Make sure you do all four corners, even if you think one of them seems less relevant – it may be that an insight from one area can help build one from another.
    Which have the ability to create step change in the brand? Which of these do you have most energy for? What ideas for the brand, and what it could stand for, seem to have the most potential?

You may need to let the issue of 'Grip' be something you and your team live with for a little while – initial points of grip may seem at first uncomfortable or unnatural to some in the group. It is easy to forget now that some of what gave Avis its grip in the 1960s was how fresh the notion of celebrating that they were number two was at the time – to the point that initially some of the agency account team did not want to present the idea at all, on the grounds that it was un-American to want to be something other than number one.

Behaviours and Qualities to consider: Outlooking.

Visioning

Once you have identified the Insights of Opportunity you want to pursue, you will need to have more than a positioning. To create a genuine culture, you will need to have a very clear sense of where you stand and why you stand there – probably projected in a point of view about the world, and how it is or should be, if your brand had its way. In this, understanding what you are against will be as important in generating richness and texture as understanding what you are for.

To get you started, ask yourself:

- What does this brand believe in?
- What would it change about the world if it could?
- Think Camper, and 'Walk Don't Run'. What is it for? What is it against?

One further point – as you explore the notion of antipathy, what you are against as well as what you are for, bear in mind that though powerful, it is important to see personal antipathy as a starting place, rather than an ending place. Part of Urban Outfitters' early sense of itself was the 'anti-Gap' mindset; so too also the clothing and furnishing store Anthropologie, when it began, thought of itself as the 'anti-Banana' – but it was careful to move on from that initial sense of simply being a counterpoint to something else. This was, in effect, something to push against that seeded the original sense of the brand – but the culture evolved into being something uniquely its own.

Behaviours and Qualities to consider: Pushing will obviously be important here. Does what you have go far enough? What happens if you push it further?

Get a Clear Understanding of What it Will Mean for Your Brand to Be a Challenger

You also need to start thinking about how you are going to need to engage with the marketplace. This will have important implications for your relationships with functions like packaging, PR, and so on. This is something we don't think about upfront nearly enough; we tend to leave it to the advertising to define it for us. But it is going to be very important in defining our character.

Let's use this rather crude tool[3] to help us discuss this within our team. We shall call it 'The Map of Consumer Engagement'. It has two axes. The first, the horizontal axis, is this:

discover, seduce, empathize, help, encourage, champion, challenge, confront

Our brand can engage with our consumer through any of these – on the right-hand side, it can leave the consumer to discover it (Absolut), it can seduce (innocent, Lush), it can empathize (Saturn), help (the Orange 'Learning' campaign), champion (Think Different), challenge (Mini, Camper), confront (Diesel, fcuk).

The second axis is: Public vs. Private – does the brand seek a public stage to reset the agenda, or does it seek to do it in an apparently more personal and understated way? (see Figure 4.2.)

There are a number of clarifications we should make so that we can use this properly. The first is that a popular misconception about Challengers is that they always live over on the top right-hand corner – as public, in-your-face confronters of the brand leader or us. Some, like Wasatch, do indeed occupy this territory; Diesel is another.

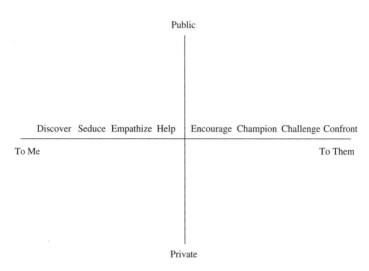

Figure 14.2   **The Map of Consumer Engagement 1**

But many don't. Snapple, I would argue, seduced. innocent succeeded through creating discovery; Absolut, too (and indeed most super-premium products) are not confrontational, though they can be Challengers. Orange and Saturn achieved huge initial success, though they were not aggressive. This was partly, perhaps (particularly in Saturn's case), because the rest of the car industry was seen to be crudely confrontational in its hard sell already.

The second clarification is that having a strong position, opinion or belief system on something doesn't necessarily put you in the top right-hand corner. Camper's 'Walk Don't Run' philosophy is most powerfully argued in their 'Magalogue' (a cross between a magazine and a catalogue) on 'The Walking Society', distributed in their stores, but their retail space is not militant with issue-related posters in the way that The Body Shop's was from time to time (see Figure 14.3).

And the third is that the choice is not a simple one between the bottom left (quiet, personal discovery) and top right (very public challenge). Snapple occupied a very successful position at the top left here with its Wendy advertising, and Diesel's provocative print advertising, websites and store material allow it to play very powerfully at the bottom right (though its TV takes it top right).

A final point to note is that not every brand in your world will fit on here – I am deliberately putting up a map where the only dimensions

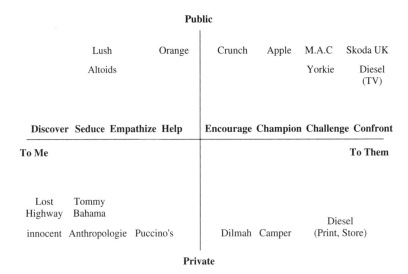

Figure 14.3   **The Map of Consumer Engagement 2**

are to do with *a desire to positively engage* the consumer emotionally in some way, because that is what most Challengers have to do to succeed. But not all brands do this, particularly certain kinds of market leaders (the bigger airlines, for instance), or certain kinds of fashion brands. However, it is something we may well want to be looking for ourselves.

So look at where you think your brand will need to play (and clearly one will draw both on how the other brands in the category are behaving and the other brands your consumer is drawn to, in order to find a differentiated place here). Now look at the implications of this for people we need to align and the marketing skills we need to cradle tightly within our team. If you are on the bottom left, for example, you will want to use packaging and 'quiet' media in very intriguing ways; if you are top right, you will need a PR company that excels in idea creation (as well as having a good list of contacts), and a risk-amenable CEO.

What would it mean to put your brand and yourself in two or three different places here? If you have time, play each of these out a little: you will want to find something that is right for the brand, your appetites as a team, and the amount of exposure or subtlety your organization will encourage or tolerate.

Behaviours and Qualities to consider: Projecting. Leaning.

The Articles – A New Kind of Contract Between Your Team

Write a new set of Articles with all the team, including your business partners: how are you going to behave individually and in terms of the relationships between you, going forward to get what you want? Note that this 'way of living' will be complementary to any structure or architecture for defining the brand your company may use – its thrust is how you need to *behave* in order to deliver this sense of the brand. This is something most brand teams in companies never really discuss, yet it is probably the most important dimension of the job. So let's draw up a new kind of contract between ourselves – and our business partners. (Remember Avis and DDB, in case you think we are getting too touchy-feely at this point.)

Divide the room into two groups. Show both the Pirates' Articles beforehand, and explain that we are going to define the spirit of how we are going to go forward, how we are going to operate as a team in order to genuinely deliver the brand as we think it should be delivered.

Ask each group to go into a different room and write a set of Articles – no more than ten, and preferably less. When they come back, look at the common areas that sing out and make those the ones at the top; add those others from either group that strike you as powerful and important. Cut away all that is left. This will be your 'Way of Living'.

If you are feeling theatrical, you can ask everyone to put their signature to it. This may seem pushing it too far for some, but in effect you are simply doing as Lexus did. And they asked everyone to sign it, and then carved those signatures in stone. Hard to argue with where they ended up.

Behaviours and Qualities to consider: Binding.

Giving it Meaning and Support

Parallel Lines

Having defined our vision, we are now about to see two different kinds of activities play out. One is Wrapping our brand vision – giving it all the texture it needs. The other is engaging those around and above us that we need to engage.

Wrapping

We are now at the bit in the process usually referred to as 'Brand Expression' or 'Brand Offerings'. But as we saw in Chapter 4, many of these Pirates seeking a different kind and intensity of relationship with their consumer – one encouraging a participation in their culture rather than simply purchase – have more layered and detailed expositions of what their brand stands for than are usually captured by notions of 'advertising', 'promotion', or 'relationship marketing', these being the usual convenient silos our briefs fall into.

And we saw in exploring the concept of 'Wrapping' that it takes the form of a number of layers wrapping outwards from our core beliefs – what we hold important that differentiates us from other countries and peoples:

- Our culture and customs – the way we do things. What characterizes our citizens internally – the kinds of border control we practise. Our particular habits and rituals that emerge from all of this.
- The way we speak, verbally and visually – our language and iconography.
- The things we have that no one else has. The sensory and physical cues, the sense of offer.
- The manifestation of all of this in Experience.
- The manifestation of all of this in how we create Folklore.
- The manifestation of all of this in Communications.

Some Inspirations

You're on your own here, you and your business partners; there is no easy ABC methodology for producing powerful cultures and expressions of those cultures. But if you work from the inside out, rather than leaping from the vision to the communications, and if you push your exploratory thinking at each stage, and look to project your beliefs and sense of self in the components of each layer, the elements will come. And bear in mind that they will not all come straightaway – cultures grow organically, and build on themselves over time. But you have to give them places to start, and early expressions to build from.

What you can do, though, is constantly look for inspiration from outside your category to feed your imagination and 'provocate' the possibilities. In that spirit, let us offer three more examples, all from subcultures within larger companies.

The first is the way the culture was expressed in terms of engaging with the trade. Now if you are a packaged goods marketing director, and you present to the multiple retail buyer, you present on their terms. You go to their office, you sit on the other side of their desk, and you show your presentation to them, and try to get them excited about all the things you are doing to make your brand vibrant and dynamic. And they get any number of people coming in every week and saying exactly the same thing.

But Tango weren't happy with this: they wanted to be thought of as a brand in their own right, rather than just another part of the Britvic portfolio, and they wanted the trade to understand exactly what their brand was about. So they created an environment they themselves could control – one that would not be that which the buyer sat in day after day, and one that would really make the brand stand out in that buyer's mind.

So they took a jet-black Bentley Continental, put a tow bar on the back, and attached an equally black caravan. Both vehicles had the word Tango written all over them in huge letters; the Bentley also flew little Tango flags from either side of the bonnet, like an ambassador (a real brand ambassador). Then they drove to the retailers to make their pitch.

So now let us put ourselves in our audience's shoes. Imagine that you are the carbonated soft drinks buyer for a major grocery retailer. You receive presentations week in, week out, in your office, or perhaps a meeting room, and what tells you which brand is which is the logo they have at the bottom right-hand side of their Powerpoint charts. And then one day this team from Tango come in and tell you that they don't want to present to you in your office, they'd like you to come out to the car park. You are a little surprised, but you get up and walk to the car park, where you see this enormous black Bentley and its incongruous caravan. Hmm, you think, I wonder what the caravan looks like inside? You find out – because once through the caravan door, you have entered Tango's world. Lemon ceiling, apple and orange seats, a blackcurrant table (the four flavours); plastic fruit everywhere.

Now here's the interesting bit. Because when you get past the Bentley, into the caravan, have pushed aside the piles of orange plastic fish that were the emblem of the current promotion and sat down in front of the computer on that blackcurrant table, what you get is a hard-edged commercial presentation ('as if written by McKinsey') about why thinking of Tango in this way is better commercially for you, the retailer, and better commercially for the brand (and therefore the shareholder). So the Tango team did parade their culture to all audiences, not simply to the consumer – but in a spirit of 'noisy bilinguality': recognizing that the sole purpose of all of this was to build a brand that offered a better return.

The second example is the relaunch of the chocolate milk brand Yoo-hoo. We have already seen that their distribution base prompted them to rethink their 'Vitamins and minerals' approach to Moms, and turn instead to teens. The team discovered that Yoo-hoo was the favourite drink of Joey Ramone (who knew?) and became part of the Warped Tour, complete with Cutlets and Shoo-hoos. But equally interesting is the way they have taken that into their working environment. At one level this is about the creation of one's own working culture – calling the central area of their working space 'the mosh pit', the music is provided by the Marketing Director herself, from whose office a torrent of punk loudly emanates. To ensure that any passer-by is fully aware that this is the territory of the Yoo-hoo team, they have hung a large banner up above their space left over from an OzzFest sponsorship, across which an animated 'spokeswoman' in a skimpy leather halterneck and skirt was crawling, and to which the Marketing Director had added a painted anarchy symbol of her own devising for good measure.

But creating such artefacts that represent and cue to your team and those around you that you are a different kind of brand is only half of it, because the team leader is not just a transmitter but protector of this culture. Take as an example that anarchy symbol on the banner above the 'mosh pit' within Snapple. After a while the groundswell of complaints from those around in other brands who thought it was a satanist symbol grew too loud for Snapple management to ignore, and they told Kristin Krumpe this. So in her shoes one would be faced here with something of a dilemma: they see it as a satanic symbol, you see it as anarchy. What do you do? They are genuinely upset. It seems only fair to take it down, surely.

Krumpe's reaction? 'Frankly, my reaction was that they need a bit of education about the difference between a pentagram and an anarchy symbol'.

This is exactly what you need. And, of course, it is the results that continue to justify the need for this culture: while the rest of the category struggles to grow 1% a year, Yoo-hoo was up 9% in 2003.

And the third example is one of how we might want to approach the development of the external manifestations of the brand, in this case looking at the PepsiCo brand Mountain Dew. In developing the launch plans for their new cherry variant, the brand team came up with a number of possible names, from Cherry Swirl to Cherry Rush to Code Red, and put the names as elements in a possible launch mix into two kinds of research, one exploring purchase intent and the other exploring communication. They found that the names explicitly mentioning cherry as a flavour performed better in terms of Purchase Intent, whereas the darker romance of Code Red cut through in terms of Communication, with its connotations of 'danger' and 'emergency'. Which way should they go? Jim Nordgren, the Research Director on the brand:

> For the common names like Cherry Dew, there wasn't any imagery besides 'a cherry flavour added to juice'. Even Cherry Rush was … nowhere near [Code Red] in terms of the intensity of the communication. It was tough for us, because we thought, 'Oh God, is the intent really going to be lower? Is the appeal really going to be lower?' [But] it was much more important to deliver imagery on that brand than it was the product descriptor of the flavour.

Nordgren and the rest of the brand team decided that for a brand like Mountain Dew, with such a strong image and equity among its target, the need to have a name that strongly projected the brand and built real equity meant they should pursue 'Code Red', even though it apparently might mean sacrificing some purchase intent. In the end, the final mix proved hugely successful, and the dilemma Nordgren mentions was overcome, but the choice they initially made is an important one to understand for a Challenger that aspires genuinely to Wrap, rather than simply relies on advertising to put forward a message or image.

Behaviours and Qualities to consider: Wrapping. Projecting.

Articulate the Changed Model to the People You Need to Influence

In terms of selling the vision and changed model to those you need to influence, always make sure the strategy and the ideas travel together. Don't ever, *ever* allow yourself to get lured into an elevator speech – the 'just give me what it's about in ten minutes' kind of thing. Regard such meetings as recruitment, rather than communication. Remember the MCA Matrix in Chapter 6 – all you are interested in is creating champions. Bystanders are useless.

Articulate the model and be clear that you still have a model: it is simply a different – and in its own way equally rigorous – model, and one more suited for this kind of brand challenge.

Help senior management in particular remember that they are not the target audience. Show them the kinds of brands and communications that their target audience really responds to, particularly across other categories. Establish this as a necessary filter for them before reviewing any work you are showing to which you need approval or response.

Critical here is to avoid dilution. Dilution kills. This is where the Denter's ability to accept some tension, and the group's unity, may be tested. Dilution usually occurs when the group finds their initial clarity and boldness gradually watered down by a series of internal approval presentations, reviews from coordination groups, fine tuning by one-size-fits-all research methodologies and corporate guidelines about legal clearance and the like.

Behaviours and Qualities to consider: Binding. Denting. Leaning.

Keeping it Going

Ongoing Activities

Once you are going, there are a number of key things we will want to do at regular intervals.

(i) Keeping the Beat

Have regular meetings when you get your cross-functional teams together. Make these immovable in their diaries. Note the successes you are having, however small initially. Join the dots of success and movement for your team – they may be too close to see the progress during periods of That Difficult First Year.

Ensure the five key disciplines (or however many there are in your company) continue to feel as one on this brand, and continue to hunt as a pack.

Where things are not moving, identify whether they are stuck or static. If they are static, the group simply needs to redefine its priorities. Where they are stuck, you will need to invoke the Smokejumper.

(ii) Looping in the Smokejumper

Keep them informed. Warn them of impending smoke. Never stop recruiting them.

(iii) Avoid Dilution. Remember the Gap

You will have found the story of Clarissa in Chapter 2 charming, but too far-fetched for you. But it may well take theatrical acts of exactly that sort to prevent the dilution that naturally occurs.

What you have to do is help your group and those supporting your group to remember the gap between what we see as different (marketers close to the category, spending every day thinking about and looking at it) and what the consumer sees as different (spending 3 seconds twice a week in front of the shelf at the store). Don't stop Pushing as part of your approval system.

Behaviours and Qualities to consider: Binding. Denting. Leaning. Taking it Personally.

The Navy Drift

The longer you go on, and the more people you involve, the stronger and more insidious will be the potential drift back to the Navy. If you fall asleep at the rudder, the undertow will just pull you back to the Navy way of thinking that you are trying to leave.

There are a number of factors that can drag us and our brand adrift. Some will be self-induced: because the brand team rests on its laurels, lets their heads come up. Others will be to do with personnel change at a key level and the newer people becoming progressively more conservative – or slowing the process down because they want to add value by tweaking the centre. This is where one needs to have a firm hand to keep from drifting back to the Navy.

My partner in San Francisco, Mark Barden, used to work on a carnival. At night, as they drove the big trucks through till dawn to the next destination, his job was to sit in the cab and tell the driver stories, to keep him awake, keep him from drifting across onto the wrong side of the road. I like that. We are all at that wheel, at once driving and being driven. We are all in danger of falling asleep and watching others do so. Resist it.

Tell them stories. Keep them awake.

Keep. Them. Awake.

Feeding the Beast

We talked above about having an Idea Hamster on the team, and it is interesting to note how many of the Challengers we looked at in the first half of the book have their own creative resource inside the company: both Puccino's and innocent have a person each whose sole job it is to write the continually evolving packaging and email newsletter (Dan at innocent) or write the continually evolving packaging and retail 'conversation' (Jim at Puccino's).

But another way to do it is not to have a single person but instead a commitment to making ideas flow through the team in a more systematic way. Let us close this chapter by looking at Target, who are a great example of an enormous company creating a systematic way of doing just this.

In the 1990s Target reached a strategic crossroads where their expansion was starting to take them into geographies where they would be up against Wal-Mart, and the company was divided on how they should compete against this formidable bear of an adversary. Half the company thought that they must compete on Wal-Mart's territory of 'Low Low' prices. The other half thought they would never win such a battle, but what they should be trying to do was give their 'guests' more than they expected at a price that was less than they expected.

The highly successful strategy for Target that emerged is based on two simple, directional pieces of thinking. The first is a belief: Bob Ulrich, the CEO, believes you don't have to have money to have taste (hence their celebrated initiatives in persuading famous designers to create ranges of everyday objects and clothing at Target). And the second is the sense of their personality: they are 'Fun, Fast and Friendly'. And one of the key implications in putting these two together is that not simply do they 'wrap' their retail environment in all kinds of ideas, display material and playful uses of the Bullseye icon, but that those ideas and materials change frequently – indeed, the original intention was apparently that something in the store would change from visit to visit each time you came.

So Target have become an ideas culture. They have a room, which every two weeks is filled with new ideas, and every two weeks the CEO and the Marketing Director walk through the room and review them. They review these ideas in a very pure way – there is no set-up when they are presented. They don't want decks or charts, they just want the ideas. They don't want to be sold something; their view is that if the idea can't speak for itself, it's probably a bad idea.

The two of them are looking for slightly different things in reviewing these 40 or so ideas. The CMO is essentially looking for:

- the 'Wow' factor;
- whether it is on Brand;
- whether it is Smart and Good.

And the Chairman and CEO Bob Ulrich is looking to answer the question: 'Do I want the company to be going in this direction?'

The budgets flow where the ideas are, and the best idea wins.

From their redefinition of value, Target's results are of course justly famous: over five years Target stores grew pre-tax profits almost 100%, from $1.3 billion to $2.5 billion – and this from a discount store (in 2001 54% of all the items Target promoted in print advertising cost under $10).

Now filling this room with 40–50 ideas every two weeks is a formidable task – the group of people underneath the two of them call keeping the ideas flowing through the room 'Feeding the Beast'. And most of us will not clearly require this quantity of ideas. But we will require a steady flow, we will have a beast we need to feed in order to maintain our momentum once we have it. So we will need to have our own, smaller-scale version of that room and that process.

And, of course, that desire.

Shunning the Conventions of Society

The bonfires and skinny dipping I will leave to you.

15

That Difficult First Year: Emotional Preparation

How do you make God laugh? Tell him your plans.

Old Jewish joke

The first year in creating the breakthrough is a long one, whether you are in a large company or on your own. These are the hardest days for a Challenger individual: others around you are overtly sceptical, and yet you need to have the confidence to make decisions and commit to spending precious resources and energy, without yet any bankable evidence that you are right. It can be very hard. A cold and lonely place.

So how does one slay the dragons of doubt during that difficult first year – in others and in yourself? How does one resist pressure from above and around to change or undesirably modify? What is the role of one's partners? Of design? Of research? Of involving other kinds of business partners earlier rather than later?

Accept It Will Be Difficult: Things Won't Go Quite to Plan

Knowing what one needs to do oneself is only a small part of making it happen, of course – there are so many other people to influence. And there is a slight temptation when one is within a large company to assume that things would be somehow easier if we were doing this on our own. If we had our own company, we think, we would be able to do *whatever we liked*. How much faster we could move . . .

It can be salutary to realize how infrequently in the real world, even for the more recent successes, this is true. Let us look at some of these so-called 'free' Challengers and the problems they faced.

Perhaps You Can't Source the Product

Sometimes the very first step on the journey turns out to be the hardest. Richard Reed of innocent:

> So we take our idea, and we go and speak to every single player in the juice market in the UK, from the smallest to the biggest, including really lofty companies such as Tetra Pak. And to a person they were incredibly helpful and pleasant and forthcoming. They'd go, 'OK, well, we've got some amazing new strawberry flavouring, we've got E38210, which you are going to have to use. It's brilliant, you know – it gives one of the best strawberry tastes on the market', and we're like, 'Well, actually we are going to just use strawberries.' And they would say, 'Yeah, but unfortunately it doesn't work like that. You don't understand.' And our answer was, 'Well, actually it's you that doesn't understand, because we've only got one idea. Our idea is to be the one company that makes completely natural fresh healthy drinks. So I know a concentrated juice is going to make it cheaper and is going to give us a bigger margin. I know it is going to extend the shelf life and therefore make for easier production logistics – but actually I'm drinking this thing myself, so I just want something that is made from strawberries and bananas. And that means, yes, we are going to have to make it every day; and that means, yes, we are going to have to hand select and buy fresh fruit every day; and that means, yes, we are going to have to bottle away at night and distribute it in the shops the following morning; and, yes, it is going to have a short shelf life; and, yes, it is going to be hard to sell; and, yes, it's going to be dah dah dah . . .'

Because they stuck to their idea and the underlying principle behind it, it took them nine months to find someone who could make their product the way they wanted it. And nine months was hard because they had financially anticipated it taking only one. By the end of the nine months paying the rent was the least of their issues – they were eating cereal three times a day because they had abandoned their day jobs and run out of money. Reed describes it as 'a very, very bleak period' in his life.

But those hard nine months were also an important part of their company's life – because out of that insistence on doing it the right way, rather than compromising, came their success: in no small part due to the recognized quality of that product, they now have a rate of sale of 3 to 1 in their favour against the historic market leader, in spite of a 30% premium. And although hard at the time, from that refusal to compromise or dilute their idea during the first nine months came a real strength and confidence later on:

> I guess each one of those times to go back to that original core thing and say 'No, *this* is what we are about', and not to compromise when there was everyone telling us to, and every sort of personal and business pressure encouraging us to do so . . . for me, that was such an incredibly good thing to have happened. To have actually come through it, and stuck with it, and to realize now, three years on, that the only reason why we are a success is because of that. At each one of those stages I guess we could have got confused, and thought, 'Well, actually the main thing is getting out to market.' But *actually* the main thing was about getting the drinks right – and everything else is going to have to wait until we get through it.

(Compare this to Dave Illingworth's remarks in Chapter 6 about the power of the Lexus Covenant only really kicking in when Lexus was tested.)

The Consumer Doesn't Seem to Agree with You

Even when the manifestation of your sense of the brand is coming together, there is the balance to strike in using what the consumer says to inform our decisions. We need confidence on the one hand (and to give confidence to those above us) – which can come from a warm consumer response – and yet we mustn't dilute a vision the consumer has yet to fully experience when we put incomplete pieces in front of them. So we saw earlier (in Chapter 8 on Refusing) that Lorenzo Fluxá had chosen to go with the name he felt was right, even though the groups chose something else.

But sometimes the setback is not that your desired consumer prefers a different *element* to the one you were thinking of before launch – it is that they apparently reject the entire idea. Charlotte Semler of Myla:

> We had this idea of creating a luxury sex brand aimed at women. It really just came from magazines, you know, looking at the cover lines on *Vogue*, *Elle*, *Cosmo*, *Marie Claire* – and they're all about sex. And it made us think that there were a huge number of women out there who were very interested in sex, and were very style and fashion conscious, and had quite a lot of disposable income. And once you've written those three bullet points, the rest is incredibly simple.

Well, it should have been. After nine months of rejections, they finally got backing late in 2000 – and shortly afterwards their first distribution point, which was to be the upmarket London department store Selfridges. Just before they launched in September 2001, and after they had finalized every aspect of the product range and marketing mix, they decided to put the packaging into research. The researcher was a friend of one of the founders, someone who understood the concept well, and the groups were recruited exactly on brief. Yet the results were not those a fledgling brand hopes for – and the consumers' issues went well beyond the packaging:

> It was specifically intended to be packaging research, but it came back trashing everything we'd ever said. And because of that it was too late to change the packaging as substantially as they were asking for.
>
> They [the consumers] wanted it to be boudoir: you know, they wanted velvet, and gold taps, and fluffiness and lace and all that stuff. They didn't want – they didn't understand – modern design and the kind of contemporary concept we were aiming for.

How did Semler react? With the gung-ho stoicism of the hardened entrepreneur?

Oh no, no, we were upset. I mean, particularly I was upset. I think Nina has more of a tendency to go 'Oh, fuck'em', but particularly because I came from a research background, I was like 'Oh, God.'

Yet it was too late to change anything – they had to hold true to their original vision.

And if the consumer seemed against them, so did world events – they launched their range and first store on the day that terrorists flew two planes into the Twin Towers, precipitating huge economic uncertainty and a cold retail climate. But two and a half years later they are a dynamic brand, expanding beyond the UK and the USA, and still successfully following the brand vision that the consumer groups rejected before they launched. Three years in, sales are still doubling every year.

However, all this is not to advocate a wilful ignorance of every input that comes our way; clearly, there are things one sometimes needs to hear in what the consumer says, and input one needs to incorporate: thus we saw Paula Moss responding to the poor response in her new packaging by recognizing that there were some historic visual equities that they had walked away from, and which the consumer still needed in order to recognize the brand they had known till then.

The point is the very obvious one that all good researchers and marketers always make, and one of those concepts that is known but rarely used – ultimately, decision-making in marketing, particularly when your brand is trying to do something new, is all about judgement. What makes such judgement particularly hard for a Challenger, who is trying to do something unproven in that difficult first year, is the sense of unbelieving scrutiny from those around you – and sometimes from those above.

Your Boss Has Other Plans

Of course, your superiors often have a keen interest in the project, and are keen to offer their own views – which don't always coincide with your own. Chris Moss, the Marketing Director of a new mobile communications company owned by Hutchison, used a consultancy to help develop a positioning and a range of possible names for the new venture. In the end, they narrowed them down to a choice of two names – Microtel or Orange. Hutchison and indeed Moss's CEO were very much for Microtel: they knew from consumers that it at once signalled it was a communications company, but also cued convenience and modernity through the 'Micro' prefix (and we should bear in mind that this was at a time when cell phones were the size of bricks). But Moss believed that if they were really to aspire to be more than just a follower, they needed the courage to adopt a name that genuinely cued a whole new set of values in their chosen market. Against the initial wishes of his CEO, the board and the parent of the new company, he fought for Orange. In this case, stubborn conviction in one's vision wasn't all that was called for – he needed to think laterally as well. When the legal people told him that he couldn't register Orange as a trademark, he asked why; they replied that one couldn't trademark a colour. At which point, I suspect, most of us would have stopped – we've researched it, we've fought for it, and in the end we just couldn't register the damn thing. Fate was against us. But Moss didn't stop. He asked if, in that case, they could register it as a fruit. The legal people went away and explored it – and found the precedent in Apple. Orange was registered – and a whole new telecommunications brand was launched.

Compare this to the story of Mr Ishizaka proposing that Project F become a new luxury car brand rather than a flagship model for Toyota. Both these now iconic brands owe a key part of their success to the stubborn vision of a key individual at a pivotal stage in their development. What would the new company's fortunes have been if it had been named Microtel? With exactly the same people at the helm? Would it have changed the way telecommunications companies thought and marketed themselves? I'm sure your view is the same as mine.

Critical to this kind of ability to push for some aspect of the brand one believes in, even if it appears to run up against the view of one's superiors at key moments, is in fact understanding one's consumer much better than the other person – think of Kristin Krumpe and her 'intimidating' understanding of her consumer, even to those above her. This is *informed* judgement, not simply blind vision.

And Moss, interestingly, comments that this need to be able to push back when one meets the word 'No' from above reframes what it means to be a good CEO or boss as much as a good employee. A key characteristic of a good boss, he suggests, is not necessarily that they recognize a great idea straight away, but that once they have been persuaded it is a good idea, they are able to support it as vociferously as they once argued against it.

Your Government Has Other Plans

In launching into his first important market, Australia, Merrill Fernando of Dilmah was told by the Australian retailer he was trying to persuade to carry Dilmah that the Australian consumer did not need another tea:

> When I first saw Coles in Australia, which is the biggest chain there, and talked them into (or tried to talk them into) stocking my Dilmah tea, they said, 'Merrill, you have no chance, because the big boys know what the consumer wants and that is what is on the shelf. Consumers don't want any new brands on the shelf because they are very happy with what is on the shelf now.' So I told him, 'I do not agree with you, pardon me, but the consumer or the consumer's option is restricted to what is on the shelf and what is on the shelf is what the *brand owner* thinks is what he should give the consumer, making certain that he enjoys his generous margin of profit.' He said 'No, no, no', he wouldn't agree with me.

Fernando just had to keep going back and back, convinced of the quality of his tea, and that the Australian consumer would want it if they just got the chance to try it: 'Finally, after about a year, he agreed to put two packets of Dilmah tea on the shelf . . .'.

The trade resistance you can prepare for – though it demands the kind of persuasive tenacity that Fernando demonstrated. What is harder to find your way through is even being discouraged by your own government from pursuing this ambition. Fernando again:

> I was the fourth largest exporter of bulk tea [in Sri Lanka], but I realized that bulk tea had really no future, because my own customers all over the world moved away from Ceylon tea to other cheaper sources of tea. So I knew before long I would not have a substantial business, and I decided that I would go into value-added tea exports. That's how it started, and

even my old importers and importers in different countries of bulk tea and packers didn't even want to recognize me, didn't want to know me. And all those incidents and experiences made me more and more bitter, until I realized that my mission must be fulfilled one way or the other. And that is what gave me so much determination towards success.

And in my own country, the tea trade people, other people in the trade, were against me. And our own government was very worried, thinking that the big boys would stop buying Ceylon tea because we are now exporting value-added, finished product. In fact, representations were made from the major buyers and they came to say, 'You should not start exporting value-added teas, you are competing with us' and I had to meet and pacify our own government to say I was doing the right thing, 'Let me do it my way all alone'... But they discouraged me and they were concerned.

As he says, it made him bitter – yet he managed to turn that negative emotion into a positive determination, and one that gave him the tenacity to fight through a number of key obstacles over a long period of time.

And Then Someone Starts Laughing at You

So things are not going your way. So what you really need now is some cast iron support from those you know and respect to nurse you through. But what in fact you get at best is lack of encouragement and a disappointing commitment in those around you. And at worst – well, laughter is not as unusual as one might think.

Michael Kuhn, the former head of Polygram, was responsible for greenlighting every movie Polygram made on his watch. Some of them were easy to approve, some less so – and one of the latter was *Being John Malkovich*. This is Kuhn's version of how the team behind the film made the original pitch to him:

This is about a young guy who is an unemployed puppeteer. His wife is nuts, likes monkeys and is also unemployed. The hero gets a job as a filing clerk in an office that is only half a floor high. He finds a hole in the wall, which leads to John Malkovich's head. He then exits on the Jersey turnpike.[1]

For some reason Kuhn is underwhelmed by this as an idea for a film, but procrastinates on his decision by making various demands of the prospective filmmakers – all of which demands they inconveniently proceed to meet. Eventually, in a bid to clinch the funding, the producer invites Kuhn to a 'wonderful' (his words) house deep in Mexico and, several margaritas into a party, finally persuades Kuhn to agree to do the movie.

Kuhn goes on to describe an encounter shortly afterwards with one of the lead actors who had been cast in this movie, behind which he has just put millions of dollars:

> Filming was underway. I attended the Toronto Film Festival and there was an airline strike, which meant that someone had to hire a jet to get stars in and out of Toronto. I hitched a lift on one of the planes going back to Los Angeles. On board was Cameron Diaz. During the course of the trip she discovered that I was putting up the money for *Being John Malkovich*, which she was returning to Los Angeles to film. She broke up with laughter at the thought that anyone would finance this film.[2]

Kuhn goes on, laconically: 'It did not inspire confidence in me.'[3]

For those that find the film world too distant from their own jobs, consider the story of Chris Hawken at Skoda, a European car marque with a historically calamitous reputation for build quality and reliability. Skoda had a poor reputation even within its parent, the VW group, where it was apparently known as 'the big green chicken brand' after the bird that made up its logo.[4] Just after signing up for the Skoda job in 1988 in the UK (their third largest market, and where the image problem was most acute), Hawken went to a reunion of old university friends:

> We were all in a French farmhouse, baby monitors hissing away. Toward the end of the evening, when everyone was a bit pissed, I announced that I was going to Skoda. They just fell off their chairs with laughter.[5]

Of course, the fact that other people laugh at you is not in itself a sure-fire guarantee that you are onto a brilliant idea. And however confident you are, however much you try to buttress your self-belief, you will always have moments when the questioning of others gets to you, when your outer walls are breached by that faint suggestion that there is always the possibility that they may be right.

So although one has one's own fierce belief, there are always moments of doubt. So how do you give yourself the best chance of being strong? How do we find that confidence again when you find yourself starting to waver?

In Hawken's case it was in assembling a great team around him – particularly his new advertising agency:

> I think if you met the people, if you met the team that we have at [the agency], you can really have confidence when you're working with people like that. I met some people who I just thought, 'Blimey, it's got some brilliant people here, who are really going to sort it out.' When you are working with people like that you can really have great confidence, I think.

We should remember that in order to get this team in place, he had to fight to fire the previous aligned agency, in difficult circumstances, against the wishes of a European Head whom he thus alienated, and in doing so got himself banned from the Skoda Marketing Communications Council. He fought for the team that would give him the work – and the confidence – to make the difference the brand needed. And they made that difference: sales rose 64% in the following two years.

Equally interesting is that it is the *people* Hawken is drawing confidence from here rather than the insight or the strategy or the initial work per se, all of which had yet to be developed. Indeed, when the initial creative work arrived, he was at first disappointed in it – though it later turned out to be the work that ran and began to turn the brand around.

Sources of Strength

So what are the sources of strength running through the above examples during That Difficult First Year? We see in these stories and those like them a number of commonalities:

- The critical importance of a very clearly understood idea: a brand centre, sense of purpose (as with Dilmah). Something that one believes strongly in, and acts as a touchstone for decisions – and getting this right is more important than hitting a launch date (as with innocent). Sometimes this brand vision expressed in something concrete, like the Lexus Covenant.

- A sense of tenacity and bloody-mindedness. Persuasive and inventive tenacity, but tenacity all the same.
- An ability to use things being against you positively – look at Merrill Fernando using his bitterness to fuel his determination.
- An ability to draw strength from having been through the fire – Scott Lutz commenting on a Denter getting their rigidity from being dented back.
- Surrounding yourself with great people (Skoda).
- By no means last, an absolute confidence that one has the product the consumer will really appreciate (Dave Illingworth's confidence in the quality of the Lexus LS 400, for instance).

Finding the Moment of Personal Belief

These sources of strength need to be enough to keep you going until that moment when you have found the moment of personal belief and confidence and broken through to (in the words of Richard Reed) 'the sunlit uplands'.

'They Bought it!'

Eventually, the first ever batch of innocent smoothies was produced – this product that had taken them so much time and emotional energy to bring to life. And precisely because the juice was so pure and fresh, time was naturally very critical – as soon as they got the product, a countdown of eight days began before it went off; after that eight days it would be worth nothing at all. So one might imagine that, as soon as this precious first batch of product came in, the three founders would be sprinting for the van, gunning the engine and working out how many potential distributors they could hit by close of play.

But in reality something very different happened. Because what the three of them emotionally needed to know now above all at this point, after all this effort, was whether the stuff would sell: would, in effect, their idea and business model work? They knew people liked the product, and they knew the packaging was good – but would people actually notice it on a shelf? Would they pick it up and pay a premium price for it?

'We were just petrified.'

So what they did was invent a small-scale test market of their own. There was a man in the office complex they were renting who ran a sandwich shop called 'Out to Lunch'. On the Thursday morning, they gave him 24 bottles free, on the condition that he sold it over the next 24 hours in his shop at a certain price. He agreed – hell, it was free.

For the next day and a half the three of them sat around waiting. They knew the clock was running down on the rest of those 376 bottles in their precious first batch, but they found themselves unable to do anything until they knew whether it had worked in Out to Lunch. Finally, on the evening of the following day, the three of them went to see how many of the bottles were still left in the fridge in the sandwich shop. They had written a business plan based on the projection that each outlet would sell 4 units per day – how many of those 24 would Out to Lunch have sold?

> If you ever go to this place called Out to Lunch, it's in an old bus depot. The windows are really high and you can't see in, so we got these old bread crates and piled them up and so we were like little kids trying to see into a football match, peering in to see if any bottles had been sold ... And [we see] there are only 4 left out of the 24 – so in a day and a half we had sold 20. So, you know, that just reduces the paranoia slightly. You think, 'OK, we've at least sold 20 bottles ... we've got the business off the ground, we've sold 20 bottles'... It's amazing what confidence that gave us: 'We sold some, we've got the money, somebody has bought them.'

And it was only then that they did leap into the van and gun the engine, confident that it worked.

Energy from the Internal Consumer

The physical development of the Discover 2GO ® key chain credit card took many difficult years. At one critical point David Nelms was forced to take the cross-functional team off the job and assign them to another project, as the initial prototyping that they were trying earlier came to an end. The prototype had thrown up a further problem – the keys the card was attached to scratched the card and the magnetic stripe: they had yet another obstacle they were going to have to overcome. But in this potentially awkward hiatus for the project, Nelms had a pleasant surprise from one of his 'guinea pigs' – when he asked his own wife to hand back the prototype card, she refused to give it to him: she loved the convenience and the effect it had when she used it in store. Shortly afterwards Nelms assigned a fresh team, they found a way to sheath the card in a protective cover, and the Discover 2GO ® key chain card was launched. Within two years of launch, it was in millions of consumers' pockets and bags; the first real innovation in physical credit cards since the magnetic stripe.

The First Signs that the External Consumer is Pleased to See You

Merrill Fernando of Dilmah, on what happened when Coles finally agreed to stock his product after a year of Fernando pestering him:

> So finally … he took in two of my products. Lipton's market share was then about 45%, the market leader, and their price was $1.99 for 100 bags. So I said I want to price my tea 100 bags at $2.19 because my quality is far better. That day, they wouldn't hear of a new product coming above the market leader, so I tried to talk him into it. He said 'No, you have to accept the market leader is the best tea.' I said, 'It's not so', but he wouldn't take this so I said, 'All right, I'll price my tea at $1.89.' Then within three, four months, Lipton's on promotion brought their price down to $1.49 … that was intended to kill my business. So when I talked to the buyer I told him, 'Well, the game is up.' But he said: 'Merrill, you're lucky.' I said 'Why?' 'The number of phone calls and letters we have received from our customers, thanking us and thanking Dilmah for bringing Ceylon tea back to the shelves,' he said, 'is unbelievable.'
>
> That is why [he kept us on], and I thank him very much for giving the consumer that opportunity. And that was the turning point in my commitment. Then I got stronger, and I knew that my dream about

marketing my own brand of tea was, in fact, because I had Ceylon tea in my hand, and I was right.

All of these are moments of personal breakthrough drawn from some kind of consumer reaction, but none of them are formal evaluative testing in research, though that was also part of the process in the development of Discover Card, for example. And it is not to suggest that the moment of recognition when one sees the first ad, or piece of packaging is also not enormously powerful and sustaining; the point is that as a human, rather than a marketing machine, you will not necessarily find that source of emotional energy in the usual places. Draw your strength from whatever works for you; that they seem unusual to others is irrelevant if it gives you the confidence and energy to push on.

Feeding the Belief, and the Value of the Team

You may need sources of strength even after the first year: sometimes it is hard to see the progress you have made. These sources of strength often have a more talismanic nature to them.

Scott Lutz was an officer of General Mills, who had a considerable track record in Innovation. But the efforts of launching 8th Continent, of denting and being dented, led to moments of gloom and doubt. The following is from an email Lutz sent me, containing a note that was sent to him by one of the people who was part of his team, and which provided a touchstone for him in moments of darkness:

> Attached is the note from Kymm Pollack, a young manager who was an early employee of 8th Continent. As I told you, when things got dark for me, I would read this note, as she had instructed me to do, and I would be recharged. I think this is a great example of how a more open leadership style can result in more of a 2-way relationship – very key in stressful start-up situations.

Dear Scott

Now that I'm officially off the Continent, I can look back and realize just how far we managed to come. I'm amazed and humbled by what the team accomplished. Although the jury may still be out on whether or not the world will credit 8th Continent as a success, I can say that for the 20 or so people on our team who made it happen the experience remains 'once in a lifetime.'

How often can anyone claim a 'once in a lifetime' experience? I hope you remember this statement in your darkest days when you despair about the future of innovation. Or that you have yet to make your mark on the world. The fact that you created an environment that touched and changed many lives for the better is an extraordinary, 'once in a lifetime' accomplishment. You envisioned it, nurtured it, allowed others to leave their mark on it.

I hope you take out and re-read this letter every time the going gets tough. I hope you remember the lessons of 8th Continent. In my mind these are:

It's the little things that make a difference. This counts for drinking soy milk and it counts for touching lives. Each person who worked to found 8th Continent was changed in some fundamental, positive way, by his or her own admission. Some examples:

- Several people made significant improvements in their personal health, from losing weight to more regular exercise.
- Some people connected *for the first time* with feeling passion for their work.
- Many people took time to look inside themselves and ask in which direction they are heading. I think we'll see the results of these introspections in the coming months.
- Many people forged bonds with team members that will last a lifetime.
- Many found courage to stand up for something they believed in.

In my own life, here are some of my accomplishments thanks to you and the Continent:

- I have a leadership map. I can articulate my leadership philosophy.
- I can recognize and build consumer intimacy.
- I have learned to function – even thrive – in an ambiguous environment.
- I understand my gifts and my core purpose.
- I can recite every word from Chapter 11 of 'Built to Last' from memory. (Just kidding . . . but I'm probably close.)

None of the above is trivial. This is why you can never say out loud that you are discouraged by the legacy of 8th Continent, whatever the share number.

8th Continent's true legacy will not be known for a long time. Each person, each life that leaves transformed or even just slightly changed, will take a piece of 8th Continent into the world with them. It's the 'Pay it Forward' model. The acorns you have planted need time to grow. In time, I think you will be very proud of your 'Forest.'

And the second major lesson of 8th Continent . . .

It's the journey, not the destination. As our consumers and Ann Bancroft know, glory and satisfaction lie in taking steps toward reaching a goal, regardless of whether or not that goal is achieved. How many times did we repeat that? It's Bob and Rita sacrificing the candy that has nothing to do with increasing cholesterol, but they feel better anyway because they're taking action. Remember this as you evaluate 8th Continent – and your – success against the achievement of 'guaranteeing the future of innovation.' Core purpose is a guiding star, never meant to be fully achieved. I have no doubt in my mind that you are making *significant* inroads toward this core purpose. You ooze this from your pores. It's in the air around you. You are on the right path.

You are perhaps one of the most courageous people that I have ever known. I have never met someone who goes after and embraces new ideas and new ways of thinking the way you do. I have never worked with someone so committed to changing the world. Your courage and passion are the foundation of 8th Continent, the experience that touched so many. I hope you realize what a gift you've given us all in the creation of the Continent. I hope you realize the role you've played as the catalyst for so many positive changes in people's lives.

I look forward to serving as a member of your board of directors and keeping you honest!

Figure 15.1 Reproduced by permission of Kymm Bartlett Pollack

Pollack's emotional generosity here responds to the personal commitment Lutz has put into the brand and his team. She understands that even a passionate and outwardly confident team leader needs strength and encouragement to fuel them, and that they may well not get it from those above them. Lutz's emphasis at the beginning on the value (and importance) of a two-way relationship in this kind of venture is a deeper insight into the value of hunting as a pack – not simply are we putting a united set of shoulders to the door, but we are recognizing that during the stress of the journey there will be times when each of the team, including the leader, will need recharging. And it becomes each member of the team's responsibility to watch for and help deliver that.

Again, this is about more than professionalism, and doing a good job. It is about 'taking it personally', and recognizing that others are – and will – as well. I had a client who used to remind me that 'we are human beings, not human doings'. Even if the organization sometimes may forget that, the team should not.

Courage – Its Importance and Its Limitations

Peter Drucker observed that whenever one saw a successful business, someone there had once made a courageous decision. And while it may seem strange to some to talk about a concept like courage in the world of marketing (nobody is dying here, and there are plenty of people in other jobs who do require real courage every day to get from one end of it to the other), nevertheless there will be key moments along the journey which will of course take courage.

It may be in fighting for the initial concept, like Mr Ishizaka of Lexus, who made a recommendation even though he believed it could endanger his career. It may be an act of faith in implementation – like the launch team at Orange, who went ahead with launching the brand in 1994 without a billings system able to collect the money from their customers at the end of the month. They needed to hit a launch date and Richard Brennan, the IT Director, committed to completing the billings system within the month that followed – while the launched company was already letting customers use the service. This must have taken enormous courage from him, and courage from those around and above him: if he and they had failed, it would have been disastrous for the business.

And there are some brands who actively promote courage as a specific virtue in everyone who works on them. Just beyond the reception of

Diesel Industries, the denim and fashion clothing brand, is a wall bearing a large bas-relief of a Mohican Head. Above and below the head are written the words 'Only the Brave'. You cannot enter a lift, or walk through to the ground floor of the main building without passing this image. Somehow, in Diesel, it does not seem glib. Here is a company that has a history of brave decisions, and that is effectively reinventing itself twice a year in products and advertising.

There's a thin line between courage and stupidity, of course, and the mere possession of courage, while necessary for a Pirate, is not enough. But it is necessary, and we need to understand ourselves, our team and our brand in order to know where we are going to find it during That Difficult First Year.

Conclusions – Of a Sort

In 1996 I saw Oliver Stone being interviewed on the US show *Charlie Rose*. Stone had recently finished making the movie *Nixon*, and Charlie Rose asked him (in effect) what on earth had possessed him to make a movie about the disgraced US President. Stone's answer was very simple: he wanted, he said, to let people just walk with Nixon for a while.

I hope there are different kinds of uses for this book – some will find the stories stimulating, others will be interested in the aspects of personal behaviour, and others will want to focus on the practicalities of establishing a Challenger Brand culture within their organization (writing a set of Articles, for example).

But this chapter will probably be the most polarizing. Some readers will find it frustrating – where are the practical steps to draw on, they will ask? Particularly for my journey within Behemoth, Inc? But others, I hope, will draw a different kind of sustenance from it, and perhaps not an immediate one: the sustenance of simply having walked a little with some of these Challengers in That Difficult First Year, and knowing they went through some of the highs and lows that you will go through, or perhaps are going through. And in that respect, at least, it will have a value of its own, and one to come back to.

The Future of Piracy

Part V will conclude the book by offering a view on what kinds of organization 'licensed Piracy', in the sense we have been talking about it, would be important for, and indeed the stage in their development at which they should be thinking about encouraging it. It will close with a reflection on the nature on the personal choice facing an individual who wants to risk being a Pirate, and the kind of individual for whom that decision will and will not suit.

Chapter 16   Pirates, Privateers and the Emergence of the BSC

This chapter looks at the future for Piracy. It begins by arguing why certain kinds of large organizations should be deliberately moving to being a cradle of 'licensed Pirates', in the form of promoting brand-centric subcultures, and closes the book by looking at what kinds of individual the life of a Pirate or Challenger is and is not suitable for, particularly when they find themselves within a large organization.

16

Pirates, Privateers and the Emergence of the BSC

> A privateer was an armed vessel, or the commander and crew of that vessel, which was licensed to attack and seize the vessels of a hostile nation ... The privateer captain was expected to keep a journal and to hand over all ships and goods seized to an Admiralty court to be assessed and valued. A proportion went to the sovereign, the rest went to the ship's owners, her captain and crew. In theory an authorized privateer was recognized by international law and could not be prosecuted for piracy, but ... privateers were often no more than licensed pirates.
>
> *David Cordingley*[1]

We said at the beginning that what this book is really about is Necessary Pirates. They do not need a licence if they are running their own company (though they often seem to market themselves as though they have a commission from the consumer). But they do need a licence – and should be given one if there is a strong case to be made – if they have a corporate parent. And the role of Part III of the book has been to lay out how it is possible to be a Challenger within large organizations, and how to make the case for that licence to the admirals who have it in their power to grant one.

We have also started to explore the idea that the intelligent use of 'Brand subcultures' is also the source of revitalization for the broader culture for large, multi-brand companies, and in this final chapter we will play out this idea to a conclusion. In this sense, then, Piracy can be regarded as potentially 'necessary' for *both* sides: for one side as the only way to realize the specific brand opportunity, and for the other as the only way to make quantum jumps in the way they think about building more powerful consumer relationships through marketing or communications.

But before we explore the idea of the progression of large multi-brand companies, it would be worth first taking stock of some of the key conclusions and arguments so far:

(i)   Brands – and particularly Challenger brands – are built primarily by people and the qualities they display. Not just in famous single brand companies where the founder is sovereign, but in any organization, by every marketing person. The behaviour and personal qualities in what they push for and against (obviously provided they already have a sound knowledge of marketing principles) are what makes the real difference. While some powerful work has been done by respected academics in building disciplined structures for understanding and developing brands, such structures walk past the point that Bill Bernbach made 40 years ago – that the fortune of brands, like ideas, depends entirely on the quality of the people that rub up against them, and the qualities they choose to display in managing those brands and ideas.

(ii) If we are a Necessary Pirate, there seem to be nine of these key personal qualities and behaviours concerning the relationship between ourselves, our brand and our company which we need to foster. These are:
      Behaviours
      • Outlooking – A Different Kind of Insight Seeking
      • Pushing – A Different Kind of Approval
      • Projecting – A Different Kind of Consistency
      • Wrapping – A Different Kind of Communication
      Personal Qualities
      • Denting – A Different Kind of Respect
      • Binding – A Different Kind of Contract
      • Leaning – A Different Kind of Commitment
      • Refusing – A Different kind of Passion
      • Taking It Personally – A Different Kind of Professionalism

And finally. . ..
- Brand-centricity

(iii) The only focus for the application of these qualities and behaviours is the specific nature of our brand's vision and opportunity; it is not our own political ambitions, or a random desire to be different for different's sake.

(iv) Pursuing this brand vision and opportunity means that we may well have to do things differently from the way other people in the category are doing them, from the way other people in the company are doing them, and indeed from the way things have been done in the past. In this sense, we are a 'Necessary Pirate' (rather than a Vanity Pirate) – our success depends on behaving in this way.

(v) There is much that we can learn from those that have passed this way before. Being such a Pirate is not the same as being an anarchist: it does not mean tearing up the rulebook, but invoking a different kind of rulebook – for ourselves, our team and the way we interact knowingly with the parent organization if we have one. In this regard, we will not be throwing aside a respect for Insight, or Rigour, or the resources of the parent company – we will simply be evidencing and drawing on them in a different kind of way.

(vi) Allowing brand-centred subcultures within a larger corporate culture – although apparently counterintuitive, might in fact be regarded as the only correct way to maximize shareholder value. Because it optimizes the chance of the brand delivering against its identified opportunity, and it creates a group of highly motivated people driven by what is right for the brand. As such, it is, in fact, the only responsible framework to build for the future.

(vii) Recognizing the importance of allowing such subcultures to flourish around brands is the last big marketing and brand jump that organizations have to make: a cultural jump. A recognition that Brand Culture is something to be fostered and invested in.

While apparently straightforward, this line of thinking has some important implications, particularly if we turn our telescope around, and look at what it means from the point of view of the corporation looking down on its brand portfolio, rather than the brand looking up at the parent. How do marketing-led companies progress, and where does or should this fit into their future?

The Progression of Marketing-led Companies, and the Emergence of the BSC

Being a Challenger is essentially a matter of mindset, rather than size or environment. And in the past I used to talk rather polemically of how in the future there would be only two kinds of companies – Challengers, and what the West Coast of America at one point called rather charmingly 'BDCs': Big Dumb Companies. And the first decision we had to make, I used to say, is which of these we wanted to be.

But what the line of argument we have been pursuing suggests is that in reality for large multi-brand companies this was a wilfully simplistic distinction. Small is not necessarily good – the dot com boom showed that dumbnessm need not be solely the province of the Big Company; there were (and are) many Small Dumb Companies as well, it just takes less time for them to disappear. So my question may have worked as rhetoric, but the desired drama masked a more interesting development that lay between the two choices.

Because in reality many multi-brand companies actually need to go through 'the Navy Phase'; it is a necessary stage of their evolution. The reason is that they have a host of brand and marketing people in a variety of geographies and markets, each doing their own thing without enough discipline or structure, and the result is the tide of mediocrity we see on our television screens and in the newspapers on our breakfast tables all around us. So organizations do have to raise the standard of their marketing output, and that only comes from imposing some discipline through the enforcement of common ways of doing things, and an emphasis on methodologies and templates as a way of ensuring that this discipline has been gone through.[2]

What I am suggesting, though, is that this raising of the standards is an interim step, rather than a final destination, for such a company. That there are in fact four stages such companies need to think of themselves as going through as they progress.

Phase 1: Freebooting

Characteristics: No model. Undisciplined individualism

This phase represents the 'Bad Old Days'. In this phase, every brand group does its own thing in its own market, and frequently without real knowledge of the consumer, or indeed very much discipline in the way they develop insight, strategy or communications. In this phase, marketing is very hit or miss; there is the occasional runaway success, but it is very random. Communications are blunt.

Many pharmaceutical companies, one could argue, are just starting to emerge from this phase now.

Phase 2: The Navy

Characteristics: One benchmarked model. An emphasis on consumer under-standing, discipline and rigour. One size fits all.

Many FMCG companies have moved into this phase by now. By developing a set of models, methodologies and processes for each stage of the process (with appropriate gatekeepers) they are reducing overall wastage, and increasing the overall efficiency of money spent. Certainly they have fewer disasters (and perhaps fewer runaway successes). More focus is given to understanding the consumer.

A 'command and control' model, encouraged by globalization, can drift into over-processing.

Phase 3: The Navy, Plus Selected Privateers

Characteristics: One model, plus selected exceptions. In these exceptions, emphasis is often on youth or upscale targets. Some transference of learning from this exception within the rest of organization, particularly if they have been initiated or championed at some point by senior management.

Some companies in this phase are starting to have at least one licensed exception within their portfolio. Usually it is an acquisition, or sometimes an experiment to try to reach a young or upscale target market that resists mass marketing the way the company does it on the rest of their brands. It is not often a global brand – usually it has started as a local 'Pirate', whose very local nature has allowed it to escape the scrutiny of large rooms until it had a proven mix, and its success brought it a wider notice.

The 'different' brand will, like some of those we have looked at, often have an internal brand culture that differs from those around it. The nature of its 'difference' from the rest of the organization will vary. In some cases, it will be the communications and research models alone (as with Axe); in some cases it will be the Business Model (Hovis moving away from price promotion to a nourished brand again); at its most ambitious it will be Communications, Business and Sales Model (OK Soda, perhaps Kiehl's).

This brand, though relatively small, will have unduly high salience, and even Thought Leadership within the company as a whole. It thus may well feature in the CEO's speeches, and PR to Wall Street. The 'jury' of other managers within the larger company, however, may well be out on how much one can learn from this 'different way of doing things'. Some of these managers may be actively critical.

(Note: Movement through these four phases is not one-way. Some of the companies in Phase 3 will have a setback on their hands, such as that of Saturn within GM, which may have encouraged the rest of the organization to retreat back to Phase 2. Others, conversely, will have a number of managers encouraged by the success of selective subcultures and looking for experimentation on their own brands, effectively moving forward to Phase 4.)

Phase 4: The BSC (Big Smart Company)

Characteristics: Different, coherent 'bilingual' models for different brand opportunities. An emphasis on differentiated internal brand cultures as well as differentiated consumer marketing. A sharing of, and profiting from, learning across brands.

In this phase, marketing-led companies have moved to a model where each brand is in effect a 'Republic' within the whole – having its own model, and its internal own culture, supported by the resources of the parent.

Since this is a new concept, let us unpack the benefits and difficulties of this phase for a large organization a little more.

The BSC: A New Era for Marketing-led Companies

A BSC is a multi-brand company which accepts that to genuinely deliver the real opportunity for the brand (and therefore the optimum financial return to the shareholder), the brand has to be allowed its own culture within the organization. That recognizes that this culture will therefore effectively be a subculture distinct from that of the parent, with its own model of how to get to market and how to behave internally. Not all of the subcultures will be radically different from each other, but just because they are in the same category does not necessarily mean they will be close.

The BSC might, in effect, look like this (Fig 16.1):

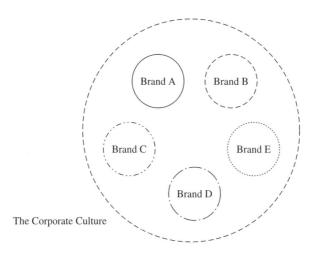

Figure 16.1   **BSC Inc.**

Here every brand has, in effect, its own model. How different they are from each other, in terms of the 'Communications Model/Business Model/Sales Model' range we looked at above, will vary according to their situation and needs.

How would life be different within a BSC? Let's play out how these five brands might differ from one another and what implications being part of a BSC might have for a number of different disciplines.

HR/Career Management

A BSC will need to rethink how it manages career paths. Just because I have done a great job on Brand A (which is all about female empathy) does not mean I am right for Brand B. Brand B is about passion and brio and, while I have many good personal qualities, those are not my most obvious ones. And the career path will not be left solely to the benign powers on high in HR: the team on Brand B will have the right to expose me to whatever their 'trampoline' is – and if I don't seem right for the group, I will not (and should not) get on the brand.

Instead of the career structure automatically progressing towards general management, the BSC recognizes that one can advance to a very high level within the company by staying within one's discipline (in particular Marketing/Branding).

Research

We will almost certainly need more than one model. Brand D, a youth brand which relies on high production values in its finished commercials, may not want to evaluate its emerging ideas in the same way (or at the same stage) as Brand C, a TV brand with a straightforward product advantage to communicate. And both of these will be different from the PR-seeking activities of our Challenger value detergent, Brand B.

Trade Marketing

While we cannot have an entirely different trade team for each brand, there will be times in particular brands' lives when we need to create our own Bentleys and caravans. Make them sit up and understand what makes this brand – and this brand opportunity – different and special, and not just another brand for the shelves from Behemoth, Inc.

Packaging

We are used to maximizing packaging efficiencies across all our brands. But Brand E, which is going to seed itself and grow based on the idea of the consumer 'discovering it' for themselves, is going to model itself on innocent, and use packaging as its primary medium of communication. It is going to change pack copy every two months, and have three versions in market at any one time. We will need to think entirely differently about how we cost this, and what 'efficiency' means for this kind of packaging; it may also have implications for different ways we are going to distribute our marketing funds between packaging and advertising.

Perhaps 'plate change' costs for packaging come to be seen like 'production costs' for advertising–something that should fall under the remit of marketing budgets, rather than operations. This would considerably facilitate the deployment of packaging as the marketing tool it has the potential to be.

Legal Department

They will need to be closely involved with everything Brand B does – it is going to sail very close to the wind to generate buzz, and it needs to feel the legal department is on its side. A Smokejumper may well be important in brokering some of these decisions.

Innovation

Brand C, a long-established brand, whose core category consumers now think is tired and dull – the choice of a previous generation – is going to look at dramatically recasting its core product icons for a limited period every year before withdrawing them, much like Burberry does with its iconic trench coat. Its objective is to get people to rethink products they had thought they knew all too well. Brand D, on the other hand, is a recently introduced brand which needs to be a Thought Leader in its categories to compete with three very strong existing players; it is therefore going to push five entirely new innovations through in the next three years. By pushing the boundaries of how the consumer thinks about the category, it will have a higher degree of risk attached to it, and it will accept that it will have a failure rate as a part of this innovation strategy because there will not be 'copper-bottomed' ways of being sure of success before one launches. But this will not slow it down or stop it innovating in this way.

Communications

Brand D is going to be a Fame brand, accept the challenge of 'Madison and Vine', and move the majority of its marketing budget into a much more embedded relationship with entertainment content. As such, it will need a completely different kind of business partner from Brand E, our discovery brand, which will need partners who can help it seduce and entice.

Environment

Each subculture would be encouraged to manifest that culture in the nature of its working environment. Currently if one walks down a corridor in most multi-brand companies, and someone had taken away the packaging and products out on display, one could be walking through a firm of lawyers for all the difference that is visible between one brand team and the next. In a BSC these cultures would be 'their own countries', and the colours and artefacts and noise and people reflecting this would be immediately apparent, if not striking. This lack of physical and cultural uniformity would be actively encouraged by the parent, as further fuelling the team's personal pride in, and connection to, the brand.

Brand Definition + Discipline

Although not strictly a department, we should note one other important distinction about the way the information on the brand was formalized. Whether one uses Pyramids or Bullseyes to formalize one's brand values, the existing frameworks are only currently capturing *what* the brand is about. They are not capturing *how* the brand and the brand team need to behave to realize that sense of the brand, nor are they capturing an aspiration towards the richer textures of 'being our own country' – to the consumer or internally. Insofar as they can, such structures would evolve to capture both these additional imperatives.

There would, however, still be a real rigour and discipline in the way brand development was approached—even if 'one size fits all' processes no longer dominate. Consumer intimacy is still paramount, and the key brand development questions are asked and answered. There is an emphasis on judgement, and an emotion-based vision, but it is informed judgement, and a strategically powerful vision. This is not Freebooting.

And so on; one could clearly tease out more. The point about all of these is that besides being individually right in order to really help drive the brand, they also have the ability to create leaps of learning for the company of better ways of going to market. One looks at the success of

Mini in the USA through a variety of highly visible and well publicized ideas, using every media but television, and one cannot but believe that at the top of BMW they are sitting down and looking at how to try some of that model on some of their other launches.

What remains in the BSC, then, of the corporate culture? Well, of course, moving to a BSC may not mean complete slash and burn – there may be certain accounting procedures one retains across all brands, for instance, and clearly there are efficiencies in production and sales to be discussed. But in the main, it means looking for a new kind of balance between what companies have historically been good at, and what they need to become good at. I sent a paper on the topic of Brand Subcultures early in its life to David Fong, an ex-adman and colleague of mine when he was based in Singapore, and who now runs his own business. He sent back the following, talking about just this balance:

> The problem for large corporations with the idea of a subculture is that no one really addresses how the two co-exist productively. The tendency is for one to tolerate and/or eventually subsume the other.
>
> Coming from the brand ethos side we tend to see and hope (explicitly or implicitly) that the Brand Subcultures become the igniters of total organization change. Moreover we believe that this cultural change is powerful for the health and future of the business.
>
> However, I question this. I think that organizations need *two* types of forces to be successful.
>
> One force is Brand Subcultures because of the quantum leaps they are capable of creating.
>
> The other force, however, is equally vital and that is the ability to extract full incremental value out of a brand. This requires resources, structure and talent to be able to lower costs, fight for dominance in channels, build growth through line extensions, etc. When you look at the extractive ability of Unilever, Nestlé, P&G, you can't knock their ability to wring full incremental value out of their brands. With the Apples of this world it's where the wheels start to wobble.
>
> The conflict between the two forces is obviously grounded in their different disciplines. The former live in the world of conceptual thought, the latter in the world of prescriptive action. I wonder if the evolution for marketing is to understand that with the speed of change and the ferocity of competition organizations need to be capable of morphing

between 'yin and yang' (the ability to extract incremental value and the ability to create quantum value) at any moment. If this is accepted, then the issue is to find structures that foster this morphing – and in turn the resulting cross-fertilization and benefits.

And there are other balances to be struck, too, that have not been answered here. How do you ensure your people have enough grounding in the discipline and methodologies represented by Phase 2 above, so that you can be confident that in moving to more individual brand models they will bring a refined model rather than no model to the table? I am not pretending that being a BSC is not without challenges, or that there are not more questions to be answered. But that is the nature of progress, after all.

Are Brand Subcultures Right for Our Company?

What the four phases above show is that in reality a move to a BSC will not be right for every company, and certainly not now. Some companies will be currently focused on progressing from Phase 1 to Phase 2 properly – all this will seem a long way off. Others will be in Phase 2 with an R&D powerhouse behind them, highly profitable year-on-year growth, and no apparent business need to move on. Others again will be in Phase 2 with a brand and a brand manager they want to give some leeway to, and for whom one subculture seems important, but frankly quite enough: dipping a toe into Phase 3 is as far as they are planning on going.

Yet I would argue if one does see one's brand genuinely as one's assets, rather than as the tools to leverage massively efficient R&D, production or sales systems, then the senior management of most companies should be building the idea of the BSC into the way they are developing the management of their people and brands over the next five years; that this is the future for marketing-led companies. Peter Drucker remarked that business only had two functions, marketing and innovation; all we are proposing here is for senior management to apply one to the other, and foster a further innovation in marketing – proposing that in effect, the CEO of Behemoth, Inc needs to see this as a form of innovation:

cultural innovation. And, like all innovation, it needs to be set not in a climate of occasional exploration, where one retreats and regroups from mistakes, but one of continual and underwritten experimentation. And perhaps just as an ambitious brand will have several innovations in a test market at any one time, so an ambitious brand company will be trying new ways of going to market, new kinds of brand culture – because they may need more than one model to succeed. And this commitment and support must come from the very highest management in the company. Simon Clift argues, with some passion:

> Brand Management is too important to be left to the Brand Managers. The management of brands ought to be at the same level as the management of the company.

Because, in effect, the management of brands and the cultures around those brands lies at the centre of the future success of the company. It optimizes the return to the shareholder by making each brand as powerful as possible; it retains the best people within the organization because they are personally aligned to brands and challenges they care about; and it gains the most from their best people's potential by using them where they are at their most passionate. As well, of course, as rippling the beneficial effects of any learning in each case across the rest of the organization.

As such, it could and should herald a new era in marketing-led companies.

Is It Right for Us Personally?

Yet even if there is a case to be made for moving to Phase 3 or 4 being right for the company, is it right for us personally?

I was originally going to end the book on an unequivocally uptempo note. Renzo Rosso of Diesel had said in his interview:

> If you only live once, you are obliged to enjoy your time. You need frustration, you need mistakes, because that is how you learn, but you have to be happy at work.

I had felt that this spirit, the spirit of taking it personally, was really where the heart of the book lay. Historically we have tended to think there is a fork in the road – either we can go and do our own thing in our own company and really care about it, or we can work in a large organization and leave it all behind when we walk out of the door. And in between are the large single-brand companies with a clear and appealing ethos like Southwest or Apple, which represent some kind of halfway house on that scale.

But in listening to the people we talked to, I had a strong sense that it was surely time to redefine what it means to be 'professional', whichever size or kind of organization we work in. Because we have to align ourselves with brands we care about, that matter to us. And it is in both parties' interests to make sure this happens – which means that both the company and the individual need to be initiators.

So I had read an interview with Ellen MacArthur, the diminutive yachtswoman who had sailed single-handedly around the world, in which she mentioned that her motto was the French slang expression 'A donf!', which means 'Go for it!'. I had liked this, and had felt it was a suitably piratical exhortation with which to close the book. I was going to juxtapose this with Churchill's 'KBO', and close by suggesting that these were the two choices we had: 'KBO' or 'A donf' – how did we want to live our lives?

But in the last three weeks of writing, I had a final conversation with Brian Lanahan, the man behind OK Soda, which made me realize I had been too glib about the issue of exposure. Although I try to dismiss it as the Third Excuse for the Navy, the fact remains that while most companies are in Phase 2, or even 3, being a Challenger within a multi-brand environment is a risk; it can go wrong. And you need to think about how each side would handle that. After we spoke, Brian sent me an email, describing his journey home through the January snow of Minneapolis, reflecting on what it meant to be someone pushing for change before an organization was ready:

> Adam,
>
> Had a think about our conversation on my walk home last night. It occurred to me that if your book is written for people called to the Challenger role inside companies, then I didn't really speak to a personal insight that came out of the OK [Soda] experience for me. I think it goes on the order of defining what success looks like for you on a personal level as you enter a Challenger assignment.

I recall complaining a bit that Coke should have been more committed to the process of challenging industry conventions, rather than just waiting to see if OK 'worked'. But in fact I doubt most large companies are able to make such commitments beforehand, hence it's a 'challenge' to take on projects that go against the grain. If there was full commitment, then there wouldn't be much of a challenge.

Point here is that in my experience, the big challenge of these types of projects is more inside the company than it is in the marketplace. As such, in running one of these endeavors you are inherently going against the grain of the system that surrounds you. So you must live with a daily friction and lack of 'attaboys' that the system provides. We humans are tribal creatures; it's taxing to live in subtle conflict with those around you. So it's important to know why you are doing this on a personal level, since you may not get a lot of external support.

One of the things that really bonded the OK team was that we all wanted to change the way soft drink marketing was done. I also wanted to change the culture at Coke; and saw OK as a way to demonstrate that the company could do marketing differently and treat people differently. In hindsight it feels like I was tilting at some pretty big windmills. So we were all rebels and idealists and that's what motivated us and sustained us in the wilderness. But it also made it very hard to re-enter the mother ship. Interesting that only one member of the 8 member team from W+K and Coke was still at their respective employer three years later. It was hard to go back.

So my advice to would-be Challengers is to spend some time getting clear on why you are doing this. What does success look like for you? What happens if you succeed; what happens if you fail? You will probably need an intrinsic motivation to sustain you, and yet you must beware of the Challenger energy so shaping you (and your team) that you can't reconcile with the system you've been challenging. Perhaps that's just in the nature of this work. Hard to stay grounded amongst the passions. This way lies drama, for better or worse.

Take care,

Brian

(Reproduced by permission of Brian Lanahan)

This is a book about brands and companies in transition; as such, it is not a book about certainties, but a book about uncertainties. Attempting to do things in a new way within a company will create, as Lanahan says, drama – within the brand, within the company, within your working and personal life. The people we spoke to varied in terms of how they responded to this drama: some clearly drew enormous energy and strength from it, enjoyed playing the maverick; others accepted it as necessary, but found it much more stressful and difficult.

Either way, if you do 'take it personally', it will create drama in your personal life, with dramatic consequences, for better or worse – and perhaps pushing you off the steady gradient of a predictable career path in your present company.

To take a small sample of the people we have looked at in the second half of the book, on the one hand Scott Lutz and Brian Lanahan have moved on from General Mills and Coca-Cola respectively to fulfil themselves in good jobs in different companies. On the other, Simon Clift and Chris Hawken were promoted within their companies, presumably to encourage more of what made them successful in the process. Kristin Krumpe is still feistily at bat.

So what I am proposing is a more sober self-examination. Is being a Pirate, a Challenger, right for you? Do you care enough about the brand, or the company, to put yourself in a position of risk? Do you feel you have had enough of being a prisoner of your category's history? Of being handcuffed by your company's culture? Because if you have, and you want to do something about it, you have to be able to manage the downside as well as the upside. When Carly Fiorina was chosen to run HP in 1999, she was asked why she had been successful up to now; she replied that part of it was due to the fact that she was prepared to take risks 'and accept that failure is also possible'.[3] This way lies drama, for better or worse.

Now I think there are a number of reasons why many of us are so drawn to a sentiment like that of Jobs, in spite of all the risks – why there will probably come a time when we want to be a Pirate, rather than stay in the Navy. Perhaps it is that we find a brand or a consumer we feel passionate about. Perhaps we reach a point of professional crisis: we don't want to be just another corporate veal, being fattened for retirement. Perhaps we share the view of one of our interviewees, who said 'Few of us are hurting for money, but most of us are burning for significance.' Perhaps it is that we relish the chance to stretch ourselves, to push outside our own and other people's comfort zones, to drive our world forward. We may even share the view of Henri Cartier-Bresson, that life should be about intensity, not longevity. There are all sorts of good and bad reasons why it might be appealing to us.

However, I'll leave you with one final thought as to why some of us may be Necessary Pirates, risky or not. In *Born to Rebel*, Frank Sulloway's seminal study of the effect of birth order on personality types, he concludes that there is a key difference between firstborns and those who are born second or third.[4] Those born first are most likely to find their place by adopting the parent's values, and identifying with authority. But for those born second or third in a family, that space and way of surviving is already taken – they have to find a different way. The consequence is that these second and third borns are not simply more likely to find their place in the family (in terms of getting the attention and space they need) by rising up against the existing family mores, but that they are also significantly more likely to challenge the conventional wisdom of their time – whether their fields of challenge are those of Darwin, Franklin or Voltaire. It is these second or third born, Sulloway concludes, who tend to be the ones who move on our whole society's thinking through these very challenges.

So perhaps some of us just have to be Pirates. Either as individuals, because we are wired to be that way and it is the only way we know to grow and find meaning in life, or because our brand is not the big 'First Born', and needs to rise up a little within the corporate parent and shout to get the attention from the sales force and the factory manager that it needs to flourish. If so, then maybe this book should really be for those people – who know all the risks, but are just going to do it anyway. And the merit of adding 300 pages to that elegant one-line quote of Steve Jobs is that perhaps, if we need or want to be Pirates, by understanding those that have been this way before, we can try to shade the odds of success a little more in our favour.

So if you would let out the Pirate Inside, be a different and considered kind of Pirate. Outlook. Dent. Be noisily bilingual. Get the lawyers on your side. Take it personally. Stock up on celery. Write and live by the Articles for your brand.

And remember the words of Dave Hieatt: Beware the person who believes what they are doing.

Postscript

Last week, at an international conference in Havana, a Soviet officer gave conclusive proof that the 'underlying forces' theory of history is bunk. One man, the officer revealed in his testimony, can make history. One man can save the world. It happened back in 1963 in the heat of the Cuban Missile crisis, when a Russian submarine patrolling the seas off Cuba was attacked by an American destroyer. Unbeknown to the Americans, the sub was equipped with nuclear torpedoes, one of which was immediately readied for use. Two officers were prepared to give the go ahead for Armageddon, but under Soviet rules of engagement it requires three to sanction a nuclear strike. Thankfully, the third refused.

And so it came about, as one US security expert put it this week, that 'a guy named Arkhipov saved the world'.

Jeremy O'Grady[1]

Acknowledgements

People in business that you meet will sometimes tell you that they want to write a book. They don't really mean that, in fact: what they usually really mean is that they want to attend their own book launch party. Which is, of course, an entirely different thing, because in between them imparting this information and the first sushi canapé being handed round is the whole ghastly business of actually writing the wretched thing.

The ghastly business side of writing this book was made from time to time enormously enjoyable by three things. The first was the huge stimulation one gets from interviewing people who have really moved the needle in their work: the Challengers we interviewed, many of whom were extraordinarily generous in the time, ideas and hospitality they shared with us. I have acknowledged them individually at the beginning, but this book is really a stitching together of their thinking, rather than mine: a kind of patchwork, if you like, sewn from the bright and fascinating material they each gave. I found, and continue to find, them inspiring, and I hope a little of the energy they gave me comes through in the voice I have tried to give each of them in the book.

The second thing that made this book a pleasure to write was the help of Olivia Knight. Olivia started off in eatbigfish, the company in which I work, as the researcher for the Challenger Project, the ongoing study into Challengers on which all our thinking is based. As such, she was in theory also going to be the researcher in the book – help dig some examples out, develop some case histories that argued for or against the hypotheses, set up some interviews, format the book, and so on. But her influence on the book has been profoundly greater than that. I could mention all the ways she has contributed – the suggestions of people we should interview, the bringing of questions and ideas to the table, her delightful but firm intolerance of the easy option, her ability to help re-see and restructure chapters to whose faults I had become entirely snowblind, her stimulating companionship along a winding road. But

I will say none of these things. I will say simply this: Olivia made everything better. She was my Isabella Blow. Thanks, Liv.

The third happy resource I had to draw on was that of my fellow crew at eatbigfish. Hugh Derrick did much of the initial research and conceptual mapping of the themes of the book with me, and acted as backboard and idea pusher throughout; my most regular partner in the workshops I do, I am constantly learning from his acuity in how and when to push a room. Mark Barden and Peter Field, my partners in San Francisco and London respectively, both gave me pivotal feedback on the book at a draft stage, which particularly influenced the introduction and the last chapter; the five years of eatbigfish have been infinitely richer for knowing them both. Robert Poynton has been a general source of ideas, knowledge and philosophy during the writing of the book, and my primary partner in one of the great Internet pleasures, meme tennis – though I fear he is a couple of sets up. Teresa Murphy managed our everyday business around the book writing and helped create the temporal and emotional space to give it the focus it needed; no one can run interference like T. Eve Noiret-Ryan, lover of Puccino's, managed me and us immaculately through the frothy last few months of completing the book: I have high hopes for her ideas on Wrapping it.

Helen Lewis, Andy Bird, Matthew Shattock, Neil Munn and Brian Lanahan all generously read versions of the book in the last two months, and offered polite but firm advice that has significantly coloured the structure and flavour of the book, as well as helping me constructively edit and sharpen the final version. Andy Bird has also been a considerable influence in the thinking that continues to develop on Brand subcultures.

The interviews in the book would never have taken place at all without the help of a number of individuals within the organizations concerned: Melinda Speck at W Hotels, Mike Wells and Jill Dittrick at Lexus, Dilhan Fernando at Dilmah, Sylvia Rebuli at Diesel, Beth Metzler at Discover Financial Services and Ruth Coughlan at Camper. Robin Asiz was also instrumental in setting up a number of the UK interviews. And I am also grateful to Keith Yamashita and Tessa Graham for making it possible to use two of the more important quotes in the book.

That I was able to talk about those people and brands we couldn't get direct access to is largely due to Alexandra Uhlmann and Ashridge

Business School, who have been generous enough to allow us to use their online business library to help research key brands and areas of thinking for the book. The thinking and content would have been considerably leaner without their support.

I'd like to thank Kate Marber, who first introduced me to the ideas of Challengers, and Alasdair Ritchie, for incubating a fledgling challenger. And in terms of developing my thinking, I would like to thank the clients I have had the chance to work with in the past five years, from whom I have learnt an enormous amount about strategy, brands, and the power of the group. My gratitude too to those, such as Marianne Reuterskiolde of the Swedish Marketing Federation, who have given me the opportunity to explore the thinking in parts of the book in speeches over the last couple of years. From the happy pressure of standing up and talking to a paying audience come the convulsive jumps that make me develop and push the thinking.

And finally, of course, my gratitude to my family. To Ruth, twice over – who as a member of the book team tenaciously pushed through the enormous task of tracking down all the rights to the images and permissions for the quotes that appear, and who as my wife pretended not to notice as in the last month of writing I turned the house into a homage to the Post-it note, and myself into a homage to the last years of Howard Hughes. Who over the past five years has put up with my admiration for Constructive Piracy, and the freedoms it brings and the freedoms it sometimes takes away. And whose support has helped make eatbigfish an adventure, rather just than a business.

Finally, no voyage would be complete without my 9-year-old boys, Will and Louis, who know nothing about business, but an alarming amount about piracy, and even more about what to do with the answer 'No' when they get it. Book's over, boys: tonight we sail for Tortuga.

Notes and Sources

A significant number of the quotes used in this book are from interviews carried out by the author; see the Dramatis Personae for a list of these interviewees. All other sources are referenced in this section.

Introduction: Necessary Pirates

1 Steve Jobs quoted by John Sculley in *Odyssey* (1987) Harper and Row.

2 Kevin J. Clancy and Jack Trout, 'Brand Confusion', *Harvard Business Review*, March 2002.

3 Captain Charles Johnson, *A General History of the Robberies and Murders of the Most Notorious Pirates* (reprinted 1998), Conway Maritime Press.

4 David Cordingley, *Life Among the Pirates: The Romance and the Reality* (1995) Abacus.

Chapter 1   Outlooking: A Different Kind of Insight Seeking

1 'Elmore Leonard didn't become the world's greatest crime writer by doing things differently. He just does them better,' Stephen Amidon, of *The Sunday Times*, quoted on the back of *When the Women Come Out to Dance* by Elmore Leonard (2003) Penguin/Viking. Mind you, you have to be as good as Elmore Leonard to pull this off.

2 Adam Morgan, *Eating the Big Fish: How Challenger Brands Can Compete with Brand Leaders* (1999) John Wiley & Sons. Page 156.

3 Jonathan Ive, quoted by David Kirkpatrick in 'The Second Coming of Apple', *Fortune*, 9 November 1998.

4 Shonagh Walker, quoted by David Robertson in 'Only Natural', *Far Eastern Economic Review*, 10 January 2002.

5 Andrew Gerrie quoted by David Robertson, ibid.

6 One interesting side benefit of the idea is the elimination of waste: 'We are also cutting out as much packaging as possible. By selling solid shampoo, rather than bottled, we save two tonnes of plastic waste a year' (Andrew Gerrie, ibid.). What a great way of thinking about conventions we take for granted – why should shampoo be liquid? Why should it need a bottle at all?

7   Mike Beirne, 'Taking a Licking', *Brandweek*, 23 November 1998.

8   Edward de Bono, *Tactics: The Art and Science of Success* (1984) Little Brown & Co.

9   Perhaps our fundamental notion of Insight needs to change just as our notion of intelligence, for instance, has changed. Until recently the concept of 'intelligence' was taken to mean one kind of intelligence, specifically IQ; now, however, people tend to believe in Multiple Intelligence Theory – the concept that there are a number of different kinds of intelligence that a child or adult can manifest, from musical intelligence to spatial intelligence to kinetic intelligence, and that each of course has its own equal validity.

Chapter 2   Pushing: A Different Kind of Approval

1   This is obviously not a real English word, but it is wonderfully evocative.

2   Kingsley Amis, *The Old Devils* (1986) Hutchinson.

3   Isabella Blow, Philip Treacy and Hamish Bowles, *When Philip Met Isabella*, Assouline, 2002.

4   Theodore Spencer, 'Fitness Goes Berserk', *Fortune*, 20 March 2000.

5   David Finnigan, 'Brother, Can You Spare a Dime?', *Brandweek*, 12 November 2001.

6   Mike Hoffman, 'A Brand is Born', *Inc.*, December 2001.

7   Clark Collis, 'Back to the Future', *The Guardian's The Guide*, 29 June 2002.

8   Danny Ecclestone, 'Hello, French Polishers? It's Just Possible You Could Save This Band!' *Q magazine*, April 2002.

9   Gregory Gregory, *Universe of Design, Harry Winston, Rare Jewels of the World* (1998) Universe Publishing and The Vendome Press.

Chapter 3   Projecting: A Different Kind of Consistency

1   Source: www.maurice-abravanel.com.

Chapter 4   Wrapping: A Different Kind of Communication

1   Orlando Figes, 'Birth of a Nation', *The Guardian*, 14 September 2002.

2   F.G. Fowler and H.W. Fowler, *Pocket Oxford Dictionary*, 5th edition (1969) Clarendon Press.

3   'Style Notebook', *The Sunday Telegraph Magazine*, 28 July 2002.

4   Ibid.

5   My thanks to the incomparable Chris Abel for coming up with the term 'Border Control'.

6   Gina Morris, 'Mordor, He Wrote', *Word*, April 2003.

7   Gavin Martin, 'Rock and Roll Animal', *Uncut*, May 2003. The album was recorded at Toerag Studios which famously only uses analogue recording equipment, and which boasts a 'filth button'.

8   Our Lighthouse Identity, for those who have read *Eating the Big Fish*.

9   Quoted by J. Bloom, in 'Upstart jetBlue Marketer of the Year: Airline Experience, Low Prices Prove Potent Sales Tools for Fliers', *Ad Age*, 9 December 2002.

10   Captain Charles Johnson, *A General History of the Robberies and Murders of the Most Notorious Pirates* (reprinted 1998) Conway Maritime Press.

11   Andrew Rolfe, quoted by Andy Milligan and Shaun Smith, *Uncommon Practice* (2002) FT Prentice Hall.

12   John Harris, 'The Odd Couple', *Q magazine*, April 2003.

Chapter 5   Denting: A Different Kind of Respect

1   John McEnroe (with James Kaplan), *Serious* (2002) Little Brown & Co.

2   Thanks to Dave Bonaguidi for the anecdote.

3   Stephanie Strom, 'Pushing the Envelope at Sony: A Japanese Corporate Rebel with a PlayStation Cause', *The New York Times*, 4 May 1999.

4   Ibid.

5   Speech at Lexus Dealer Conference, San Francisco 2002. With thanks to Lexus for permission to quote.

6   W. Chan Kim and Renee Mauborgne, 'Tipping Point Leadership', *Fast Company*, April 2003.

7   Jamie Oliver, quoted in 'The Food Section', © *The Guardian*, June 2003, author Merope Mills.

Chapter 6   Binding: A Different Kind of Contract

1   David Ansen and Jeff Giles, 'Don't Mention the Oscars', *Newsweek*, 4 April 2002.

2   Bill Bryson, *Mother Tongue* (1991) Avon.

3   Henri Holmgren and Peer Eriksson, *A Book About the Classic Avis Advertising Campaign of the 60s* (1995), in-house publication.

Chapter 7   Leaning: A Different Kind of Commitment

1   Schirf, quoted by Donna Fein, 'Honeys, Hand Me A Polygamy Porter', *Inc.* August 2002.

2   Ibid.

3   Speech at the Lexus Dealer Conference, San Francisco 2002. With thanks to Lexus for permission to quote.

4   David Hochman, 'Lance the Legend', *Men's Journal*, October 2003.

5   Peter Biskind, *Easy Riders, Raging Bulls* (1998) Bloomsbury. The same open crew and actor scepticism was apparently also to be seen on the set of *Star Wars*. Lest we find Spielberg's reaction unusual, Biskind recounts that throughout the shooting of *Mean Streets*, Martin Scorsese was so tense he had to wear white gloves to stop himself biting his nails.

Chapter 8   Refusing: A Different Kind of Passion

1   Paula Moss, quoting her predecessor.

2   Reminiscent of Richard Branson's celebrated line when he gets impatient of analysis paralysis: 'Screw it, let's do it.'

Chapter 9   Taking it Personally: A Different Kind of Professionalism

1   Ann McFerran, 'A Life in the Day', *The Sunday Times*, 2 February 2003.

2   W Hotels. Book. W Hotels in-house production.

3   PETA Press Release, 30 April 2003.

Chapter 10   Brand-centricity

1   Steve Jobs, quoted by Gary Wolf, 'The Wired Interview', *Wired*, February 1996.

Chapter 11   Red Pill, Blue Pill: Learning from Success

1   John Deighton, 'How Snapple Got Its Juice Back', *Harvard Business Review*, 1 January 2002.

2   Jon Gisby created this expression.

3   Will Smith, quoted by D. Ansen and J. Giles, 'Don't Mention the Oscars', *Newsweek*, 4 April 2002.

4   Gareth Edmondson-Jones, quoted by J. Bloom, 'Upstart jetBlue Marketer of the Year: Airline Experience, Low Prices Prove Potent Sales Tools for Fliers', *Ad Age*, 9 December 2002.

5   Amy Curtis-McIntyre quoted in ibid.

6   Lindsey Owen-Jones, quoted by R. Tomlinson in 'L'Oréal's Global Makeover', *Fortune*, 30 September 2002.

Chapter 12   Why Brand-centred Subcultures Fail: Learning from Failure

1   Tim Burt, 'Aston Martin Chiefs Told to Change Out of Bondage Gear: Branded Pens and Briefcases Will Replace Suggestive Merchandise', *Financial Times Weekend*, 26 January 2002.

2   Mark Luce, of S.A.B. Miller, remarks, 'God save me from agencies who just give me what I want.' This is reflected in the view of an Account Director I used to work for who told me that the role of a good Account Manager was to understand what the client wanted, understand what the client needed, and help them want what they need.

3   Greg Farrell and Jennifer Comiteau, 'The Big Red Machine', *Adweek Eastern Edition*, and interview with Brian Lanahan, 9 January 2003.

4   Dominic Rushe, 'New York Party May Be Over for Boss Man', *The Sunday Times*, 2 June 2002.

5   Ibid.

6   SaturnFans.com News Service, 12 November 2003.

7   Doris Mitsch, 'A Different Kind of Company to Keep: Saturn and the United Auto Workers Union', for Stone Yamashita Partners, June 2002 – with thanks to Doris Mitsch and Keith Yamashita.

8   Ibid.

9   Ibid., and Jack O'Toole, *Forming the Future: Lessons from the Saturn Corporation* (1996) Blackwell.

10   Doris Mitsch, 'A Different Kind of Company to Keep: Saturn and the United Auto Workers Union', for Stone Yamashita Partners, June 2002 – with thanks to Doris Mitsch and Keith Yamashita.

Chapter 13   Biting the Other Generals: The Wider Benefits Successful Subcultures Bring

1   Stephanie Strom, 'Pushing the Envelope at Sony: A Japanese Corporate Rebel with a Playstation Cause', *The New York Times*, 4 May 1999.

2   John Gorham, 'Twang of Nostalgia', *Forbes*, 6 August 2001.

3   Alexis Petridis, 'Friday Review: Hold Tight the Massive', *The Guardian*, 22 November 2002.

Chapter 14   Writing the Articles in Our Own Organization

1   John Sculley, *Odyssey* (1987) Harper and Row.

2   Frank Rose, *West of Eden: The End of Innocence at Apple Computer* (1989), Viking Penguin.

3   It is crude in the sense that the elements are not an accurate scale of gradation – 'discover' and 'seduce' involve different types of engagement with the consumer, rather than different degrees of the same one but it is simply a way of visually representing various possibilities for positioning ourselves.

Chapter 15   That Difficult First Year: Emotional Preparation

1   Michael Kuhn, 'Are You Pulling My Leg?', *The Guardian*, 5 July 2002.

2   Ibid.

3   Ibid.

4   Matthew Arnold, 'Marque of Respect', *Marketing*, 9 August 2001.

5   Ibid.

Chapter 16   Pirates, Privateers and the Emergence of the BSC

1   Daniel Cordingley, *Life Among the Pirates: The Romance and the Reality* (1995) Abacus.

2   This chapter was considerably influenced by the thoughts of Andy Bird of Brand Learning.

3   Simon London, 'Profile: Carly Fiorina', *The Financial Times*, 20 January 2004. Fiorina would, I imagine, laugh at the notion that it is only the first year that is difficult; but then she has been working her way through a rather larger series of challenges than most of us are facing.

4   Frank J. Sulloway, *Born to Rebel: Birth Order, Family Dynamics and Creative Life* (1996) Abacus. My thanks to Mike Daniels of DDB for suggesting the interesting connection between Sulloway's work and Challengers to me.

Postscript

1   Jeremy O'Grady, *The Week*, 19 October 2002.

Index